Principled International Criminal Justice

Commencing its search for a principled international criminal justice, this book argues that the Preamble to the Rome Statute requires a very different notion of justice than that which would be expected in domestic jurisdictions. This thinking necessitates theorising what international criminal justice requires in terms of its legitimacy much more than normative invocations, which in their unreality can endanger the satisfaction of two central concerns – the punitive and the harm-minimisation dimensions. The authors suggest that because of the unique nature and form of the four global crimes, pre-existing proof technologies are failing prosecutors and judges, forcing the development of an often unsustainable line of judicial reasoning. The empirical focus of the book is to look at JCE (joint criminal enterprise) and aiding and abetting as case-studies in the distortion of proof tests. The substantial harm focus of ICJ (international criminal justice) invites applying compatible proof technologies from tort (causation, aggregation, and participation). The book concludes by examining recent developments in corporate criminal liability and criminalising associations, radically asserting that even in harmonising/hybridising international criminal law there resides a new and rational vision for the juridical project of international criminal justice.

Mark Findlay has written extensively on trial transformation in international criminal justice. For decades he has been a leading global figure in the development of critical global criminal justice and procedure, arguing new ways of perceiving the international trial process. As the author of 28 books and more than 150 refereed publications he has an established reputation in regulation and global governance, international criminal justice, globalisation, and crisis thinking. He is Professor of Law at Singapore Management University and holds honorary chairs at the Australian National University, and the University of New South Wales.

Joanna Chuah Hui Ying reads law at Singapore Management University. Her research and writing interests include international and comparative criminal justice, humanitarian law, corporate and environmental law. Joanna advocates for and contributes articles on human rights and environmental sustainability issues to media and activist civil society organisations in Singapore.

International and Comparative Criminal Justice

This series explores the new and rapidly developing field of international and comparative criminal justice and engages with its most important emerging themes and debates. It focuses on three interrelated aspects of scholarship which go to the root of understanding the nature and significance of international criminal justice in the broader context of globalization and global governance. These include: the theoretical and methodological problems posed by the development of international and comparative criminal justice; comparative contextual analysis; the reciprocal relationship between comparative and international criminal justice and contributions which endeavor to build understandings of global justice on foundations of comparative contextual analysis.

Series Editors

Mark Findlay, Law School, Singapore Management University, Singapore
Ralph Henham, Nottingham Law School, Nottingham Trent University, UK

Also in the series

Developing Restorative Justice Jurisprudence
Rethinking Responses to Criminal Wrongdoing
Tony Foley

The Exclusionary Rule of Evidence
Comparative Analysis and Proposals for Reform
Kuo-hsing Hsieh

Policing Undocumented Migrants
Law, Violence and Responsibility
Louise Boon-Kuo

Principled International Criminal Justice
Lessons from Tort Law
Mark Findlay and Joanna Chuah Hui Ying

For more information about this series, please visit:
www.routledge.com/International-and-Comparative-Criminal-Justice/book-series/ICCJ

Principled International Criminal Justice

Lessons from Tort Law

Mark Findlay and Joanna Chuah Hui Ying

Routledge
Taylor & Francis Group
LONDON AND NEW YORK

First published 2019
by Routledge

4 Park Square, Milton Park, Abingdon, Oxon OX14 4RN
605 Third Avenue, New York, NY 10017

Routledge is an imprint of the Taylor & Francis Group, an informa business

British Library Cataloguing-in-Publication Data
A catalogue record for this book is available from the British Library

Library of Congress Cataloging-in-Publication Data
Names: Findlay, Mark, author. | Ying, Joanna Chuah Hui, author.
Title: Principled international criminal justice : lessons from tort law / Mark Findlay, Joanna Chuah Hui Ying.
Description: New York, NY : Routledge, 2018. | Series: International and comparative criminal justice | Includes bibliographical references and index.
Identifiers: LCCN 2018004296 | ISBN 9780815367000 (hardback)
Subjects: LCSH: International criminal law. | Torts.
Classification: LCC KZ7050 .F56 2018 | DDC 345—dc23
LC record available at https://lccn.loc.gov/2018004296

ISBN: 978-0-8153-6700-0 (hbk)
ISBN: 978-1-351-25836-4 (ebk)

Typeset in Galliard
by Swales & Willis Ltd, Exeter, Devon, UK

Contents

Preface

The higher order purpose in the analysis to follow is to interrogate justice as conceived in the international criminal trial jurisdiction. Set out in the Preamble to the Rome Statute, the foundation instrument for the International Criminal Court (ICC) are inspirational aims that necessitate justice dispensed by the court to recognise both conventional criminal justice rationales (such as deterrence and retribution) as well as more radical concerns for peace-building and victim satisfaction. The essential focus of the Preamble is the protection of the global community from the destructive consequences of criminal atrocity. As such, international criminal justice (ICJ) is both a legal and a social project. We will argue that the emphasis on harm caused by global crime and the need for its prevention does and should have a unique influence over the processes of legal reasoning in the international courts and tribunals.

The task for the judiciary in dispensing international criminal justice is both unique and extraordinary. The Rome Statute requires that individuals should be prosecuted for identified crimes, no matter how expansive these atrocities may be in the combination of perpetrators and victims. The law on which such prosecutions rests is a hybrid of domestic procedural traditions containing technologies of proof often better suited for crimes much more contained in their reach. Adapting these pre-existing criminal proofs to the context of global criminal trials naturally results in distortion and abstraction.

The juridical challenge of ICJ can be dismissively reduced to result-oriented reasoning, or little more than an exercise in hegemonic political pragmatism, but to do so misses two other important critical themes aligned with justice and proofs that the book will interrogate. International Criminal Court judges must, among other concerns, determine an accused's *responsibility*. This evaluation was consciously threaded through the Preamble and the Rome Statute to recognise that international criminal trial deliberations must reflect on the liability of the accused for alleged offenses AND on the harm these crimes caused to victims. In nation-state criminal justice the latter consideration would only surface, if at all, after the verdict was settled, and sentencing issues enabled the consideration of victim suffering and community outrage. In addition to these more expansive responsibility interrogations pre-sentencing, the nature of the crimes coming before the international criminal courts and tribunals are vastly different from those which are the common concern for domestic criminal courts. These unique crimes, in terms of perpetration, victimisation, and consequent threat to individual dignity and global order, position humanity as the constituency and deliberative focus for international criminal trial decision-making. As such the book suggests the need to explore a new international criminal jurisprudence that will facilitate a radically different mission for international criminal court prosecutors and judges.

A novel direction in public international law is the adoption of a prosecutorial model focusing on individual criminal responsibility such as prevails in the ICC. The profound challenges posed by the individualisation of international criminal justice underpins the book's critical framework. Crimes against humanity, war crimes, genocide and crimes of aggression are no run-of-the mill criminal phenomena necessitating the proof of a single act or an individual's mental state. Along with these more limited liability questions, the collective, organisational and contributory nature of perpetration, and mass victimisation complicate conventional juridical[1] methodologies.

Aligned with this individualised justice paradigm are the elaborate and inclusive aims for justice propounded in the Preamble. Their scope, we believe, inextricably directs international criminal jurisprudence to consider the significance and priority of confronting atrocity in a wide realm of responsibility, one which cannot be contained within the present proof realms of nation-state criminal procedure, particularly as they concern participation and secondary parties. Further we will argue that the victim harm focus of ICJ means that damages along with liability lean toward the logical amalgamation of comparable tortious principles of causation and contribution.

It is a consequence of the unique formulation of ICJ, we argue, that in terms of its statutory constitution the ICC has no alternative but to exhibit a more expansive approach to judicial decision-making and concepts of trial justice than would ever be realistically aspired to in the national jurisdictions. To fail this task would significantly jeopardise the legitimacy of the ICC project, at a time when cost/benefit analysis finds its role in ending impunity an adventure in utopian thinking.

Unfortunately, if there currently is originality in international criminal jurisprudence and the proof procedures it exhibits, this seems to degenerate into the difficult and often unconvincing manipulation of techniques in reasoning designed for another world of liability. International criminal law (ICL) is intended to emerge from the harmonisation of national substantive and procedural traditions. Achieving this is a tall order, even if limited to developing as a hybrid of Anglo-American common law, and continental European civil law, with all the compromises this entails. Add to this climate of give-and-take the much contested principle of complementarity, and the concurrency of national

1 Throughout the analysis to follow, where *juridical* is used it is intended to designate the civil law intersection of responsibilities between prosecutors and judges as officers of the court.

and international interests over the manifestation of justice in addressing global crime is fraught with uncertainty and potential partiality.

It is our argument that, while being committed to determining individual responsibility, the international criminal trial (ICT) faces much greater tests than presently are being recognised and resolved in the judicial decision-making coming out of the international criminal courts and tribunals. The collective nature of the crimes within the jurisdiction of the ICC (and their context) have led to difficulties in satisfying the traditional criminal law proof requirements such as *mens rea*, *actus rea*, coincidence and causation. Consequently, the international courts have stretched the principles of participation and association up the chain of command, to accommodate the need realistically to apportion responsibility for international crimes leading to a body of fragile jurisprudence particularly around core concerns of mental state such as knowledge and agreement. This book answers *why* the proofs are being applied in a manner which might be diminished as undermining some of the central traditional requirements for conduct and mental state as they are perceived in domestic jurisdictions. In so doing, we reflect on the unique expectations that could be directed toward the outcome of judicial reasoning in atrocity trials, and propose a logic to underpin a more convincing, rational and principled international criminal jurisprudence. This development will better complement the emergence of a new vision for juridical reasoning shaped by international criminal justice as a notion not so much concerned with individual rights or collective responsibility, but more particularly about systematic abuses of power and the need to have responsibility repositioned through the recognition of obligations and duties not to endanger humanity.

We contend that constructing a stronger and more robust legal reasoning when prosecuting and adjudicating responsibility for the four international crimes within the ICC's jurisdiction will never be possible while the interpretation and application of concepts associated with secondary participation and complicity are dependent on principles and proofs designed for conduct and contexts in the national sphere. Yet, through identifying this potential complication of logical and principled legal reasoning we are not impugning the outcomes that are their product. To a large degree, the judges in international criminal trials are faced with perpetrators whose responsibility can be established, and whose punishment is in line with the aims of ICJ, even if they are not the sole or even the most significant authors of horrendous crimes. Indeed, if the courts were to insist on the strict and narrow application of national criminal law proof requirements, neither liability nor responsibility might be determined and as such the application of a prosecutorial model for achieving international criminal justice would fail. The function of the ICC to protect present and future victims would cloud in the eyes of those whose confidence and faith in justice is crucial to the court's legitimacy.

It is incorrect to read the purpose of the text as an apology for lax reasoning, or as a pragmatic argument that the ends justify the means in ICJ. Our critical lens is turned specifically against the gaps in the process of legal reasoning and the application (or lack thereof) of essential proof requirements resulting from novel situations of criminality which only abstractly mirror traditional criminal law principles as they may be understood at the national level. Particularly, we will reveal that the use of tort/crime proof hybrids is a creative solution to these gaps, which open a path for new forms of principle and practice much better suited to the exigencies of the four crimes. Up to this point of time there are just too many *exceptional* cases in the international trial jurisprudence demanding flexible interpretation, even contortion, for individual criminal responsibility to be imposed.

We will lay out the limitations and indeed the possibly dangerous consequences threatening a credible international criminal law (both in substance and process) resulting from the failure to creatively evolve an international criminal jurisprudence purpose-designed for its novel proof contexts. This critique is intended to move from appreciating the collective nature of crimes within the international jurisdiction, the problems presented by options to prosecute nationally or internationally, the inadequacies of using national proof technologies to address the unique proof challenges in international crimes, and the manner in which fundamental principles of criminal law jurisprudence are at risk along the way.

Some of the specific platforms the analysis will construct in order to seek out a convincing notion of international criminal justice both as a jurisprudential and an actual paradigm will include:

- The need for a purposeful understanding of justice in the global context which recognises the wide goals of the Rome Statute and their victim constituency.
- The unique frame and context of international crimes, both in the collective nature of their perpetration and victimisation, along with the tangential context that deterrence and retribution must have effect within the global community.
- The strains caused by requirements only to prosecute natural persons (literally interpreted) who exhibit individual criminal responsibility in the more collective context of perpetration and victimisation.
- The challenges to central features of justice such as certainty, finality and fairness posed by the operation of complementarity and the possibility of prosecution in parallel jurisdictions.
- The judicial interpretations of proof which seem to be drifting away from the highest levels of mental state when it comes to holding an individual responsible for collective crimes.
- The tendency through conviction-driven justice expedients to see a merging of criminal liability and tortious responsibility in case-by-case rationales rather than a new and cohesive jurisprudence.

This book is a pocket-sized exposé of *some* profound problems. The ICC set sail earlier than most expected and somewhat rudderless, with anything but a sophisticated jurisprudence to guide its initial rocky years. As with its forebears, the Nuremberg and Tokyo military tribunals, the laws and procedures are a work in progress. Even the mode of justice the court was to market seemed big picture and beyond its capacity. The first indictments were tainted with self-interest and political partiality which would provoke the more recent accusations of continental bias. The court is chronically under-funded and it is small wonder that it took over a decade to resolve its first case. Decisions to investigate and prosecute cannot be broken free from *Realpolitik.* Witnesses recant and prosecutors bungle with ill-conceived applications for non-disclosure. The picture could be accused of cut and paste.

In a minor way, we offer a window through which the court can envision its future. So much is asked of it and so much maligned. Our contention is that with a pathway to a new jurisprudence, the court will break free of nation-state thinking on proof that is designed for another world of criminality. We assert this can be achieved without any violation of the foundation statutes, and conceptualisations of ICL. The court's burden to create and interpret the particulars of international criminal law and procedure without support from any a priori detailed and conventionally evolving codification, or the constant niggling of parliamentary legislative reform, would be heavy even for the best-resourced national court. We propose a simple recipe. Settle the nature of the justice to be delivered, contain the procedural poisoning of those principles that parallel jurisdiction sourcing risk, and take up the possibilities of the tort/crime hybrid but beyond the expedients of case-by-case reasoning.

In summary, Chapter 1 conceptualises international criminal justice relative to the aspirations of the Preamble, differentiates these from national traditions, explores issues such as constituency and conflicts over presumptions, looks at realist interpretations of individual responsibility pitted against peace-making, touches on other jurisprudential interpretations of individual rights against collective responsibility, and speculates on how atrocity trial decision-making might thereby be explained. The enunciation of international criminal justice then governs the critique of ICL as it is developing, of contemporary proof technologies in more collective contexts, and of the potential for new proof technologies through an appreciation of the harm dimension of ICJ and the novel characteristics of global crime to stimulate a more rigorous perspective for juridical reasoning at the global level.

Chapter 2 directs attention specifically to complementarity and discusses how the choice of jurisdiction, preferred offenses, differential punishment regimes, the possibility of double jeopardy, and challenges to certainty represent preliminary procedural impediments to the achievement of ICJ as a predictable project. More than this, the chapter is a brief indictment of the flawed thinking in substantivist local-looking directions for the translation of national procedural traditions into the management of collective responsibility and victimisation. Such approaches to international criminal jurisprudence are the product of political pragmatism and compromise but because of their inapplicability to global criminal responsibility will not thwart exploring the possibilities of tort proofs as they operate in these same procedural traditions. The chapter concludes with an invitation to see complementarity in terms of overarching justice principles, and not more narrowly as struggles over jurisdictional minutiae.

Chapter 3 looks at the mystification of individualism through comparative empirical case-law analysis emerging from the international criminal tribunals. Targeting joint criminal enterprise and aiding and abetting first as national proof constructs and then developed now in the international criminal trial practice, the analysis exposes the fissures and distortions in technologies of proof through a method of case-law deconstruction emerging from the international court and tribunals. This chapter is the essential precursor to the tort/crime hybrid enunciation in Chapter 5.

Chapter 4 notes the unique nature of the four crimes over which the ICC has jurisdiction so that the importance of atrocity context can further explain the manner in which proofs engage with collective perpetration and victimisation. Focusing on genocide, the analysis suggests that the unsatisfactory and often unrealistic application of a prosecutorial model to events of this nature which evolve historically and are congenitally contested and contingent, pose a genuine risk to the legitimacy of ICJ in the eyes of victims, and fuel the derision that the ICC is only a process of the powerful. Unless these issues are met through a more robust and creative trial procedure the fragile emergence of a new mission for international criminal jurisprudence, and more particularly for the global juridical project, is conjectural.

Chapter 5, our second empirical exercise, takes up the exposé of proof in Chapter 3, and the contextual justifications for a new approach beyond strained purpose and constructed knowledge in Chapter 4, naturally then revealing how tort/crime hybrids around the proofs of causation and contribution offer a better path to satisfy extensive and endemic requirements of responsibility rather than employing the more limited reasoning in domestic criminal liability determinations.

Building on this, Chapter 6 speculates a case for a new jurisprudence by looking at corporate criminal responsibility and criminalising organisations through association, as case-studies for how in national jurisdictions, new crimes invited unique proof technologies which exceeded the limits of contemporary criminal liability thinking. From there we invite a visionary judicial reasoning where both perpetrators and victims surpass the individual locked in space and time, and where uniquely conceived international criminal justice and global criminal responsibility receive principled and logical interpretation.

In the words of a reviewer, the book tells the story of a trial frustrated by the imperative to assess collective violence through individuated lenses. Storytelling such as we rehearse throughout the text, the stories of horror and hope, are personal, historical, and actual, specifically intended to add to the analysis of the structural and the systemic. Judges adjudicate stories with tools of reasoning designed to determine responsibility and manage its consequences. For ICJ this is an instrumentalist pursuit more than any rarified game of legal interpretation. International criminal justice needs to prohibit *and* protect. Our commitment to the realisation of such justice without sacrificing reasoned principle, interrogates rather than supplicates international criminal trial justice and in so doing strengthens its resolve.

1 Conceptualising international criminal justice

Introduction – the aspirations of the Preamble

In searching for a convincing notion of international criminal justice (ICJ), the Preamble to the Rome Statute of the International Criminal Court (ICC)[1] is an obvious starting point. The Preamble initially paints its justice constituency as the 'delicate mosaic' of the global community,[2] which atrocity crimes[3] can shatter at any time, and anywhere. With these considerations in mind, the core foci for international criminal justice[4] are the communitarian consequences of atrocity.

Unfortunately, while identifying such grave crimes threatening the peace, security and well-being of the world, the Preamble consciously down-plays the role of the nation-state in such endangerment, preferring to locate responsibility[5] on individualised perpetrators. This approach is consistent with the deterrent goal of ending impunity,[6] however we will argue in Chapters 3 and 4 as a perspective for justice in such formidable crime settings it presents a fundamental tension within the 'mass' nature of atrocity crimes, in terms of victimisation and perpetration. This tension plays out in a potential and prevailing crisis of legitimacy, one where recognition of legitimate victim interests can lead to outcome-oriented trial reasoning and the attendant risks for due process.

1 UN General Assembly, Rome Statute of the International Criminal Court (last amended 2010), 17 July 1998, Preamble.

2 As will be indicated throughout this book, the term 'global community' is so ill defined in the literature as to have reached the state of metaphor. Consistent with the purposes of the analysis to follow we represent community not in terms of temporal or spatial location but rather through bonds of trust. In a global context, to speak of community we reject the duality determined by hegemonic legitimacy (see Findlay, Mark, *International and Comparative Criminal Justice: A Critical Introduction*, Routledge: Oxford, 2013, Chapter 5). Global community should be an inclusive phenomenon central to considerations of justice which gives political, economic and social form to 'humanity'.

3 Stover, Eric, *The Witness: War Crimes and the Promise of Justice in The Hague*, University of Pennsylvania Press: Philadelphia, 2005, p. 51.

4 International criminal justice is a governance frame which recognises political, economic and social entities distinct from public international law's conventional intercourse between nation states.

5 As within the Rome Statute, and across the analysis to follow, 'responsibility' may incorporate liability, but more importantly recognises the significance of duty and obligation which attend on harm and damage.

6 Rome Statute, Preamble.

Atrocities are committed against communities of humanity.[7] The perpetrators predictably act in organised groups exhibiting cultures of violence way beyond the culpability of the individual. It is not hard to understand in such contexts, when charged with protection and peace-making[8] as well as proportional punishment, judges in the international criminal jurisdictions are moved by the widest outcome-oriented deliberations (see Chapter 3).

The Preamble particularises victims[9] of atrocity over the centuries (in order of significance – children, women and men) having suffered so as to 'shock the conscience of humanity'. Therefore, justice has a broad and inclusive moral audience. Peace-building is a primary higher-order consequentialist priority for international criminal justice. This notion will be guaranteed through the inculcation of a 'lasting respect for and the enforcement of international justice,' however determined (discussed in Chapter 6).

The Preamble returns to more conventional aspirations for criminal justice in affirming that such serious crimes *as a whole* must not go unpunished. Effective prosecution is identified as the medium for punishment.[10] The domain of punitive justice is seen first as national, enhanced through international cooperation. How jurisdictional (and we later argue, principled) integration and cooperation is to evolve remains unclear, and as the empirical focus of the next chapter evidences, often through politicisation proves contentious. In theory at least, the admissibility of jurisdiction functions within and if necessary beyond the conventional international law adherence to state supremacy, overlaid by the jurisdiction of a permanent international criminal court in relationship with the United Nations system,[11] having jurisdiction over 'the most serious crimes[12] of concern to the international community as a whole'. When considering the punitive dimension of international criminal justice it might be argued that the unique features of global crime[13] necessitate a novel understanding of the penal personality beyond

7 At the invitation of the Rome Statute we adopt humanity as the constituency for international criminal justice.

8 Peace-making is also read in light of the Preamble as a legitimate aim for international criminal justice, linked to retribution, through the protection of humanity against harm and the prosecution of those who harm humanity. So defined, justice has protective and preventative ends.

9 Victimisation in the context of the Preamble is inclusive, not exclusive, and as such the legitimacy of victim interests are not to be determined against hegemonic authority, but rather within the vast scope of humanity.

10 Stahn, Carsten, and Sluiter, Goran, *Emerging Practice of the International Criminal Court*, BRILL: Leiden, 2009, Vol. 8 of Legal Aspects of International Organization, Part III Prosecutorial Policy and Practice.

11 Maogoto, Jackson, "A Giant without Limbs: The International Criminal Court's State-Centric Cooperation Regime," *U. Queensland Law Journal*, 23, 2004, pp. 102, 133.

12 Security Council Press Statement on the contribution of courts and tribunals in the fight against impunity, 2012, SC/10700.

13 For the purposes of this analysis, distinctions between global and international are conscious. Global is a dynamic metaphysical which refers to the interconnection of humanity beyond time and space. International, on the other hand requires the 'national' as its referent.

the penal state,[14] and certainly adopting humanity as the constituency for international criminal justice challenges the link between crime and punishment in this sphere, back to the nation-state. The harm prevention paradigm for ICJ exacerbates the strain between national and international justice considerations, while at the same time offering new opportunities for international criminal law (ICL) and procedure to create a novel and more fit-for-purpose global criminal jurisprudence.

The potential for inconsistent understandings of justice and its aims between nation-state and emerging international criminal justice traditions is much more than a simple consequence of the procedural compromise that is complementarity, or the artificial sourcing of international criminal law tied to some influential domestic criminal law traditions (see Chapter 2). International criminal law is anticipated to emerge from the harmonisation of the major procedural traditions world-wide. In fact the process of constructing an international criminal jurisprudence is more of a hybridisation of rules and procedures ill-suited to the proof of global crimes (Chapter 4), and not purpose-designed to recognise the peace-making, victim-oriented aims in the Preamble.

While responsibility might be individualised in ICL, the determination of harm through international criminal justice is required in adopting the most expansive vision of actual and potential victims. Victim-focus beyond their obvious interests in punishment and penalty means that in determining responsibility, judges and prosecutors must be moved by the massive injury caused and damage inflicted through perpetration.[15] This approach we later argue (see Chapter 3) presents the necessary predisposition for augmenting proof technologies in international criminal trials, while presenting possibilities to engage comparable proof challenges from other fields of law such as tort (delict) where harm determination predominates (see Chapter 5).

Consistent with nation-state primacy, the Preamble calls on every State to fulfill its duty in exercising criminal jurisdiction over 'those *responsible* for international crimes'. The document re-iterates that in so doing, states cannot challenge the territorial integrity of another state. So the pursuit of ICJ is foremost in the hands of states and the sectarian security interests of national governments (which should be subsumed by duties to action criminal responsibility) will only be trumped where the 'ends' of international criminal justice, and 'for the sake of present and future generations,' necessitate that the ICC should intervene. The discourse of public international law resonates in this inculcation, but the operational problems it invites plague the consistent realisation of ICJ.[16]

14 In this regard, one may draw an analogy to corporate criminal liability and its unique task of penalising entities which have no soul or body on which to inflict punishment, but can be made responsible for harm: Bucy, Pamela, "Corporate Ethos: A Standard for Imposing Corporate Criminal Liability," *Minnesota Law Review*, 75, 1991, pp. 1095–1184; Bucy, Pamela, "Trends in Corporate Criminal Prosecutions," *Am. Crim. L. Rev.*, 44, 2007, pp. 1287–1306.

15 Ciorciari, John and Heindel, Anne, "Victim Testimony in International and Hybrid Criminal Courts: Narrative Opportunities, Challenges, and Fair Trial Demands," *Virginia Journal of International Law*, 56 2, 2016, pp. 236–338.

16 Drumbl, Mark, "Pluralizing International Criminal Justice," *Michigan Law Review*, 103 6, 2005, pp. 1295–1328.

Clearly espoused by the Preamble, prevention is the guiding purpose for punishment. It is, but not only, to be achieved through an end to impunity for the perpetrators. Both individual and general deterrence are stipulated as the influences on individual, collective and possible perpetrators to realise the Preamble's retributive and protective functions.

Within the body of the Rome Statute, Article 22 locates the exercise of justice against persons determined by the court to be criminally responsible. Article 25 specifies (in summary) that:

> The Court shall have jurisdiction over ***natural persons***[17] pursuant to this Statute . . . A person who commits a crime within the jurisdiction of the Court shall be individually ***responsible and liable***[18] for punishment in accordance with this Statute . . . if that person:
>
> (a) Commits such a crime, whether as an individual, jointly with another or through another person, regardless of whether that other person is criminally responsible;
> (b) Orders, solicits or induces the commission of such a crime which in fact occurs or is attempted;
> (c) For the purpose of facilitating the commission of such a crime, aids, abets or otherwise assists in its commission or its attempted commission, including providing the means for its commission;
> (d) In any other way contributes to the commission or attempted commission of such a crime by a group of persons acting with a common purpose.[19]

In this light the processes and consequences of justice are dependent on the actions and mental states of individual persons, whether operating independently or in certain contexts, collectively.[20] An obligation of the court in determining

17 Regarding the apportioning of criminal responsibility, the analysis to follow does not operate under an assumption that this term is limited only to individuals. Natural persons comprise culpable collectives and organisations, even giving life to the body corporate; Krings, Britta, "The Principles of 'Complementarity' and Universal Jurisdiction in International Criminal Law: Antagonists or Perfect Match?," *Goettingen Journal of International Law*, 4 3, 2012, pp. 737–763.

18 The determination here, we read as consciously requiring responsibility for victimisation, necessitating punishment. Liability is relevant, therefore, in apportioning and calibrating punishment. Other consequences for the harm caused can be visited on the convicted party through punishment and other nominated means consistent with the aims of ICJ.

19 Interestingly, intention in respect of common purpose is determined in the article as the aim of furthering the criminal activity or criminal purpose of the group, where such activity or purpose involves the commission of a crime within the jurisdiction of the Court; or the knowledge of the intention of the group to commit the crime. At this level, the proof platform for secondary participation and complicity sits at the broadest end of comparable nation-state traditions and challenges a literalist interpretation of subjective mental state.

20 Jain, Neha, "Perpetrators and Accessories in International Criminal Law: Individual Modes of Responsibility for Collective Crimes," *Journal of International Criminal Justice*, 13 4, 2015, pp. 896–897.

justice is to consider the *responsibility* of the individual for the commission and the consequences of atrocities. International criminal trial procedures reveal a growing trend toward the proof of conduct and causation above the intricacies of subjective mental state.[21] The importance of foreseeability and risk of consequential harm drawn from the purposes, knowledge and behavior of other connected criminal actors, and the organisational context of the criminal enterprise resonates with the tortious applications of negligence as sufficient proof of liability (Chapter 5).

Justice is individualised, responsibilised and potentially contributory. As we will argue later (in Chapters 3 and 5), the use of the notion of responsibility instead of the commonly understood (in criminal law parlance) *liability* is much more than a drafting preference.[22] As such, responsibility can be determined through parallel legal disciplines like tort, recognising contribution to the harmful act and focusing on the nature of damages caused rather than more narrowly on the subjective fault of the perpetrator.

The role of peace-building and security

To draw the threads of justice from the Preamble it is necessary to make some simple but no less profound connections. The first mentioned peace-building aims link in with the end to impunity and on to victim's interests. These objectives can be viewed at the individual level (child, woman, man) as offering protection from the harm caused by crime which an end to the perpetrator's impunity is intended to secure. The difficulty with this subjective paradigm is that the crimes, their perpetrators and victims are uniquely contextualised in collective action and authority. Therefore, proof principles such as joint criminal enterprise and aiding and abetting (see Chapters 3 and 5) are borrowed and extended even further from their tenuous subjective determinations at the nation-state level, in order to suit the unique situations of global crime (Chapter 4). What we are witnessing as a result is the development of a sporadic and sometimes-unpredictable international criminal jurisprudence, crafted to fit the collective peculiarities case-by-case for proving atrocity allegations (Chapter 3).

Communities of victims are also offered protection from crime's potential to shatter common bonds, cultures and shared heritage. Aligned to this aspiration for security is the spirit of compensation which is taken up in the body of the Rome Statute.[23]

21 There are several judgements out of the international criminal tribunals that might be seen as indicating a return to the vaunted common law maxim that 'a man might be seen as intending the natural consequences of his actions'.

22 There is no mention of liability in the Rome Statute.

23 Rome Statute (1998), Article 75 states: 'The Court shall establish principles relating to reparations to, or in respect of, victims, including restitution, compensation and rehabilitation. On this basis, in its decision the Court may, either upon request or on its own motion in exceptional circumstances, determine the scope and extent of any damage, loss and injury to, or in respect of, victims and will state the principles on which it is acting.'

At this point, with the focus on protection from identified harms, and the restoration of peace, security and world well-being, justice is assuming much more than that for which conventional criminal justice at the national level would lay claim.[24] Our contention, forming a recurrent analytical theme through the text to follow, is that such expectations of justice might be more at home in a tort claim, rather than a criminal trial. Add to the interest in harm, damage and restitution,[25] the ICC's facility to award reparations, and the tortious analogy is strengthened. So saying we are not suggesting that the international criminal jurisdiction would be abandoned in favor of some civil damages paradigm. The strong retributive dimension of justice as declared in the Preamble would not countenance such a transformation, and nor do we. Rather our argument is for a rational, predictable and principled international criminal jurisprudence that:

- recognises the unique features and circumstances of global crimes; and
- adopts proof technologies particularly related to causation and complicity which are not reliant on the already-stretched calculations of secondary liability in nation-state procedural traditions.

Procedurally (see Chapters 3 and 5), justice is to be achieved within a trial context where the victim voice is strong, independent and recurrent. Victim participation in an ICC trial may extend well before the sentencing stage which usually provides the limited arena for victim participation in national jurisdictions.[26]

Differentiating international criminal justice from national traditions

Common to principles of criminal justice as generally understood in national jurisdictions is individual deterrence through ending the perpetrator's impunity. It is not drawing the bow too long by assuming that general deterrence is also envisaged in ending impunity, certainly if the proactive protection emphasis of the Preamble is recognised, and the hierarchical nature of criminal conduct is understood. Therefore, international criminal prosecutions are meant to punish perpetration, satisfy legitimate victim interests for restitution, and to prevent future victimisation though the deterrent impact of ending impunity (or more realistically increasing its random likelihood).

24 Rome Statute (1998), Preamble states: 'Recognizing that such grave crimes threaten the peace, security and well-being of the world.'

25 Klass, Alexandra, "Punitive Damages and Valuing Harm," *Minnesota Law Review*, 92, 2007, pp. 83; Rabin, Robert L., "The Pervasive Role of Uncertainty in Tort Law: Rights and Remedies Symposium: The Limits of Predictability and the Value of Uncertainty: Sixteenth Annual Clifford Symposium on Tort Law and Social Policy," *DePaul Law Review*, 60, 2011, pp. 431–1229.

26 Garbett, Claire, "The Truth and the Trial: Victim Participation, Restorative Justice, and the International Criminal Court," *Contemporary Justice Review*, 16 2, 2013, pp. 193–213; Tibori-Szabo, Kinga, and Hirst, Megan, *Victim Participation in International Criminal Justice: Practitioner's Guide*, T.M.C. Asser Press: Heidelberg, 2017.

In national jurisdictions for decades the dominant criminal justice rationale has been retribution embodied in state monopolies over prosecution. The role of the prosecutor in the ICC still envisages a community (humanity) representation at least by recognising the shock to the conscience of humanity caused by these crimes and the resultant collective moral investment in their prosecution. That said, the ICC has specifically ruled that prosecutors' interests and those of victims may not necessarily coincide.[27] Understanding that these interests may compete, as we see it, implicitly diminishes the dominion of retribution at least as it might be said to motivate the prosecutors' energies and reflecting nation-state rationales.[28]

Another argument favoring the diminution of retribution as a rationale for ICJ[29] is the shift in the constituency for justice.[30] Despite the recognition in the Preamble of some primacy of State interests, there is no suggestion that the State is the principal justice recipient. Indeed, the initial references to all the peoples of the world, of humanity and of victims makes clear the intention that a justice constituency should be seen in these terms.[31] Humanity involves complex estimations of victimisation, along with a deep conviction that the harm is against the human and the humane.

With this shift in constituency from the state, or at least individualised victims or limited communities at the national level represented by state agency, it might be assumed that the bond between criminal justice and governance[32] is lessened (if the state's monopoly over justice is so diverted). We do not intend to interrogate this complex synergy here past the recognition that if international criminal justice and governance remain connected it clearly is a more communal governance realm than that in which justice is contested at nation-state levels.[33]

The restorative themes in the Preamble envisage peace for populations, people and polity. In other places we have asserted that ICJ needs, for the sake of its legitimacy, to be accessible, inclusive and integrated.[34] The argument for this presumes outside models of fairness through access, expanding towards the imperatives laid down in the Preamble that demand justice in action protects and preserves people, their communities and their humanity.

27 Garkawe, Sam, "The Victim-Related Provisions of the Statute of the International Criminal Court: A Victimological Analysis," *International Review of Victimology*, 8 3, 2001, pp. 269–289.

28 Bibas, Stephanos and Burke-White, William, "International Idealism Meets Domestic-Criminal-Procedure Realism," *Duke Law Journal*, 59, 2010, pp. 637–704.

29 For a more general argument about the demise of retribution as a justification for contemporary justice paradigms see Findlay, Mark, "Harmonising Global Criminal Justice for Peacebuilding," in Kerry Clamp (ed.) *Restorative Justice in Transitional Settings*, Routledge: New York and Abingdon, 2016, pp. 152–172.

30 Findlay, Mark, and Henham, Ralph, *Beyond Punishment: Achieving International Criminal Justice*, Palgrave Macmillan: Basingstoke, 2010.

31 Rome Statute, Preamble.

32 Gevers, Christopher, "International Criminal Law: Recent Cases," *South African Journal of Criminal Justice*, 26 3, 2013, pp. 431–438.

33 Findlay and Henham, 2010.

34 Ibid.

Underlying principles and presumptions – tensions between the national and the international

There has been much written which criticises the threat to defence primacy and due process in the international criminal trial posed by the position accorded to victim interests through representation.[35] The Rome Statute, and its Rules and Procedures[36] reiterate essential criminal justice presumptions such as:

- the accused is innocent until proven guilty[37]
- the accused cannot be tried or punished twice for the same facts and offense[38]
- participation in criminal enterprises requires for responsibility to be established, an appropriate causal association, and some satisfactory coincidence between conduct and the actual mental state of the accused. As will be discussed later, both these caveats have come under considerable strain within the developing international criminal law jurisprudence (Chapters 3 and 4).

In procedural actuality, all such presumptions at the international level must be read against the raised significance of victim presence and preference in all aspects of the trial,[39] and the impact this has on whose interests are pre-eminent and in what contexts. It is also important to note that certain what might be considered cornerstone protections for the accused at the national level (such as the protection against self-incrimination), are not expressed at the international trial level.

In Chapter 4 we discuss the unique features and contexts of the offenses within the ICC's jurisdiction. Obviously the proof requirements attaching to these offenses will implicate considerations of justice. In particular, under common law in cases such as *DPP v Smith*[40] and *Woolmington*[41] the historical ascription to presuming an accused intended the natural consequences of his act, was rejected. However, in Chapters 3 and 5 we reveal the primary importance of conduct in establishing the four global crimes, and the manner in which inferences about subjective notions such as purpose, knowledge and agreement are more liberally drawn from conduct in judicial reasoning at the international level.

The relevance of less definitive presumptions and a lower level mental state proof requirement will have profound influence in constructing international

35 Gillet, Matthew, "Victim Participation at the International Criminal Court," *Australian International Law Journal*, 16 1, 2009, pp. 29–46.

36 Rules of Procedure and Evidence, International Criminal Court (2nd ed., 2013).

37 Rome Statute, Article 66 states: 'Presumption of Innocence: Everyone shall be presumed innocent until proved guilty before the Court in accordance with the applicable law.'

38 Finlay, Lorraine, "Does the International Criminal Court Protect Against Double Jeopardy: An analysis of Article 20 of the Rome Statute," *U. C. Davis J. Int'l L. & Policy* 15, 2008–2009, pp. 221–248.

39 Garbett, 2013; Tibori-Szabo and Hirst, 2017.

40 *DPP v Smith* [1961] AC 290.

41 *Woolmington v DPP* [1935] UKHL 1.

criminal justice, particularly from the accused's position. Most obvious of these is the move away from individual rights protections (exemplified in the accused's presumption of innocence) in preference for the recognition of complex collective rights (of victims, victim communities, and of humanity). As a result expectations for justice like trial fairness will not be confirmed only in terms of due process and the equality of arms.

Accepting such repositioning will also go some way to explain the flexibility of judicial reasoning at the international level (discussed in Chapters 3 and 5), which appears to be more predisposed to prosecution success than is the case in many nation-state criminal jurisdictions. We later speculate that international trial judges may feel driven to recognise responsibility for contribution to atrocity, over finite distinctions concerning what the accused knew or intended regarding the consequences of individual or collective conduct (Chapters 3 and 6).

Realist interpretations of international criminal justice – who is it for and how is it legitimated?

There is rich commentary concerning the envisioning of justice as an interactive framework of rights and responsibilities.[42] In the major procedural traditions which inform international criminal law the pre-eminent rights, until otherwise denied, are those of the accused. In fact, the procedural justice of these traditions in large measure rests on the recognition of the rights of the accused.[43]

In the international jurisdiction, rights as a feature of criminal justice represent a more variegated terrain. The Rome Statute identifies a focus on individual persons for the purposes of prosecution. Along with this, and it could be argued contesting at a higher level, is the need to protect victims, as individuals and as communities which extend out to humanity at large. This pluralist approach to the concerns for the rights that international criminal justice should respect, presents difficult questions of pre-eminence and balance when seeking to achieve justice in an adversarial trial context.[44] For instance, the harms produced by atrocity crimes, particularly war crimes and genocide are collective in their consideration because

42 Caplan, Russell, "Professor Dworkin's Jurisprudence," *American Journal of Jurisprudence*, 22 1, 1977, pp. 118–159; Westmoreland, Robert, "Dworkin and Legal Pragmatism," *Oxford Journal of Legal Studies*, 11 2, 1991, pp. 174–192.

43 Baum, Lynne Miriam, "Pursuing Justice in a Climate of Moral Outrage: An Evaluation of the Rights of the Accused in the Rome Statute of the International Criminal Court," *Wisconsin International Law Journal*, 19 2, 2000–2001, pp. 197–230.

44 We should be clear at this point that the trial, in our view, is not the only or the dominant arena for achieving ICJ. Obviously, the considerations of this text focus on the delivery of formal trial-based justice, but what has come to be understood as transitional or alternative justice styles offer much by way of expansive opportunities to achieve the aims enunciated in the Preamble, see: Findlay, Mark, "Contemporary Challenges for the Delivery of International Criminal Justice: Where to the ICC?," , in Arlie Loughnan and Thomas Crofts (eds), *Criminalisation and Criminal Responsibility in Australia*, Oxford University Press: Melbourne, 2015, pp. 292–311.

the perpetrators may be motivated by intentions to damage communities as much as their individual members (Chapter 4).[45] If rights are to be restored to communities of victims through international criminal justice then the conceptualisation of such rights demands a collaborative understanding along with individualised manifestations. Legitimate victim interests flowing from atrocity crimes require mediation in their collective form. Against these, the rights of perpetrators may also need to be collectivised in recognition that offenders associate through, and exhibit networks of control in order to achieve their criminal enterprises.

Even in an instrument as sparse in its detail as the Rome Statute, rights issues are sometimes confounding. For instance, Art. 7 (3) in defining crimes against humanity, expresses:

> For the purpose of this Statute, it is understood that the term 'gender' refers to the two sexes, male and female, within the context of society. The term 'gender' does not indicate any meaning different from the above.

A literalist reading might suggest the trans-gender persons and others within LGBT communities that don't fit so neatly into this gender duality, and who may as much need the protection of the court from harms directed to men and women victimised by such atrocities, are facing a denial of rights.[46] Justice, if it is to defer to equality of outcomes would eschew such an interpretation.

In addition, if we move from an individualist-rights understanding, and entertain customary or communal rights, which the Rome Statute does in many places, then the nature of rights and their correlation with justice needs a richer understanding. Generally, the issue of rights in criminal justice theory is difficult and often dissatisfying. Instructive in examining international criminal justice as a rights paradigm, Hohfeld's position on rights[47] suggests that rather than looking at different rights in substance one should consider different rights' recipients. For instance, if an international criminal court is determining the rights to be protected of a child soldier as a witness that is a right's form both individual and consistent with the UN convention position[48] at an international level. On the other hand, when approaching rights in the customary and collective context, such as those of the community harmed by child soldiers, these are complex, shared and interrelated rights. If we think of justice being delivered to different

45 Schwartz, Sarah, "Wartime Sexual Violence as More Than Collateral Damage: Classifying Sexual Violence as Part of a Common Criminal Plan in International Criminal Law," *University of New South Wales Law Journal*, 40 1, 2017, pp. 57–88.

46 Knight, Charlotte, and Wilson, Kath, *Lesbian, Gay, Bisexual, and Trans People and the Criminal Justice System*, Palgrave Macmillan: London, 2016.

47 Lazarev, Nikolai, "Hohfeld's Analysis of Rights: An Essential Approach to a Conceptual and Practical Understanding of the Nature of Rights," *Murdoch University Electronic Journal of Law*, 7 205, 2005, p. 9.

48 Leveau, Fanny, "Liability of Child Soldiers Under International Criminal Law," *Osgoode Hall Review of Law and Policy*, 4 1, 2014, pp. 36–66.

kinds of rights recipients then it is not necessary to see alternative forms of rights as competing or one above the other. Rather they can co-exist and that is the challenge for the international criminal justice as a human rights endeavor.

Another instructive example to extend rights and justice thinking here is responsibility and victimisation in forced marriage settings.[49] Concerning customary marriage rights which approve sexual unions with girls under the standard age of consent (in major criminal law traditions) the contested rights of the parties only can be respected insofar as they don't deny the rights of the child to self-determination and protection as universally understood. In reconciling different forms of rights, the experience of how the UN dealt with the cultural rights positions in the discussions over CEDAW (Committee on the Elimination of Discrimination against Women) is edifying from the point of viewing justice as a universal human expectation.[50]

The legitimacy of justice is crucial for its impact and reach. Advancing the principles and processes of justice may be more influential in achieving fundamental and deep compliance with rights inculcations, than refining effective enforcement strategies or being defeated through their conditionality.

Participants in the justice process will approach justice outcomes with different expectations. The Preamble makes it clear that dominant amongst the potential legitimators of international criminal justice are victims and their communities. However, victimisation in atrocity contexts may be far from straightforward to distill. The valorisation of certain victims above other claimants will calibrate the capacity for victims to legitimate justice outcomes.[51]

Measuring individual criminal responsibility against the end to impunity and peace-making – is it just politics?

In concluding these reflections about the justice component in ICJ, it is useful to note the instrumental attachment of responsibility (individual or otherwise determined) and the wider aims espoused in the Preamble to specifically identify the reach that justice intends. The Preamble does not espouse individual deterrence alone as an objective for prosecuting responsibility. The expectation is that by prosecuting individuals responsible for atrocities, there will be an end to an atmosphere of impunity which pervades generations past, present and future that employ, experience and are endangered by atrocity crimes. The expansive aims for the prosecution of ICJ means that both its expressive and facilitative functions are vast and various.

49 Gill, Aisha, and Anitha, Sundari (eds), *Forced Marriage Introducing a Social Justice and Human Rights Perspective*, London: Zed Books, 2012.

50 United Nations Population Fund, Child Marriage. Link: http://www.unfpa.org/child-marriage; Goodrich, Herbert F., "Foreign Marriages and the Conflict of Laws," *Michigan Law Review*, 21 7, 1923, pp. 743–764.

51 Findlay, 2013, Chapter 5.

The consequentialist justice assumption is that if impunity is to end then peace will follow. And as a responsibility of international criminal justice this is not just peace understood as settling individual conflicts. The Preamble talks of the security and well-being of the world as measuring peace-making. The ICC as a central instrument of international criminal justice must, therefore, in all its functions, deliver justice that is inclusive, or otherwise 'the conscience of humanity' will not be sufficiently appeased, to concede that justice has been done.

Despite the argument that the Preamble to the Rome Statute necessitates the International Criminal Court will deliver *justice* that is more than a retributive intent might require, there is in the Preamble and the Statute a clear procedural focus for that mode of justice delivery. Even where international criminal justice is charged with *peace-making* and protective functions, this is anticipated to eventuate resulting from the end to impunity. Justice is realised through an adversarial system and a unique prosecutorial model. Even if it is accepted that the international criminal trial (ICT) may engage proceedings demonstrating a more restorative dimension,[52] the outcome of judicial deliberation is a finding of the guilt or innocence applied to an individual perpetrator. Justice may be administered for a wider victim community but as far as the court is concerned, central to this eventuality is the prosecution of criminal conduct and a verdict in terms of legal responsibility. The analysis to follow will show how the polar ends of justice are not irreconcilable through a more empathetic application of proof technologies to justice outcomes.

Just justice

This text is interested in exploring the nature of *justice* that judges, prosecutors and defence lawyers should be collectively achieving through the international criminal trial. Because the Preamble regularly re-iterates the victim-focus for such a justice exercise, it is fair to assume that criminal justice internationally will be of a different nature than that which exercises domestic criminal jurisdictions and the courts of nation states. This assumption is neither repetitious nor recurrent with earlier thoughts in this chapter. It is essential for an ongoing restatement of ICJ.

There exists both in the critical commentary, and the judicial narrative regarding ICJ, a lack of sophistication in elaborating the nature of justice at the heart of the ICC's mission.[53] Besides the Preamble, the judicial instruments giving

52 DeWolf, Harold, "Criminal Justice as Defense and Restoration of Community: Our Non-System of Criminal Justice," *Cumberland Law Review*, 7, 1977, pp. 393–412; Petrig, Anna, "Negotiated Justice and the Goals of International Criminal Tribunals," *Chicago-Kent Journal of International and Comparative Law*, 8 1, 2008, pp. 1–31.

53 Jovasevic, Dragan, "International Criminal Courts: Between Law, Justice, Reconciliation and Rights of Victims," *Medjunarodni Problemi*, 63 4, 2011, pp. 536–566; Prorok, Alyssa K, "The (In)compatibility of Peace and Justice? The International Criminal Court and Civil Conflict Termination," *International Organization*, 71 2, 2017, pp. 213–243; Meijers, Tim, and Glasius, Marlies, "Trials as Messages of Justice: What Should Be Expected of International Criminal Courts?" *Ethics and International Affairs*, 30 4, 2016, pp. 429–447.

authority to the ICC are largely silent on what justice is and how it is to be achieved.[54] The expectations for trial justice are expansive and re-iterated, but the indicia of justice remain unclear. No doubt this is a consequence of the political processes through which the ICC came into existence as the product of many compromises (as exemplified in complementarity discussed in Chapter 2). This being so, it is interesting that even when it comes to sentencing principles, the Rome Statute is mute.[55]

Perhaps one explanation for the lack of expressed interest in the nature of international criminal justice is the distraction surrounding the exercise of juridical discretion. A recent and significant challenge to the legitimacy of the ICC has been the threatened and actual withdrawal of member states from the African continent on the pretext that ICC trials reveal a discriminatory prejudice against African accused (see Chapter 2).[56] A simple consideration of the first dozen ICC trials would seem to give substance at least to this suspicion. Further, this critique chimes in with broader concerns regarding the politicality of the ICC and its potential to operate as some institution of Western hegemony.[57] Reflecting on how the United Nations Security Council (UNSC) retains power over ICC investigations and prosecutions it might be retaliated that the politically selective appearance of ICC trials cannot be blamed on the Office of the Prosecutor alone. Whatever may be the substance of claims that the ICC is politically influenced, the exercise of juridical discretion in the actualising of international criminal justice needs examination if our critical interest is to extend beyond justice being seen to be done. There is not space here to do justice to this interesting and important justice qualifier beyond saying that if the delivery of justice is the blind and bidding servant of hegemony then its legitimacy is at risk.

Similar to the ad hoc international criminal tribunals before it, the ICC in part claims its utility, if not its legitimacy, through a capacity to convict those who perpetrate the most heinous crime. The central claim that international criminal trials depend on both an expressive and facilitative commitment to retribution and deterrence through prosecution and conviction obviously influences the ICC judicial attitude to both the principles and proofs of the justice they enforce (see Chapter 3). Even the peace-making and protective aims seem inextricably linked to successful prosecution outcomes. Thereby, the pressure on prosecutors and judges to get convictions is not surprising. Recognising the allegations that these

54 Harris, Whitney, "A World of Peace and Justice Under the Rule of Law: From Nuremberg to the International Criminal Courts," *Washington University Global Studies Law Review*, 6 3, 2007, pp. 689–702. Morris, Madeline H, "Rwandan Justice and the International Criminal Court," *ILSA Journal of International & Comparative Law*, 5 2, 1999, pp. 351–358.

55 Flynn, Colin, "Sentencing at the International Criminal Court A Practice in Search of a Rationale," PhD thesis, University of Leicester, 2015.

56 "African Leaders Plan Mass Withdrawal From International Criminal Court," *The Guardian*, 31 January 2017. Link: https://www.theguardian.com/law/2017/jan/31/african-leaders-plan-mass-withdrawal-from-international-criminal-court.

57 Withnall, Adam, "Gambia Pulls out of 'Racist' ICC amid Fears of Mass Africa Exodus," *The Independent*, 26 October 2016.

convictions are the product of discriminatory show trials, the strongest critics are alleging that impunity cannot be ended through convictions that are the outcomes of political and selective prosecutions.[58] Disputation over the exercise of ICC justice focuses on what political externalities determine the selection of who to prosecute, and who to absolve. This terrain for evaluation is an inevitable if regrettable reflection on the collapsing of desires for global justice and governance which in the reality of international relations, the ICC can never alone achieve.

The text understands the critique of ICC juridical discretion, its influence on the court's legitimacy and the way in which political sectarianism may deny claims to impartiality in justice delivery. That said, we take no side in the debate beyond accepting the unavoidable conclusion that ICJ is influenced by political externalities and as such it would be impractical to say justice before the ICC can be achieved devoid of politics and power. If so, then other levels of legitimacy such as the internal rationality of judicial decision-making, the logic of proof, and the consistent application of core principles become even more important in convincing the constituency that justice can be delivered.

In the development of our analysis we also do not impugn any motivation dominating judicial decision-making that favors the prosecution case and limits the presumption of innocence in practice. These are horrible crimes and terribly extensive victimisation. We do hold views on these matters but deem them not to be essential for our substantive argument ongoing, which takes the following form. We are witnessing in the development of proofs before the ICC, from their domestic criminal law traditions, and expanded interpretations by the international criminal tribunals, risky distortions of knowledge, agreement, participation, purpose and consequent responsibility. While securing convictions, this judicial and prosecutorial thinking endangers the already tenuous connection of certain subjective domestic proof requirements to a point where individuality and guilt are all but severed. The book suggests more legitimate, if creative, cross-fertilisation of both principle and proof through the adoption of applications in establishing tortious responsibility, such as causation and vicarious liability that align with criminal law and are therefore open for incorporation and adaption in ICL. The case we make is for the emergence of a more credible and compatible international criminal jurisprudence better suited to the proof of international crimes unique in terms of their perpetration and victimisation (Chapter 4).

More than domestic criminal justice plus

As there is no template for international criminal justice beyond the broad mandate the Preamble offers, it becomes a matter of theoretical speculation to

58 Seshaliah, Shasthri, "Self-Referrals by States and Criminal Prosecutions before the International Criminal Court," *ISIL Year Book of International Humanitarian and Refugee Law*, Vol. 11, pp. 378–400; Ezennia, Celestine Nchekwube, "The Modus Operandi of the International Criminal Court System: An Impartial or a Selective Justice Regime," *International Criminal Law Review*, 16 3, 2016, pp. 448–479.

advance any preferred model for ICJ. In his article 'What Sort of Global Justice is International Criminal Justice?'[59] Frederic Megret proposes that to confine the question within a criminal law paradigm is unhelpful, and we would agree. As so far suggested, the predominant focus in many of the dominant criminal law traditions which have influence over the harmonising development of ICL is on justice as fairness determined through ensuring due process to the accused. It is also earlier argued as against the Preamble's injunctions, such an approach is not sufficient to encapsulate the expansive terrain imagined for ICJ. At the same time, Megret indicates that without a clearly enunciated notion of global justice it is difficult to advance ICJ to that level.

Megret offers a way of appreciating ICJ by investigating its distributive potential. He argues that what the international criminal courts and tribunals distribute are forms of stigma. In this, no doubt, he is impressed by the claim that international criminal justice will end impunity. For us the invitation to use justice as a distributive agency is helpful but should not be limited to the understandings of deterrence or even re-integrative shaming.[60] What international criminal justice delivers, or more instructively services, requires in part what Megret identifies as a cosmopolitan view, but again from a critical application. In another publication, we have specified what that cosmopolitan perspective may entail as an intersection between justice, morality and governance:[61]

- control – the end to impunity
- order – a power reordering between victims and offenders
- governance – the nation state and global justice ensuring victim interests
- citizenship – in the global community as a part of humanity claiming rights and dignity.

Justice, therefore, needs to be more pluralist through offering access, integration and inclusivity across a diverse and sometimes contesting population of stakeholders.[62] If formalist claims to justice as institutionalist morality are to be preferred (which we don't), justice could be said to be achieved by ensuring the rights of one stakeholder above another. In the sense of ICJ, we would observe a new prioritisation that replaces the offender with the victim. To stop at this level of constituency-derived justice, we would also argue, is inadequate for a convincing and comprehensive appreciation of ICJ.

59 Megret, Frederic, "What Sort of Global Justice is 'International Criminal Justice'," *Journal of International Criminal Justice*, 13 1, 2015, pp. 77–96.

60 Rome Statute, Preamble; Meernik, James, "The International Criminal Court and the Deterrence of Human Rights Atrocities," *Civil Wars*, 17 3, 2015, pp. 318–339; Corradetti, Claudio, "The Priority of Conflict Deterrence and the Role of the International Criminal Court in Kenya's Post-Electoral Violence 2007–2008 and 2013," *Human Rights Review*, 16 3, 2015, pp. 257–272.

61 Findlay, Mark, and Ngare, Sylvia "Sham of the Moral Court: Testimonies Sold as the Spoils of War," *Global Journal of Comparative Law*, 1 1, 2012, pp. 73–101.

62 Findlay and Henham, 2010.

As discussed above, accepting that a rights-focus for ICJ alone would not adequately recount the empowering distributive potential of ICJ, judges may still be advised to respect more communitarian rights concerns through confronting the following:

- the practical attainability of peace and security aims;
- the widening potential for peace and security through crime and rights judicial determinations; and
- the better satisfaction of legitimate victim interests through liability and responsibility adjudication frames.

The analysis to follow rejects Megret's reversion to what he determines as more classical notions of criminal justice to claim some form of transferred legitimacy. Instead the argument is to replace unproductive debates about the normative components of justice (legalist and beyond) preferencing for a more holistic and harmonious determination of *justice outcomes* consistent with a new justice constituency that has protective and punitive focus and form. In dealing with mass conflict and atrocity at the heart of global crimes ICJ needs to produce good conditions, circumstances and results for victims and their communities.[63]

Conclusion

Chapter 6 provides a window into the new and principled ICJ which the following analysis will argue for. Essential in making that case and giving some degree of particularity to the jurisprudence it will envisage, the aims for justice enunciated in the Rome Statute must be taken as a given. While it could be said that some of these aims are by any practical measure aspirational, and as such should not weigh heavy on a construction of ICJ, we would disagree.[64]

In *The Sensibility and Sense of International Criminal Law* Immi Talgren observes that the intolerable large scale of global crimes makes international criminal justice self-evident.[65] The later observations of outcome-driven judicial reasoning agree that ICC judges, for instance, seem in part motivated by a similar moral imperative. Talgren critiques the preventive determinants of ICJ as prevailing due to 'the void of alternatives, the rational ones'. A reason why at this stage we are reluctant to lay out the definitive agenda for ICJ beyond that

63 Findlay and Henham, 2010; Garbett, 2013; Tibori-Szabo and Hirst, 2017; Glasius, Marlies, "What is Global Justice and Who Decides? Civil Society and Victim Responses to the International Criminal Court's First Investigations," *Human Rights Quarterly*, 31 2, 2009, pp. 496–520.

64 Damaska, Mirjan R., "What is the Point of International Criminal Justice?" *Chicago Kent Law Review*, 83 1, 2008, pp. 329–368.

65 Tallgren, Immi, "The Sensibility and Sense of International Criminal Law," *EJIL*, 13 3, 2002, pp. 561–595.

contained in the Preamble, is in deference to an absence of utility and rationality in both its current manifestations and the achievement of its designated outcomes.[66] But beyond this caution, it is better to see ICJ as a project of hope rather than deception. Determining responsibility when it particularly involves more than liability cannot be restricted down to some disciplined, mathematical structure. That said, it is a mode of justice designed to confront chaos, social economic and political deprivation, and terrible violence, none of which are impossible of strict quantification and control. However, to achieve the justice envisaged in the Preamble, and to contain the violence which atrocities represent, requires more than a criminalisation justice paradigm. Prevention of harm, protection of victims, peace after conflict and security for the globe can grow out of determining the liability of those from whom impunity must be denied. Venturing on to reparations, restitution and the recognition of harm and damages, the insights of tort law might also inform our construction of ICJ in terms of responsibility for our fellow citizens and on to humanity.

The Preamble contains a cosmopolitan argument reasoning the court's establishment:

> It recalls during that 'during this century millions of children, women and men have been victims of unimaginable atrocities that deeply shock the conscience of humanity': and that making sure that such crimes do not go unpunished requires 'taking measures at the national and international level and by enhancing cooperation'.[67]

In this way, the court offers *resistance against unimaginable atrocities* and a *positive program to counter atrocities* through the use of legal proceedings. Gordon and Werner suggest that the atrocious, unimaginable nature of international crimes (see Chapter 4) works as the constitutive outside humanity,

> while it may be impossible to define what 'humane' or 'humanity' means. It is possible to discover when the boundaries of humane treatment are transgressed when human beings are victimised in 'inhumane' ways . . . international crimes create sense of community as a contiguous whole encompassing a harmonious image of humanity. International crimes are, to paraphrase Beck, 'an attack on our inner Mars,' from that which lies outside the now-conventional bonds of humanity, yet happens on the same globe we inhabit.[68]

66 Findlay, 2013, Chapter 4.

67 Gordon, Geoff, and Werner, Wouter, "Between the Dog and the Divine: Resistance and Conventionalism in Cosmopolitanism," *Utrecht Law Review*, 13 2, 2017, pp. 28–36.

68 Ibid.

As a final observation on a discussion which should never end here, the concern for justice legitimacy in the international criminal trial context is almost as important as the revelation of what it distributes and achieves.[69] While these concerns have important bearing on legitimacy, equally – and some might say uniquely – for ICJ legitimacy is as much an issue of perception as performance.[70] We retain the belief that the expressive power of ICJ is key to the justice it can deliver beyond the courtroom. In that respect the confidence in a process as predictable, logical and principled may legitimate in a deeply grounded way when the impact of any particular trial is long lost.

69 Findlay, 2013, Preface.

70 Varaki, Maria, "Introducing a Fairness-Based Theory of Prosecutorial Legitimacy Before the International Criminal Court," *European Journal of International Law*, 27 3, 2016, pp. 769–788; Kiyani, Asad, "The Antinomies of Legitimacy: On the (Im)Possibility of a Legitimate International Criminal Court," *African Journal of Legal Studies*, 8 1–2, 2015, pp. 1–32; Sheffield, Kai, "Speak Softly and Carry a Sealed Warrant: Building the International Criminal Court's Legitimacy in the Wake of Sudan," *Appeal*, 18, 2013, n. 163.

2 Principle and pragmatism

International criminal justice meets international criminal law

International criminal justice as the previous chapter purports is a project for humanity. The attraction of a humanity focus rests in the ability to traverse from individualised perpetration and victimisation so central to nation-state criminal liability, on to international concerns for the global community and in/humanity. It could be said, as we discussed in the conclusion to Chapter 1, that international criminal law starts out from the context of dissent (human beings acting in unimaginably inhuman ways to other human beings) formulating the components of global crimes which become the massive challenges for proof (see Chapter 4). In turn, the Preamble suggests that to fight these crimes it becomes necessary to move away from the dissent model and seek consensus over rules and institutions which can be even imperfect articulations of the cosmopolitan ideals which the Preamble imbues in ICJ.[1]

However, whether it be in the drafting of the Rome Statute, or the language of judicial decision-making in the international criminal courts or tribunals, the translation of massive suffering into legalist definitions and concrete rules, without losing the real bond between the trial and humanity, is a daunting interpretational challenge.

As the analysis develops it reveals that the paradoxes and inconsistencies in translating ICL to ICJ are more than the prescriptions of political influence; they are integral to the manner in which substantive law and jurisdiction are negotiated.[2] Later in this chapter we will assert, as a consequence of the persistent failure to prosecute perpetrators of influence in the North World, rather than in predominantly African states, the exercise of international criminal law to produce

1 UN General Assembly, Rome Statute of the International Criminal Court (last amended 2010), 17 July 1998, Preamble.

2 Roach, Steven, "The Turbulent Politics of the International Criminal Court," *Peace Review*, 23 4, 2011, pp. 546–551; De Vos, Christian, Kendall, Sara, and Stahn, Carsten, *Contested Justice: The Politics and Practice of International Criminal Court Interventions*, Cambridge, United Kingdom: Cambridge University Press, 2015.

international criminal justice is in profound tension.[3] For both international criminal law and international criminal justice to survive the impression of hegemonic bias and similar forms of imperialism and racial distortion at the heart of the crimes they confront, it is imperative to reposition global justice as for all humanity against all inhumanity, above and beyond nation-state interests. In Chapter 6 we set out a vision for the judicial transaction of international criminal justice that can occupy local sites of suffering, while at the same time advancing a principled international jurisprudence that does not float above the tortured application of nation-state law and procedure but employs its limitations to create a new way of 'doing justice.'

However, in deference to the realism which informs this book's theorising we must first interrogate the tangled paths of jurisdiction and substantive sources for ICL.

International criminal law and procedure: where from and where to?

The current era of international criminal law had its origins at vortexes of world crisis wherein unquestioned principle was not burdened by established practice, and vice versa. The first prosecutors at the Nuremberg War Crimes Tribunal were given the broadest brief to indict individuals for crimes the scale of which had never before been known in the theater of modern warfare.[4] Procedurally the trials that they serviced were military tribunals and as such did not depend on the niceties of due process and equality of arms that domestic criminal courts in the US, the UK or the other Western allied jurisdictions would have recognised.[5] The military court model set the stage for the procedures of the more recent ad hoc tribunals and no doubt influenced the dominant role of the prosecutor and the inquisitorial judge in the ICC format.[6]

3 Prorok, Alyssa K., "The (In)compatibility of Peace and Justice? The International Criminal Court and Civil Conflict Termination," *International Organization*, 71 2, 2017, pp. 213–243; Clarke, Kamari, *Fictions of Justice: The International Criminal Court and the Challenge of Legal Pluralism in Sub-Saharan Africa*, Cambridge University Press, 2009.

4 Schabas, William, *Unimaginable Atrocities: Justice, Politics, and Rights at the War Crimes Tribunals*, Oxford: Oxford University Press, 2012; Saber, Mahmoud and Sadeghi, Azade, "The Survey of Criterion of Gravity Threshold for Prosecution of Crimes in International Criminal Court: Comparative View on Other International Courts," *Majallah-i ḥuqūq-i taṭbīqī*, 6 2, 2015; Plesch, Dan and Sattler, Shanti, "Changing the Paradigm of International Criminal Law: Considering the Work of the United Nations War Crimes Commission of 1943–1948," *International Community Law Review*, 15 2, 2013, pp. 203–223.

5 Tanaka, Yuki, McCormack, Tim, and Simpson, Gerry, *Beyond Victor's Justice? The Tokyo War Crimes Trial Revisited*, BRILL: Leiden, 2010; Heller, Kevin, *The Nuremberg Military Tribunals and the Origins of International Criminal Law*, Oxford Scholarship Online, September 2011.

6 Çakmak, Cenap, *A Brief History of International Criminal Law and International Criminal Court*, Palgrave Macmillan US: New York, 2017; Schlütter, Birgit, *Developments in Customary International Law Theory and the Practice of the International Court of Justice and the International Ad Hoc Criminal Tribunals for Rwanda and Yugoslavia*, BRILL: Leiden, 2010.

Even so, there needed to be law to action and rules of evidence and procedure to guide courtroom practice at the international level. Following the exigencies of victor's justice framed in substantively ill-formed trial necessity post WWII, the UN committees charged with developing an international criminal jurisprudence were confronted with challenges inherent in synthesising the diversity of criminal justice traditions across even the most powerful member states.[7] With the UN Security Council's establishment of the International Criminal Tribunal for the Former Yugoslavia (ICTY) and the International Criminal Tribunal for Rwanda (ICTR) the prosecutors and judges in those bodies had to interpret law and process on a case-by-case basis. Despite the enabling statutes which provided the legislative framework for these bodies and gave some guidance to proof (substantive and procedural), the development of ICL in the trials that followed before these tribunals was heavily dependent on the idiosyncrasies of judicial reasoning which gave a precedent base for emerging legal principles (see Chapter 6). Judge-made law, growing through the application of precedent and the sometimes-disaggregated adaptation of international conventions, provided the jurisprudential foundations for the ICC.

With the ICTY in particular, a methodology of judicial reasoning evolved which applied crude empirical evaluations of what was the prevailing trial practice in most nation-state jurisdictions, and from this reconciliation of competing principle and practice settling determinations of the issue in question through the preferences of the judges who comprised a chamber in any particular trial.[8] Some critics of this expedient legal gestation have gone so far as to suggest that the dominant judges (or even their associates) carried the day when there arose clear divergence in how an offense was designated for proof and what evidentiary considerations should prevail.[9]

By the time international criminal law reached the courtrooms of the ICC, two drivers had become clear. The first was the continuing commitment to the evolution of principle and practice which reflected the somewhat unrealistic aspiration for an organic harmonisation between the major nation-state traditions. The belief in the possibility of such jurisprudential creativity was both lofty and pragmatic, setting the tone for political compromise and confluence to follow. In fact, some major national criminal justice traditions have been marginalised beyond this harmonisation on the grounds that they do not reflect the human rights foundations of the UN at large.[10] Others have been preferred, in contexts

7 Meisenberg, Simon, and Stegmiller, Ignaz, *The Extraordinary Chambers in the Courts of Cambodia: Assessing Their Contribution to International Criminal Law*, The Hague: Asser Press; Berlin: Springer, 2016.

8 Tanaka, McCormack and Simpson, 2010; Heller, 2011.

9 Findlay, Mark, and Bohlander, Michael, "The Use of Domestic Sources as a Basis of International Criminal Law Principles," in Michael Bohlander, *Globalization of Criminal Justice*, Aldershot: Ashgate, 2010, pp. 69–92.

10 O'Mahony, Jane, "'Not So Nice': The Treaty of Nice, the International Criminal Court, the Abolition of the Death Penalty – the 2001 Referendum Experience," *Irish Political Studies*, 16 1, 2001, pp. 201–213; Stephen, Christopher, "International Criminal Law: Wielding the Sword of Universal Criminal Justice?," *International and Comparative Law Quarterly*, 61 1, 2012, pp. 55–89.

of substantive and procedural contradiction for reasons which may have had little to do with legal persuasiveness. In reality, and due to the vastly different proof demands presented by the prosecution of global crime that we will canvass in Chapter 4, the development of international criminal law has turned out to be a realist and perhaps reactionary rather than reflective process of hybridisation as each new prosecution is presented.[11]

This text spends some time interrogating the fallacy of both the harmonisation and hybridisation paradigms in the development of a principled and logical international criminal jurisprudence. For now it is enough to highlight both the conceptual and practical impossibilities of achieving the aims for ICJ set out in the Preamble to the Rome Statute (discussed in Chapter 1) through the transmogrification of traditions crafted over centuries in the attainment of much more limited criminal justice outcomes, and for very different and particularised justice constituencies.[12] Indeed, on the basis of this understanding some commentators have dismissed the ICJ endeavor as so unrealistically burdening adversarial trial deliberations with unattainable peace-making aims, that the only answer for the future is to return to a much more conventional and constrained prosecutorial mode of adjudicating global crime.[13] We have in other writing rejected this view as failing to give inevitable recognition to what fundamentally legitimates ICJ as different from national justice traditions: victim recognition and the constituency of humanity, not the nation-state.[14] In what follows is offered a new approach to the development of international criminal law which would make possible the recognition of retributive and restorative motivations in an adversarial trial released from a process of distorting practice and procedure which is not fit-for-purpose.

The other driver that has significantly complicated both the jurisdiction of ICJ and the development of a dominant model, is the notion of complementarity. Since its invention complementarity has been an approach to resolving the tensions between autonomy and internationalism which has required much intellectual and procedural tinkering and generated critical condemnation.[15] The empirical core of this chapter will explore the concerns surrounding complementarity within the context of recent criticisms by African member states regarding what they allege is complementarity's biased and politicised applications.

11 See Chapter 4.

12 See the difficult cases decided by the International Criminal Courts which arguably stretched national law principles to cater to the unique context of international crime: *Édouard Karemera and Matthieu Ngirimpatse v The Prosecutor*, Case No. ICTR-98-44-T and Case No. ICTR-98-44-A; *Prosecutor v Milan Martic*, Case No. IT-95-11-T; *Prosecutor v Kupreskic et al*, Case No. IT-95-16.

13 Reichel, Philip, and Albanese, Jay, *Handbook of Transnational Crime and Justice*, Sage: Los Angeles, 2014.

14 Moffett, Luke, "Elaborating Justice for Victims at the International Criminal Court," *Journal of International Criminal Justice*, 13 2, 2015, pp. 281–311.

15 Stahn, Carsten, "Libya, the International Criminal Court and Complementarity," *Journal of International Criminal Justice*, 10 2, 2012, pp. 325–349; Imoedemhe, Ovo Catherine, *The Complementarity Regime of the International Criminal Court: National Implementation in Africa*, Springer: Berlin, 2017.

Without taking sides on the merits of these claims, the nature of the attack on ICC jurisdiction is important in revealing the vulnerability of complementarity in appropriately settling contentions over jurisdiction.

Investigations and prosecutions by the ICC can emerge independently of the wishes of nation-states.[16] However, as our exploration of the African debate reveals, if a nation-state refuses to co-operate with the ICC or indeed challenges and frustrates its jurisdictional claims then the likely success of the ICC's endeavors will be problematic. More than the assertion of nation-state interests against international criminal justice, we suggest it is the current interpretations of complementarity that present an impediment to the development of a principled and rational international criminal jurisprudence, and a strong and uncontestable procedural foundation on which its convictions rest (see Chapter 4).

In brief, complementarity recognises the pre-eminence of nation-state jurisdiction while at the same time confirming the ultimate determination of international jurisdiction. It was a compromise construct designed to appease those member states who were concerned about the power of the ICC to initiate independent prosecutions if states failed or fabricated their responsibilities to intervene.[17] If a nation-state has the capacity to prosecute ICC crimes then under complementarity, it is allowed to do so. Obviously, this preferences those jurisdictions which have bureaucratically developed criminal justice capacity over those that don't and thereby seems to direct ICC intervention toward fragmented and post-conflict nation-state settings.[18] If a state prevaricates in the prosecution of ICC crimes even though it has the capacity then the ICC can claim jurisdiction. Ultimately, the ICC prosecutor can investigate independently despite the pre-conditions of complementarity. In reality, the prosecutor is, as the recent indictments in Kenya reveal, crucially reliant on the cooperation of member states in so many aspects of any investigation and indictment.[19]

Particularly for the purposes of this chapter we are interested in the antimonies and paradoxes that complementarity will, or could, perpetrate. Whether it be due to different sentencing options, different crime constituents (as evidenced in the varied approaches taken to the ratification and legislation of the genocide convention), different prosecutorial conventions, different trial practices, and specific judicial predispositions and popular leanings, nation-state justice may produce outcomes unlike those which might be expected from an international

16 Brubacher, Matthew, "Prosecutorial Discretion within the International Criminal Court," *Journal of International Criminal Justice*, 2 1, 2004, pp. 71–95.

17 Brighton, Claire, "Avoiding Unwillingness: Addressing the Political Pitfalls Inherent in the Complementarity Regime of the International Criminal Court," *International Criminal Law Review*, 12 4, 2012, pp. 629–664.

18 Kai, Ambos, *The Colombian Peace Process and the Principle of Complementarity of the International Criminal Court: An Inductive, Situation-based Approach*, Springer: Berlin, 2010; Fouladvand, Shahrzad, "Complementarity and Cultural Sensitivity: Decision-making by the International Criminal Court Prosecutor in the Darfur Situation," *International Criminal Law Review*, 14 6, 2014, pp. 1028–1066.

19 Imoedemhe, 2017.

criminal prosecution. The injustice that may comparatively arise is not hard to demonstrate, even where a state is diligent in disposing of their prosecutorial responsibilities. In addition, there are the more subtle ramifications of jurisdiction shopping and double jeopardy that complicate the achievement of consistent ICJ when global crimes are adjudicated in very incompatible trial arenas.

So, the chapter has two pathways for arriving at a single analytical contention: that the application of domestic criminal law to global prosecutions, and the transferability of trial jurisdictions national to international for global crime will not achieve a principled and rational international criminal jurisprudence. The first, and perhaps more contentious, is to turn over pebbles in the road to complementarity which would make its destination to a consistent ICJ more like a dead end. The second and somewhat narrowly traversed pathway is to debunk harmonisation and hybridisation in the context of determining individual responsibility for global crime.

This consideration of interpretational limitations within ICL is commenced by briefly exploring complementarity. Such ordering is logical in that unless the jurisdictional issues are settled then considerations of the substantive criminal law to be applied in international criminal trials is moot. The discussion starts out with the African debate which we classify into three constituents, each of which is somewhat concealed in the wider hubris of alleged bias by the 'International Criminal Court against Africa.'[20] To put the debate in context it is important to recall that the first indictments before the ICC came from independent referrals, where the government of the Congo sought the prosecution of its political opponents, and Uganda wanted to use the threat of ICC prosecution as a device to force the Lords Army to the negotiation table.[21] If there was any politicisation in these indictments the more telling interpretation is the use of the ICC for the political interests of nation-state governments. The second scenario in the debate is how the Kenyan prosecutions changed from reluctant cooperation to outright resistance, with the consequential outcome being a failure for the prosecution to secure a sufficient case to answer, and perhaps in triumph for nation-state political interests and intractability. Finally, we look at the southern African initiatives to leave the ICC based around opposition to the claim of jurisdiction against serving heads of state.[22] Each of these scenarios can be viewed as the inevitable consequences of complementarity in its unnatural applications. Following these insights, the section moves to propose a new interpretation of complementarity which may better

20 Imoedemhe, 2017; Du Plessis, Max, "The Future of International Criminal Justice: Civil Society, Complementarity and the Case of South Africa," *African Security Review*, 19 4, 2010, pp. 17–30; Du Plessis, Max, "Complementarity and Africa: The Promises and Problems of International Criminal Justice," *African Security Review*, 17 4, 2008, pp. 154–170.

21 "Democratic Republic of Congo – Situation in the Democratic Republic of the Congo," International Criminal Court. Link: https://www.icc-cpi.int/drc.

22 "African Leaders Plan Mass Withdrawal from International Criminal Court –Decision Reached at African Union Summit Follows Announcements by South Africa, Burundi and the Gambia that they Plan to Leave the Court," *The Guardian*, 13 January 2017.

complement the secure resolution of jurisdictional questions and a more balanced coalition between the national and international interests in ICJ.

In the final part of the chapter we expose the operational fallibility of harmonisation and hybridisation as pathways to a logical and principled ICL. Again, this involves a new interpretation of hybridisation which is then given practical application in Chapters 3 and 5.

The African case-study – the foundations of the recent member state exodus?

A convincing understanding of the political considerations at play resulting in the Congo's initial independent referrals to the ICC, requires canvassing the nature and context of the referral as a political mechanism. In 2003, the transitional government that took power in Kinshasa was based on a power-sharing agreement among the four parties to the Inter-Congolese Dialogue – the previous government, the unarmed opposition, the RDC and the MLC.[23] The transitional government was led by President Joseph Kabila, son of Laurent Kabila, who rode the 1996 rebellion into power. Under Kabila operated four vice presidents, one from each of the primary factions in the Congolese civil war. Each of the vice presidents had a range of ministries answering to his authority. Those ministries were led, in turn, by ministers appointed by separate parties to the peace agreement. This partisan power-sharing produced a situation in which former enemies directly reported to one another, often resulting in political maneuvering and dangerous infighting.[24]

Within this framework, during the short time period before promised national elections as a condition of the settlement, the primary political actors had strong incentives to position themselves for electoral victory by undermining the legitimacy and standing of other parties to the peace agreement. Given that many of the key political actors were and are implicated in international crimes, international criminal justice offered a powerful mechanism to discredit enemies and re-shape the domestic political landscape. The potential implications of a criminal indictment by national or international courts were significant. If a senior government official were to be indicted or prosecuted, that individual might be unable to effectively compete in the upcoming balloting or might already be in The Hague facing sentencing. If used strategically, this application of an ICC indictment could have greatly enhanced the electoral prospects of the initiating opponents.

For President Kabila, the ICC thus had the potential to serve as a political power tool in the foreshadowed national elections. Kabila was at that time unlikely to be the subject of any ICC investigation, yet two of his potential electoral

23 Lemarchand, René, "Consociationalism and Power Sharing in Africa: Rwanda, Burundi, and the Democratic Republic of the Congo," *African Affairs*, 106 422, 2007, pp. 1–20.

24 Ibid.

opponents – Vice Presidents Jean-Pierre Bemba of the MLC and Azarias Ruberwa of the RCD – were among those persons of interest for the ICC prosecutor in his earliest investigations. Though Kabila's hands were not clean, as a relative newcomer on the political scene when his father died in January 2001, he had not been clearly or directly involved in the ongoing conflict in Ituri and South Kivu. Any crimes against humanity committed by Kabila would have occurred prior to 1 July 2002[25] and, as of then, there was little evidence that he had been personally involved in any of the major massacres in Congo within the Court's temporal jurisdiction. As a UN Mission in Congo (MONUC) official observed, one would have expected Kabila, therefore, to support a tribunal with jurisdiction over genocide and war crimes. Kabila's chief political rivals, however, were more directly implicated in ongoing crimes in eastern Congo and some therefore could have (as they did) found themselves the targets of international investigations, in turn strengthening Kabila's political hand in the transitional government and forthcoming elections.[26] As things transpired, following independent referral from the Congolese government Jean-Pierre Bemba was eventually sentenced to 18 years in prison by the ICC for rape and pillage committed by his troops. Although Azarias Ruberwa was not similarly charged as a result of referral, the attention he received from the investigations done by the ICC severely damaged his political and international reputation. These referrals thus served to destabilise President Kabila's political opponents and enabled him to consolidate his personal power. As a consequence of the independent referrals to the ICC from the then principal political powers in the Congo, complementarity under the ICC's procedural system was tainted by sectarian nation-state partisan political motivations. Referrals in this context complemented a governance strategy adopted by dominant leaders to secure or stabilise their power positions, and did not necessarily evolve from interests with justice considerations that would motivate the independent prosecutor.[27]

In Uganda, the Lords Resistance Army (LRA) had been a disruptive force against successive governments for decades. The context of an independent referral enabled for the government threats of ICC prosecution to bring LRA leaders into peace talks which they had up until then resisted. A condition of that participation by the LRA was the recusal from the government of potential ICC prosecution for the main participants. The Ugandan government stood to gain very secular benefits from any impending ICC intervention and its capacity as a negotiation chip, especially if that government could ensure that the ICC would prosecute only the LRA and on the government's say-so. Determined in this manner, international

25 Bocchese, Marco, "Odd Friends: Rethinking the Relationship Between the ICC and State Sovereignty," *New York University Journal of International Law and Politics*, 49 2, 2017, pp. 339–387.

26 Burke-White, William, "Complementarity in Practice: The International Criminal Court as Part of a System of Multi-level Global Governance in the Democratic Republic of Congo," *Leiden Journal of International Law*, 18 3, 2005, pp. 557–590.

27 Imoedemhe, 2017; Du Plessis, 2008, 2010.

criminalisation is an excellent strategy for states wishing to manipulate external pressure from bodies such as the ICC, and thereby delegitimate political or military opposition. Given the apparently functioning status of Uganda's judiciary at that time and the fact that Uganda was admittedly calling in the ICC only to assist in the LRA's capture, questions have been raised over whether, by accepting the case, the ICC had subsumed judicial responsibilities that Uganda could and should have fulfilled itself, but wished to pass over for reasons of political self-interest rather than domestic prosecutorial capacity. Uganda was not *unable* to prosecute certain LRA commanders, beyond its inability to apprehend them; and it was not *unwilling*, except that it preferred the ICC's intervention to more effectively legitimate the conditions of peace talks, as well as the provisions of the Amnesty Act.[28] In accepting such referrals, the ICC risked exposing itself to political manipulation by anti-democratic regimes, a charge now leveled against it from within African member states suspecting the influence of Western hegemony over ICC prosecutorial discretionary interpretations.[29]

On another front, the ICC investigations and eventual prosecutions of Kenyan political leaders highlight how complementarity is widely affected by changes in political sympathies and systems experiencing procedurally degenerating rule of law institutional environments. It might be said that Kenya signed the ICC ratification documents due to pressure from human rights groups, with politicians comforted at the time by the unlikelihood of the ICC prosecuting its leaders measured against nation-state judicial capacity per complementarity. For many decades Kenya had been the model of constitutional legality in central and southern Africa,[30] and local leaders at that time remained confident that if international criminal prosecutions were mooted they would be able to substantiate nation-state aptitude to prosecute.

When Kenya signed and ratified the Rome Statute, the ICC was still in its infancy. Although the Rome Statute was approved in July 1998, the treaty did not become binding until July 2002, following the ratification by 60 member states earlier that year. The ICC elected its first judges in 2003 and did not undertake any investigations until 2004. This followed the self-referrals to the ICC by Uganda and the Democratic Republic of the Congo in 2003 and 2004 respectively (discussed above). The court issued no arrest warrants until July 2005, when it moved against the leader of the Lord's Resistance Army (LRA), and the first pre-trial court hearing did not take place until 2006. The political authority in Kenya seemed easily distinguishable from these guerrilla leaders being prosecuted by the court. The ICC only achieved its first successful prosecution in 2012, that of Thomas Lubanga, a Congolese warlord.

Kenya's signing of the ICC treaty had no effect until it was ratified in 2005. The Rome Statute could not be applied retroactively to times before ratification.

28 Du Plessis, 2010.

29 Ibid.

30 Brennan, James R., "Lowering the Sultan's Flag: Sovereignty and Decolonization in Coastal Kenya," *Comparative Studies in Society and History*, 50 4, 2008, pp. 831–861.

Hence there was then no local political apprehension in Kenya that the ICC would prosecute President Moi and his supporters for instigating the violent tribal clashes during the 1992 and 1997 elections.

However, as a consequence of power struggles the Kenyan political hierarchy changed between 2010 and 2013. On 15 December 2010, in a surprise move, the then Chief Prosecutor of the ICC, Moreno Ocampo, named defendants in Kenya's political elite against whom he sought to have charges confirmed. Despite the ICC's insistence that it was not targeting communities or Kenyan governance, but only the six individuals indicted, the Kenyan state saw things differently. Most of those charged were high-level political figures close to President Kibaki. A few days after the ICC indictments were announced, members of the Kenyan Parliament passed a motion to withdraw from the ICC; while the President declined to sign it into law and even if he had, it would not have come into effect for a year following, the motion revealed the intention of local political power to resist the ICC's intent. Substantiating the indictments, the ICC alleged that meetings organising violence in retaliation for political unrest took place at Presidential State House, something human rights groups had claimed much earlier. As late as April 2012, President Kibaki said he was still considering options to try the ICC suspects locally, thereby questioning the need for an independent ICC prosecution, but not revealing the reasons behind Kenya's apparent prevarication.

Between 2011 and 2012, Kilonzo Musyoka, Kenya's vice president, engaged in shuttle diplomacy to numerous African countries as well as to the African Union (AU) and UN. He wanted their support for a deferral of the ICC's investigation so that Kenya could try its cases in its own courts, an option it had previously rejected. In January 2011, the AU said it would back Kenya's attempts to defer investigations. The UNSC demurred, instead advising Kenya to initiate any challenges through Article 19 of the Rome Statute on admissibility and jurisdiction. This sudden desire to activate domestic jurisdiction where the necessary ingredients of political will and objectivity could be said to be lacking, also unsettled human rights defenders and victims, who protested the Kenyan response.[31]

Other attempts to return the cases to Kenya followed, as the defendants' political vulnerability increased when charges were confirmed against four of the six suspects in January 2012. In April of that year, the East African Legislative Assembly asked that the cases be transferred to the East African Court of Justice (EACJ), followed by a request from the East African Community's Summit that the EACJ's mandate be extended to include crimes against humanity. Kenyan human rights lawyers denounced both initiatives. Nevertheless, attempts to get the cases back to the region continued, particularly after Annex D of the confirmation charges was

31 Oidtmann, Raphael, "The Responsibility to Protect and The International Criminal Court—Protection and Prosecution in Kenya," *Cambridge Review of International Affairs*, 29 4, 2016, pp. 1651–1653; Manson, Katrina, "ICC Rules Kenyatta Can Miss Part of Trial," FT.com, 18 October 2013; Abass, Ademola, "Prosecuting International Crimes in Africa: Rationale, Prospects and Challenges," *European Journal of International Law*, 24 3, 2013, pp. 933–946.

reclassified as public in September 2012, and revised ICC documents containing the charges (DCC) were released in January 2013. Both documentary pathways named the accused, something the defendants preferred to remain undisclosed prior to trial. As late as October 2012, Kenya's Attorney General Githu Muigai still insisted that the EACJ could be used to try the ICC cases while also making anti-ICC statements in a conference on the ICC in Nuremberg.

Kenya's UN Ambassador and Deputy Ambassador castigated the ICC at the General Assembly demanding that the cases be referred back to Kenya. The AU, including 34 ICC member states, followed with a near unanimous resolution for an African pull-out from the ICC. In mid-August 2013, an AU delegation went to The Hague, asking the ICC to refer the cases back to Kenya, but was politely rebuffed. A month later, following a visit by Kenya's Foreign Minister, the AU convened a special summit to discuss a possible mass defection from the ICC by African member states.

The ICC continued its investigations in the face of Kenyan national and African regional resistance. The political interests behind this resistance were clear but no less damaging to the legitimacy of an independent prosecution where powerful member states claimed jurisdictional priority under complementarity, no matter how specious might be the various assertions. For the ICC prosecutors, successfully completing a case in the face of such vigorous resistance, and therefrom effectively prosecuting cases to conviction, was an insurmountable challenge.

The Kenyan example shows the powerful impact of political forces in the ICC's struggle for legitimacy and, where there is an absence of nation-state cooperation, demonstrates severe problems for the workability of complementarity at the international level when independent prosecution is the preferred jurisdictional route. Political self-interest became a very useful umbrella under which to congregate regional support to further undermine the independent jurisdiction of the ICC which has always been seen by its proponents as the failsafe against the political foundations of prioritising national jurisdiction.

Kenyan resistance leads on predictably to the current crisis faced by the ICC associated with South Africa, Burundi and Gambia leaving the court over allegations of bias and the undermining of African sovereignty.[32] In 2016 a mass exodus of African member states was discussed during the African Union Summit.[33] Interestingly, Burundi triggered the ICC departures when lawmakers in October 2016 overwhelmingly voted to leave membership, just months after the court announced it would investigate recent political violence there, implicating a serving head of state.[34]

32 "African Union Backs Mass Withdrawal From ICC," BBC News, 2017. Link: http://www.bbc.com/news/world-africa-38826073.

33 "Democratic Republic of Congo – Situation in the Democratic Republic of the Congo," International Criminal Court. Link: https://www.icc-cpi.int/drc.

34 Anna, Cara, "Why African States Have Started Leaving the ICC," *The Jakarta Post*, 2016. Link: http://www.thejakartapost.com/news/2016/10/21/ap-explains-why-african-states-have-started-leaving-the-icc-.html.

The ease with which nation-state political self-interest can fundamentally undermine, via challenges of jurisdiction, the essential legitimacy of the ICC through intimidation and boycott reveals the dangers inherent in the complementarity compromise. The establishing of jurisdiction has become a flashpoint for deeper concerns about the viability of ICC investigations and prosecutions in the face of recalcitrant state resistance. Externally, hegemonic states can defeat ICJ simply through exercising unchallenged capacity or, if worst came to worst, through UNSC deferral.[35] Now less capable and more fragmented states align, defeating ICC capacity to investigate and mount a case to answer. Both levels of political interference, using the device of complementarity, and attacks against what is said to be the ICC's improper application of jurisdiction, are set to challenge the sustainability of ICC-based ICJ.

The case-studies outlined above reveal the ICC in a double-bind. First, the court's legitimacy is undermined either by it being used for domestic political imperatives, or on the other hand being criticised for hegemonic political influences determining the exercise of its prosecutorial discretion. The second and more pragmatic concern is the ICC's inability to effectively investigate and then prosecute unless with the cooperation, or at least not the resistance, of the member state concerned. Even though Kenya refused ICC jurisdiction, the court went ahead to prosecute senior Kenyan officials and failed at early procedural stages. This problematic and undermining outcome for the prosecutor revealed that the ICC values its independence above operational inevitabilities where its case is weakened by the machinations of a state in which the accused has power. Despite what appears to be a celebration of the court's jurisdiction above the parochial interests of state politics, in a practical sense the failure of prosecution at the first hurdles before trial, substantiates the overriding supremacy of the nation-state to subvert the power of independent prosecution. Far from being an aberration, as the case-studies detail, at the national and regional level member states can impede ICC jurisdiction, meant to be the counterbalance of accountability instituted in the principle of complementarity.

Complementarity, injustice and ways forward

In the plenary debates which led to the drafting of the Rome Statute the issue of the ultimate punishment was hotly contested. The lobby opposed to the death penalty carried the day.[36] In stark relief a possible jurisdictional contradiction

35 Bohlen, Rachel, "Questioning Authority: A Case for the International Criminal Court's Prosecution of the Current Sudanese President, Omar Al-Bashir," *George Washington International Law Review*, 42 3, 2010, pp. 687–712; Bederman, David, "International Criminal Court – Appeals Chamber – Rome Statute – Article 17 – Complementarity – Article 19 – Challenges to Jurisdiction or Admissibility of a Case – Kenya," *A.J.I.L.*, 106, 2012, pp. 118–909.

36 Horovitz, Sigall, "International Criminal Courts in Action: The ICTR's Effect on Death Penalty and Reconciliation in Rwanda," *George Washington International Law Review*, 48 3, 2016, pp. 505–547; Benedetti, Fanny, Bonneau, Karine, and Washburn, John, *Negotiating the International Criminal Court New York to Rome, 1994–1998*, BRILL: Leiden, 2013.

over sentencing is implicit: if an accused is tried for genocide and convicted in a nation-state with capital punishment he may be executed. Not so if the same crime were to be determined in the ICC. While complementary sentencing outcomes are not essential to ensure some commonality between national and international criminal justice, a richer appreciation of complementarity would see nation-states respecting and embracing the central justice principles set out in Chapter 1, when assuming jurisdictional complementarity and prosecuting global crime. The Preamble accepts the primacy of the nation-state while at the same time invoking a clear and common agenda for justice to be propagated through domestic prosecution.

There is nothing to say that the proof of global crimes at a nation-state level will be the same as that required by international courts and tribunals. Because of state ratification processes, the crimes charged for the same conduct might differ and certainly the approaches to secondary liability and participation can vary. Associated with this line of argument is the speculation that ICJ cannot be universalised when the jurisprudence of the national court and of the international courts can so diverge. If this is the case, could there evolve a possibility where double jeopardy protections become compromised? In each of these speculations resides the criticism that complementarity challenges rather than makes more viable the development of a principled and logical international criminal jurisprudence.

In the same vein as we would reconsider hybridity, a new but not unnatural approach to complementarity may promote rather than precaution the novel international criminal jurisprudence which the remainder of the book enlivens. In its current understanding complementarity plays two roles, one distinctly political (even though consistent with international law underpinnings) and one substantive:

- to give pre-eminence to nation-state jurisdictions where they are capable and willing to prosecute global crime,[37] and
- to recognise the independence of the international criminal jurisdiction (in certain circumstances) employing where appropriate the principles and practices of nation-state criminal justice traditions.[38]

With the ICC prosecutor having independent jurisdiction after and even beyond some lapse in nation-state jurisdiction then it seems illogical to require the exercise of that independent jurisdiction to mirror in all appropriate respects how the investigation and prosecution would have proceeded if the nation-state was the initiator. In practice, the ICC prosecutor employs investigation and prosecution techniques and procedures that are often quite distinct from those which might

37 Ellis, Mark, "International Justice and the Rule of Law: Strengthening the ICC through Domestic Prosecutions," *Hague Journal on the Rule of Law*, 1 1, 2009 pp. 79–86.

38 Simmons, Beth, and Danner, Allison, "Credible Commitments and the International Criminal Court," *International Organization*, 64 2, 2010, pp. 225–256.

be employed in domestic traditions.[39] So complementarity between the exercise of the prosecutor's independent power and the initiation of the nation-state can currently take the form of jurisdictional allocation rather than substantive and procedural transference of one to the other. Once the independent investigation power is invoked we believe that the prosecutor is not bound in any way to the jurisdictional peculiarities of the nation-state.

With this understanding settled it is interesting to propose another interpretation of 'complementarity' not focused on jurisdiction or allocation. Directing our attention to the nature of investigating the unique features of global crime, understanding the limitations on the office of the prosecutor, it is timely that the risky evidentiary reliances which feature in the evolution of the prosecution case are minimised as much as possible by the infra-structure of proof requirements which more practically reflect the contexts in which global crimes are perpetrated and victims harmed.

An example may be helpful here. If the prosecutor was not required to prove an accused knew that a particular crime would be committed as a natural consequence of an actual agreement, but rather that it was enough to show the suspect had sufficiently contributed to the preliminaries of crime which was then caused by the removed actions of others, the prosecutor's burden would be fairly relieved.[40] The only way that this outcome could eventuate is if the prosecutor, as is currently the practice, feels compelled to distort the proof technologies of domestic criminal law as they translate through international criminal law,[41] or argue for a new approach.[42] Complementarity between the traditions of domestic criminal justice where the proof challenges such as causation and contribution are comparable, like tort and crime, is an alternative we prefer. But how can a tort/crime cross-fertilisation occur and the spirit of harmonisation be retained? We offer the answer.

If harmonisation is to be ascribed to then the domestic development of criminal law and procedure should suggest the potential and extent of cross-fertilisation from other legal disciplines. As we intend to show in Chapter 6 with recent trends in criminalising deviant organisations and corporate responsibility, several common law jurisdictions have taken bold steps in transferring proof technologies from tort, corporate and even broader regulatory environments. It is particularly through compatible tort proofs that we see the possibility of complementarity advancing a new and more robust international criminal jurisprudence. If such alternative borrowings from nation-state criminal justice traditions is stimulated

39 Saber and Sadeghi, 2015; Defrancia, Cristian, "Due Process in International Criminal Courts: Why Procedure Matters," *Virginia Law Review*, 87 7, 2001, pp. 1381–1439; Stahn, Carsten, El Zeidy, Mohamed M., and Olásolo, Héctor, "The International Criminal Court's Ad Hoc Jurisdiction Revisited," *The American Journal of International Law*, 99 2, 2005, pp. 421–431.

40 Stahn et al., 2005.

41 Ibid.

42 Ibid.

by the proof necessities of changing crime forms, we see this as an invitation (in the spirit of harmonisation) to take a similar direction in ICL because of the unique challenges in proving global crime (see Chapter 4).

Complementarity of jurisdiction is shaped around a mechanical tension which leads to the allocation of jurisdiction. Even so, because the independent power of the prosecutor to claim jurisdiction is never forfeited by an earlier or alternate allocation to the nation-state, this can lead to various comparative instances of incompatibility in the investigation and trial process. The possibility that complementarity results in jurisdictional clashes and procedural/substantive incompatibilities rather than their rational resolution, means comparative injustice may be the consequence. Such challenges to universal justice are not overcome through a preference for international jurisdiction, because of the unsatisfactory application of national law and procedure within the international jurisdiction thwarting international prosecutorial success, or necessitating the transaction of procedure in illogical and unprincipled ways, so as to achieve it. With this in mind:

- complementarity should be understood as a process of universalising justice principles at play, however jurisdictional disputes are settled, and
- in the spirit of harmonisation, ICL should seek out the advantages of proof hybrids when deliberating on unique global crimes, in similar fashion to how nation-states have been tailoring novel proof technologies to address the crimes of corporations and organisations.

Harmonisation, hybridity and individualism

We intend to spend little or no time challenging harmonisation as a practical paradigm for the development of international criminal law. Its strongest proponents would concede that you cannot expect interpretational uniformity even within criminal justice traditions over time, let alone across traditions that have developed to facilitate different contexts of criminal liability, diverse interpretations of criminal justice and especially politically dependent utilities for criminalisation and punishment.[43] As with the more realistic concession of hybridity the actuality of both approaches in a case-by-case decision-making methodology, scarcely assisted by rich precedent, exposes personal preferencing playing an important role in what 'law' prevails, as might any vain search for the 'better' law.

43 Horder, Jeremy, *Homicide Law in Comparative Perspective*, London, GB: Bloomsbury Publishing Plc, 2007; Billing, Fenella, *Right to Silence in Transnational Criminal Proceedings: Comparative Law Perspectives*, Berlin: Springer International Publishing, 2016; Dubber, Markus, "Criminal Jurisdiction and Conceptions of Penalty in Comparative Perspective," *University of Toronto Law Journal*, 63 2, 2013, pp. 247–277; Mitsilegas, Valsamis, *Globalisation, Criminal Law and Criminal Justice: Theoretical, Comparative and Transnational Perspectives*, Hart Publishing, Oxford, 2015.

That said, there is a more obvious and as such terminal reason why both harmonisation and hybridity are distracting jurisprudential methodologies. Chapter 1 revealed in detail that international criminal justice, which in the trial location as rehearsed in the Preamble, should be the intention of international criminal law, is radically different from the aspirations of any national criminal justice traditions. Aligned with this realisation is our earlier allegation that the functional role of the juridical professional (judge and prosecutor) in the international criminal trial is unlike that of their counterparts even in more inquisitorial traditions, and indeed is more like one might find in courts hearing a tort claim. Under the Rome Statute, the determination of individual responsibility contemplates more than liability for the offense as revealed through conduct and mental state. Beyond these important considerations are the evaluations of harm caused to victims, and to the accused's operational as well as rational blameworthiness for breaking the law and harming humanity.

In the face of such incompatibilities, why persevere in believing that ICL will organically or even mechanically (or magically) emerge through harmonisation or hybridity? If the proof is in the pudding as the saying goes, then the jurisprudential result of persisting with such methodologies is abstractions and abdications of principle, particularly with the determination of secondary liability and participation (Chapter 3).

The following are reasons for the continued ascription to hybridity and harmonisation, despite their abject inadequacies as jurisprudential methodologies; the final reason will be addressed more closely in this section:

- a literalist interpretation of the proscriptions contained in the foundational statutes of the international criminal courts and tribunals (and their rules and procedures);
- a pragmatic practice which strays as far from state-based principles and practice as any appearance of subscription will allow;[44] and
- the misunderstanding that the determination of individual responsibility at the international level mirrors the determination of criminal liability in domestic jurisdictions.

Elaborating on the first two points can await the detailed exposition in Chapters 3 and 5. For the present purposes, misconceptions about individuality are enough to suggest why harmonisation and hybridity have either not been rejected or, as we prefer, been reinterpreted to the advancement of a more principled and logical international criminal jurisprudence.

The core of this misunderstanding and consequent analytical misdirection as we see it is a question of wrong focus. Prior to international criminal justice in its current era, public international law had always been a conversation

44 To some extent the international criminal courts and tribunals have been offered these approaches by the manner in which many domestic criminal court decisions have diluted the necessities of subjectivity in order to achieve policy goals of punishment where punishment otherwise seemed due.

between nation-states. The excitement which attended the repositioning of ICJ in part away from the responsibility of states to that of their individual citizens has meant that the attention on the individual rather than on the determination of their *responsibility* has suggested a better-than-actual fit between the concerns of domestic and international criminal prosecutions. Shifting away from the individual to unpacking the differences between liability and responsibility is, we assert, much more instructive as a core critique of hybridisation, in particular. And in any event, what is meant by the individual in the global criminal context more likely reveals a metaphor for individuals in consort and criminal conduct as historically emergent and continuing.[45]

In Chapter 1 and developed in Chapter 6 is the construction of responsibility in the Rome Statute as a bridge between tort and crime. Accepting this for the sake of argument, there is opening up a new role for harmonisation and hybridity, not restricted to some strained re-composition of domestic criminal law and procedural traditions, but a more holistic augmentation of crime and tort reasoning which benefits from various domestic jurisdictions historically at different stages of synthesis between the two fields of legal determination.[46] Viewed in this way hybridity in particular has a new dimension: ***between legal fields and across traditions.***

Our critics will butt in that nowhere in the legislative instruments of the international criminal courts and tribunals is such an interpretation invited. There they are wrong. Constantly throughout the Preamble the reader is recalled to the consideration of damage, harm and restitution – and not as some concessional afterthought to liability, which nation-state criminal compensation schemes might represent. Read the prosecution submissions and the judicial reasoning in international criminal courts and reference to harm and its restitution are recurrent.

Chapter 4 elaborates that the elements of global crime recount mass harm as much as they do individual blameworthiness. The spectacular imagining of atrocity is not of one bad person hurting one hapless other. It is of sinister associations perpetrating through war, genocide, aggression and the destruction of humanity, and massive tortious damage in terms of risks and outcomes. Indeed, the end to impunity is an end to a failure in calling to account those who harm others, not simply those who break the law.

45 Lehnardt, Chia, "Individual Liability of Private Military Personnel under International Criminal Law," *European Journal of International Law*, 19 5, 2008, pp. 1015–1034; Beck, Susanne, "Intelligent Agents and Criminal Law—Negligence, Diffusion of Liability and Electronic Personhood," *Robotics and Autonomous Systems*, 86, 2016, pp. 138–143; Kucher, Olena, and Petrenko, Aleksey, "International Criminal Responsibility After Katanga: Old Challenges, New Solutions," *Russian Law Journal*, 3 1, 2015, pp. 143–168; Mireille, Hector, "Enhancing Individual Criminal Responsibility For Offences Involving Cultural Property – The Road to the Rome Statute and the 1999 Second Protocol," in Nout van Woudenberg and Liesbeth Lijnzaad (eds), *Protecting Cultural Property in Armed Conflict*, BRILL: Leiden, 2010, pp. 69–76; Jackson, Miles, "Individual Criminal Responsibility," in Miles Jackson, *Complicity in International Law*, Oxford University Press: Oxford, 2015, Chapter 3.

46 Dyson, Matthew, "Connecting Tort and Crime: Comparative Legal History in England and Spain since 1850," *Cambridge Yearbook of European Legal Studies*, 11, 2009, pp. 247–288.

Following this line of argument, we can complement a policy theme central to this writing exercise: ***making international criminal justice work***. It is a somewhat pedantic pleasure to expose harmonisation and hybridity as at worst frauds and at best ineffectual. More valuable is the reconsideration of how these methods can be applied anew in order to make their methodological purchase effective for those who have to employ them in courtroom practice. In addition, under their aegis the following analysis advances ***a crime/tort proof hybrid without requiring any new law to give it application.***

Complementarity has an implicit capacity to derail our hybridisation adventure. A literalist interpretation of complementarity might hold that it is only possible to conceive levels of international criminal jurisdiction within a national criminal law tradition. Hopefully in the chapters to follow we will show how that is not necessarily so, and even if it were, hybridity across legal disciplines is already a feature of dynamic domestic criminal proof technologies.

Conclusion

As the critique develops and the case for the tort/crime hybrid unfolds it becomes clear that we are inviting new and positive approaches to hybridity and to complementarity. Harmonisation or hybridity cannot be limited to a one-size-fits-all criminal law tradition. Complementarity must be more creative than slotting in who-tries-what. As the analysis will show in Chapters 3, 5 and 6, many criminal justice traditions, historically and concurrently are much closer to the proof determinations of tort law. The explosion of interest in negligence as a 'mental state' in otherwise subjective liability traditions makes this irrefutable.[47] One doesn't need to primarily rely on Continental civil law where the tort/crime division is blurred[48] to advance the possibility of the tort/crime proof model. In fact, the focus on individualised mental state is a recent criminal law predisposition, now clearly in retreat. The days in common law where a man was presumed to intend the natural consequences of his act were aligned with a tortious focus on the negligent violation of duties determined against the mind of the ordinary neighbor.

In talking this through we should not be tarred with diminishing the subjective importance of liability, or as advancing a case for marginalising the realistic demands on the prosecution to prove their case. The argument is advanced in the context where subjective proofs are being perverted because of the need to establish illusive knowledge, illusory agreement and total liability for each and all offenders. This attitude in judicial thinking is returning with the consideration

47 Stark, Findlay, *Culpable Carelessness: Recklessness and Negligence in the Criminal Law*, Cambridge University Press: Cambridge, 2016; Alexander, Larry, and Ferzan, Kimberly, *Crime and Culpability A Theory of Criminal Law*, Cambridge University Press: Cambridge, 2009.

48 Sigler, Mary, "The Boundaries of the Criminal Law. By R. A. Duff, Lindsay Farmer, S. E. Marshall, Massimo Renzo and Victor Tadros," *British Journal of Criminology*, 52 3, 2012, pp. 676–678; Dyson, 2009.

of an accused appreciating the natural and foreseeable consequences of a common purpose (discussed more in Chapter 3). This is the language of tortious liability.

In its most expansive sense this chapter could be seen as an argument against the residual autonomy-based influences of public international law over international criminal justice. And in part it is. The drafters of the Rome Statute, through political necessity, created a near-impossible tension in the context of the harmonisation/hybridity methodology, wrapped up in complementarity as a mechanism for resolving contests over jurisdiction. This tension has fed back into the more pragmatic decision-making aversion against any brave and convincing assertion of the unique requirements of international criminal justice. But there is no value in revisionist history for a reformist project. Nor will the analysis of our more constructive themes proceed beyond the frustrations of this chapter without liquid thinking, thinking that Chapter 1 demands.

3 The mystery of individualism

Introduction

So far the analysis has set out an understanding of justice as it is, and how it should be delivered through international criminal justice processes and institutions. In so doing we have exposed the tensions assumed to exist in the *peace and justice* duality[1] and suggested ways in which these can be reconciled in order to produce a justice regime which accommodates the unique perpetration and victimisation of global crimes (as expressed in Chapter 1).

In Chapter 2 the doctrine of complementarity and the associated development of ICL through harmonisation are critiqued to reveal the inherent dangers in assuming, at one level, a seamless transition of justice paradigms from national to international traditions. In fact, the analysis projects injustice as the result of competition between jurisdictions and traditions. The chapter concludes by substantiating the Chapter 1 contention that the version of individual responsibility prevailing at the international level, as demonstrated through decades of tortuous judicial reasoning, jurisdictional contest and procedural compromise, is distinctly different than the aspiration for criminal justice through individual liability in the domestic setting.

This chapter is paired with Chapter 5 in order to provide the empirical foundation for the following assertions that:

- the unique nature of global crimes means that the proof of criminal conduct and mental state will not follow the conventional proofs employed in many national criminal justice traditions;
- the collective nature of perpetration and victimisation have required the construction of prosecution proofs and their interpretations so as to distort some already problematic domestic interpretations of individual proof in collective settings;

1 Mendes, Errol, *Peace and Justice at the International Criminal Court: A Court of Last Resort*, Edward Elgar Publishing: Cheltenham, 2010; Prorok, Alyssa K., "The (In)compatibility of Peace and Justice? The International Criminal Court and Civil Conflict Termination," *International Organization*, 71 2, 2017, pp. 213–243.

- international criminal juridical professionals (judges in particular) are motivated by concerns regarding the enormity of the crimes before them and the need to end impunity, so that they are more flexibly disposed to expansive interpretations of proof requirements;
- this confluence is creating an international criminal justice jurisprudence which seems sporadic, often unpredictable, and open to intellectual challenge; and against this background,
- there can be a more rigorous and principled international criminal jurisprudence that respects the invocation for individual responsibility, but interprets its proof through a tortious lens. Such sharing is not unknown in nation state proof developments (see Chapter 6) and better addresses the unique proof demands of global crime (see Chapter 4).

It might be suggested that the hurdle in this path is individualisation, manifesting subjectivity and totality of punishment. By this we mean if the focus of responsibility is on one perpetrator who is said to embody the criminal mind and conduct constituting global crime (which are at best legal fictions of proof modeling), then they should suffer the full and absolute force of the sanction. Again this is a completely unrealistic consideration of how global crime should be reduced to responsibility.

Article 25 of the Rome Statute requires:

1 The Court shall have jurisdiction over natural persons pursuant to this Statute.
2 A person who commits a crime within the jurisdiction of the Court shall be individually responsible and liable for punishment in accordance with this Statute.
3 In accordance with this Statute, a person shall be criminally responsible and liable for punishment for a crime within the jurisdiction of the Court if that person:

    a Commits such a crime, whether as an individual, jointly with another or through another person, regardless of whether that other person is criminally responsible;
    b Orders, solicits or induces the commission of such a crime which in fact occurs or is attempted;
    c For the purpose of facilitating the commission of such a crime, aids, abets or otherwise assists in its commission or its attempted commission, including providing the means for its commission;
    d In any other way contributes to the commission or attempted commission of such crime by a group of persons acting with a common purpose. Such contribution shall be intentional and shall either:

        i Be made with the aim of furthering the criminal activity or criminal purpose of the group, where such activity or purpose involves the commission of a crime within the jurisdiction of the Court; or
        ii Be made in the knowledge of the intention of the group to commit the crime.

There is little in this article which assists in understanding how, employing domestic proofs of liability designed for individual offenders and victims, in establishing crimes replete with collective perpetration and victimisation, liability and responsibility can be comfortably conflated in any complementary frame. That said, the article does offer for consideration the technologies of proof which form the empirical focus of this chapter and those which follow. The present chapter looks at joint criminal enterprise (JCE), aiding and abetting, and Chapter 6 (along with new trends in criminalising association) speculates on novel considerations of corporate liability (all envisaged in the Rome Statute) to chart how the associated proof conundrums have been further emasculated in ICC narrative so that collectivity might be re-interpreted as individual responsibility.[2] Following on from this, each of these proof paradigms is assisted and we say made more principled and rational through the application of well-established tortious proof technologies that align with similar proof demands in crime (such as causation). The chapter concludes by inviting, as we attempt in Chapter 5, the development of a new jurisprudence depending on proof technologies[3] which recognise the utility of association, aggregation, contribution, collectivity and criminal culture.

The interrogation of proof limitations commences with a focus on joint criminal enterprise (JCE). Current inadequate proof technologies and the judicial gymnastics they have spawned provide the referent for our argument in favor of an alternative but, we argue, both rational and permissible hybridisation frame, still respecting harmonisation.

JCE at the national and international level

JCE under national law (common law position)

In drawing as they might through the interpretational processes of hybridity and holism which are advocated in the development of international criminal law, the international criminal courts and tribunals have considered the following forms of joint liability under common law:

i D and P participate in the crime X and each contributes to the *actus reus* of the crime X. Both are to be tried as principle offenders and considered in terms of primary liability.

ii D and P share a common intention to commit crime X, wherein D aids, abets, counsels or procures P to commit the *actus reus*. Both are liable for the crime.

2 Werle, Gerhard, "Individual Criminal Responsibility in Article 25 ICC Statute," *Journal of International Criminal Justice*, 5 4, 2007, pp. 953–975; Ndahinda Mukwiza, F., "The Bemba-Banyamulenge Case before the ICC: From Individual to Collective Criminal Responsibility," *International Journal of Transitional Justice*, 7 3, 2013, pp. 476–496.

3 Throughout this analysis we use the concept of *proof technologies* to indicate not simply the legal constituents of proof but the mechanisms by which they are employed, as well as the processes of modification and development.

iii D and P participate in the crime X and each contributes to the *actus reus* of the crime X. During the commission of the crime, P commits another crime Y (secondary crime). D is jointly liable for crime Y if he foresaw as a possibility that P probably had the relevant *mens rea* to commit offense Y generally in the manner in which it is perpetrated by P (secondary liability).[4]

For the purposes of exploring the tensions associated with establishing individualised responsibility in contexts of collective perpetration where knowledge and agreement may be far from actual, the focus of our analysis will be on the third form of JCE. As in general with cases of secondary liability in domestic jurisdictions, the accused in a JCE allegation does not specifically intend the commission of the crime in question nor does he perform the *actus reus* of the crime in a complete, singular or total sense. In reality the accused, if convicted through JCE, are treated as if they committed the criminal conduct with sufficient knowledge and purpose thereby being individually liable as might be the perpetrator or any other participant in the enterprise. Knowledge and agreement that conventionally demonstrate sufficient purpose must be, to some degree, subjectively determined. On this basis, the contention that each participant can be punished in a similar fashion further argues that each is individually liable, even though in reality the crime could not be completed without the process of some collective endeavor connecting various aspects of involvement. The accused's criminal liability is contingent on his *foresight* of the secondary crime, which to differing degrees of subjective proof is contended as a consequence of adequate knowledge regarding, and agreement about, the consequent crime being effected. To be jointly liable for the secondary crime, the accused must have *subjectively* foreseen a real risk in the commission of the crime in question (consequential crime).

In determining whether the accused had foresight of the secondary or consequential crime, the courts in the national jurisdictions[5] have historically looked at the following factors: (i) the character and conduct of the perpetrator leading up to the commissioning of the secondary crime, (ii) the nature of the primary crime and (iii) spontaneous behaviors.[6]

Case law suggests that specific knowledge of the accused as to the background of the principal perpetrator would go towards showing that a particular act on the latter's part was foreseen by the accused. For instance, if the principal perpetrator had a known propensity for unpredictable violence, then it could be said that the JCE accused could not successfully deny that he did not foresee the consequential crime occurring. Even in these circumstances, the requirement

4 Ormerod, David, *Smith and Hogan's Criminal Law*, 13th edition, Oxford University Press: Oxford, 2011; Simester, Andrew, Spencer, John, Stark, Findlay, Sullivan, Robert, and Virgo, Graham, *Simester and Sullivan's Criminal Law*, Bloomsbury Publishing: Oxford, 2016, p. 245.

5 When we talk of *national jurisdictions* unless otherwise indicated we are referring to common law traditions.

6 *Yemoh & Ors v R.* [2009] EWCA Crim 930; *R v Powell & English* [1999] 1 AC 290; *R v Rahman and Others (Appellants)*, [2008] UKHL 45; *R v Mendez and another* [2010] 3 All ER 231; *R v Becerra and Cooper* (1975) 62 Cr App R 212.

that the further one is removed from principal perpetration, the more subjective and actual should be their foresight, remains a traditional proof requirement.[7] Consider this example:[8]

> P and S agree to commit a burglary. Together they break into V's home. In the course of the burglary, P is challenged by V whom he attacks and injures. S does not participate physically in the assault. However, S knew that P has a propensity towards violence and realised that P might well assault the occupier of the house were they to be confronted.

In such a situation, S is jointly liable for the injuries that P inflicted on V as his knowledge of P's background (violent tendencies) meant that foresight of the injuries cannot be imputed, but equally cannot be successfully denied.

Another significant circumstantial proof which should apply to the determination of sufficient foresight on behalf of the accused, is whether the secondary crime was *fundamentally different* from the primary crime. The logic goes that for obvious reasons, a crime which is fundamentally different from that contemplated by the members of the JCE would not be foreseen by the accused participants beyond the perpetrator, or even be foreseeable by the reasonable person in the circumstances. Whether the secondary crime was fundamentally different from the primary crime is a question of fact.[9] The case law suggests a secondary crime will be considered fundamentally different when the primary and secondary crimes do not relate to each other – in other words, the commission of the primary crime does not lead to or necessitate the commission of the secondary crime. There must be some change in weapon, action and intention on the part of the perpetrator of the secondary crime.[10] Radical or sudden acts done on part of the sole perpetrator would tend to show that the two crimes were fundamentally different. In this respect *difference* is really measured through *discontinuity*. For example, in the case of *R v Powell & English*,[11] D had joined P in an attack on a police officer using wooden posts, but during the course of the attack P produced a knife and stabbed the officer fatally. The House of Lords in favor of the defense held that the unforeseen use of the knife would take the killing outside the scope of the joint venture.[12] In *R v Rahman and Others (Appellants)* the court observed:[13]

7 Krebs, Beatrice, "Joint Criminal Enterprise," *Modern Law Review*, 73 4, 2010, pp. 578–604; Bećirević, Edina, *Joint Criminal Enterprise*, Yale University Press: New Haven, 2014; Farhang, Cliff, "Point of No Return: Joint Criminal Enterprise in Brđanin," *Leiden Journal of International Law*, 23 1, 2010, pp. 137–164.

8 Simester et al., 2016, p. 245.

9 *Yemoh*, para [140].

10 Ormerod, 2011, p. 223.

11 *Powell*, para 2.

12 *Powell*, paras 10B-D, 12A-B, 30B-D.

13 *Rahman*, para [33].

> It can . . . make no difference if A and B agree to kill their victim by beating him to death with baseball bats, but in the course of the attack A pulls out a gun and shoots him. B must still be guilty of murder: since he intended to bring about the death of the victim, B cannot escape guilt on the ground that he did not foresee that A would kill him by using a gun instead of a baseball bat. The unforeseen nature of the weapon is immaterial. If, instead of a baseball bat, in the course of the attack A unforeseeably used an explosive and killed people in addition to the intended victim, then B would still be guilty of the murder of their intended victim . . . but not the murder of anyone else who was killed by the explosive . . . [Further if] . . . Half a dozen youths engage in a fist fight with another group, but one of their number suddenly produces a knife and stabs one of their opponents to death. If the others on his side did not know that he had the knife, then they are not parties to its use and are not guilty of murder or manslaughter.[14]

Another challenge to the establishment of actual foresight in JCE (to be distinguished from objective notions of foreseeability) is in situations of spontaneous behaviors. In the case of *R v Mendez and another*,[15] the victim was attacked by a group of people. He was punched, kicked, hit with pieces of wood and metal and stabbed with a knife. He died shortly afterwards, the cause of death being a stab wound inflicted by a single unidentified person. The two defendants, who the prosecution alleged had been part of the group, were charged with murder. They denied that the stabbing had taken place within the compass of any joint enterprise to which they were parties. The court remarked that on the issue of spontaneous or semi-spontaneous group violence, it is typically fueled by alcohol and as such participants are unlikely to have thought carefully about the exact level of violence and associated injury which they intend to cause, or foresee may be caused.[16] A broad-brush judgment about the sort of level of violence and associated risk of injury that could be intended or foreseen should be made in such circumstances.[17] The case law sees it as a matter of commonsense whether P's unforeseen act (if such it was) was of a nature likely to be altogether more life-threatening than acts such as those which D foresaw or intended.[18]

The above scenario presents a difficulty with JCE crimes in that recognising the lack of a pre-existing established plan between the individuals involved in the crime, each might have their own separate and distinct intentions and motives which are unrelated to each other. This conditional knowledge is exacerbated when there are many perpetrators and more than one victim in the affray.

14 *Davies v Director of Public Prosecutions* [1954] AC 378, 401 per Lord Simonds LC, adopted by the Privy Council in *Chan Wing-Siu v The Queen* [1985] AC 168, 177E-H; *R v Anderson*; *R v Morris* [1966] 2 QB 110, 120B, per Lord Parker CJ.

15 *Mendez*, paras [1]–[9].

16 *Mendez*, para [48].

17 Ibid.

18 Ibid.

Further, a JCE member might be potentially liable for unforeseen consequences arising from spontaneous behaviors if he acknowledges the aforementioned behavior, and does not withdraw from its perpetration, or attempt to stop the commission of the secondary crime, or is complicit in its occurrence. A standard common law case in point is *R v Becerra and Cooper*.[19] There, B had given C a knife to use if anyone disturbed them during the burglary they were carrying out. When B heard someone coming he told C: "Come on, let's go" and left the scene of crime and ran off. C did not follow and instead stabbed the victim. B was held jointly liable as there was no communication of the abandonment of the common purpose, and the instruction "come on, let's go" did not in the court's view suffice as a withdrawal from the joint enterprise. The decision gave special weight to the fact that the handing over of the knife from B to C constituted a circumstance of imminent danger and as such more effective communication to end the joint enterprise was needed.[20] In so reasoning the courts arguably have drifted a little further away from the proof of actual knowledge as the immediate moments preceding the offense could not have been known to the accused. This alternative reasoning suggests a preference for what might be more circumstantial conclusions that could be drawn from what the accused does or does not do at the time, demonstrating an interest in outcome-orientation which verged on some oblique duty of care more common in tort.

Finally, in determining whether the consequential crime was foreseen by the accused, the courts will often look to the conduct of the principal perpetrator leading up to the commission of the eventual crime. The actions of the primary perpetrator must make the commission of the secondary offense a real possibility in the eyes of the JCE accused. Therefore, it would seem a central condition for proof that the conduct relied upon by the courts in establishing foresight on the part of the accused (and comprising a crucial dimension of the criminal conduct) must have been known to him to the extent that they suggested an identifiable risk. A typical scenario would be a case where the common intention between the parties was to rob the victim's home. To this end, when one member of the JCE group brings along a knife, it is understood within the group that the knife would be used to scare the victim into silence. During the commission of the crime, the victim refuses to remain silent and the knife is used to inflict grievous harm on him. The court is likely to hold that the secondary crime was foreseen, as carrying a knife into the victim's home for the purpose of threatening him, produced a real possibility that the knife be used to harm the victim if he did not remain quiet. The case of *R v Rahman and others (Appellants)*[21] involved two gangs in a fight which included the use of blunt instruments. The victim was attacked by the accused and several others but the ultimate cause of death was a deep stab wound. The

19 *R v Becerra and Cooper* (1975) 62 Cr App R 212.

20 *Becerra*, p. 219.

21 *Rahman*, paras [2]–[6].

accused's argument that he was unaware anyone had a knife, and further he had no knowledge that anyone intended to kill the victim, was rejected.[22] The court preferred that the principle perpetrator's intention to kill did not have to be known to the accused or the others in the joint enterprise. In its opinion, the real issue was whether the participants knew there was a real risk of death or grievous harm being caused intentionally.[23] This suggests that there is appearing in the proof authorities another move away from requiring the actual knowledge of the accused in referring back the intention of the primary perpetrator based on the propensity or 'real risk' of the crime occurring in the context of the case.[24]

So in summarising the common law position with proving JCE, the courts require:

- actual knowledge,
- agreement to the enterprise,
- common purpose,
- foreseen consequences and, as an extension from this,
- situations where, due to the circumstances, the consequences were a genuine risk of the enterprise.

JCE under international criminal law

Having canvassed the law on joint criminal liability at the national level of one principle tradition, we now turn to examine JCE in the international jursidiction as a technology of proof for establishing secondary or accessorial liability. In particular, the distortions of *foresight into foreseeability*, and *the liability of non-JCE members* are interrogated. An initial examination of the international criminal case law shows that there have been significant transits from each and all of the subjective proof conventions that exist at the common law national level.

There are three main categories of JCE under international criminal law:[25]

> JCE I: Where the accused shares the common intention of the joint criminal enterprise with the other perpetrators of the alleged crime.
>
> JCE II: Where the participants in the crime are each individually criminally responsible because all of the crimes committed by the group form part of the common intention, provided the participants are aware of the character of the system and if they act with intention to further it.

22 Ashworth, Andrew, *Principles of Criminal Law*, Clarendon Press: Oxford, 1991, p. 423. See also, *Rahman*, para [12].

23 *Rahman*, para [11].

24 Ibid.

25 Stewart, James, "The End of 'Modes of Liability' for International Crimes," *Leiden Journal of International Law*, 25 1, 2012, pp. 165–219.

> JCE III: Where all the participants in the criminal enterprise are each individually criminally responsible for the crimes committed by other members of the criminal enterprise and any falling outside the scope of the common plan if the alleged crimes represent a *natural and foreseeable consequence* of the common plan.

The concept of joint criminal liability for consequential crimes at the national level finds its mirror in the international law form of JCE III crimes. Similar to the common law domestic joint criminal liability approaches where the matter of foresight of consequences is at issue, JCE III crimes must be committed in the execution of the common purpose of the JCE group. The accused must know that a further crime which does not form part of the common purpose but is a natural and foreseeable consequence from it might be perpetrated by a JCE member and willingly takes the risk that the crime could occur.[26] In this extension of actual knowledge, the mental state of the accused is to *willingly participate* in a common purpose where a crime, even if not specifically foreseen, is a natural and foreseeable consequence of the common purpose and as such is invested with proof potential sufficient to replace actual knowledge and foresight. In some domestic jurisdictions, common purpose proofs are satisfied through a natural and foreseeable test but these are limited to situations where it would be difficult for the accused to rebut the assumption of knowledge if the onus were reversed.

However, the JCE III approach at the international level adopts an interpretation of foreseeability that differs from the common law national jurisdictions in two main respects:

> First, the ICC courts have disposed of the traditional need for subjective foresight on the part of the accused of a secondary crime in any initial determination before moving on to natural and foreseeable consequences, a sequence usually required to be exhausted at common law. The pre-requisite subjective foresight test at the national level has instead been replaced by an objective evaluation of the accused's leadership position and the historical as well as statistical association between the occurrence of the secondary crime as connected to the primary crime. In other words, instead of considering whether the accused had possessed subjective foresight of the secondary crimes through evaluating the accused's knowledge of the conduct/character of the primary perpetrator or whether the primary and secondary crimes were *fundamentally different*, the ICC focuses on the broader context in which the primary crime occurred and asserts *that the secondary crime was foreseeable due to the fact that they were often committed together as part of a historical or organisational conclusion*. As such, the courts place greater weight on the collective nature of the conduct in order to determine that its consequences were objectively foreseeable. Further, by focusing on the

26 Goy, Barbara, *International Criminal Responsibility Before the International Criminal Court*, Martinus Nijhoff Publishers: Amsterdam, 2012, pp. 30–31.

historical or statistical association between the primary and secondary crime, the court in substance utilises a determination of risk analysis to conclude on the issue of foreseeability. For convenience, this approach will be referred to as the *risk-analysis* approach towards foreseeability.

Second, unlike the common law national jurisdictions, the ICC prosecutors loosely frame the common intention between the parties in the broadest terms. For example, instead of delimiting the common intention specifically to perform genocidal killings the courts have permitted the common intention of the JCE to be framed as the *destruction of X race*. Mounting the common intention so broadly acts as a catch-all for a wide variety of secondary crimes. The primary crime particularly intended could have been to perform genocidal killings only, however under the broad approach the secondary crime of rape and destruction of property may also be included within the common intention as objectively foreseeable having regard to the fact that the *destruction of X race* is wide enough to encompass substantively different secondary crimes that could comprise such destructive enterprise. This interpretation will be referred to as the *broad-intention* approach towards foreseeability.

The case to best illustrate the first divergence between the national and international jurisdictions regarding the risk-analysis approach to foreseeability is *Prosecutor v Édouard Karemera et al* ('*Karemera*').[27] There, one accused, Matthieu Ngirimpatse, was charged with others in a JCE, and thereby made individually criminally responsible for the rape and sexual assaults performed on Tutsi women. Interestingly, the Chamber did not find a shared intent by the JCE members to cause serious bodily or mental harm by raping and sexually assaulting Tutsis.[28] Instead, the court referred to the third category of JCE in holding that:

> during campaign(s) to destroy in whole or in part a national, ethnic, racial, or religious group, *a natural and foreseeable consequence* of that campaign will be that soldiers and militias who participate in the destruction will resort to rapes and sexual assaults unless restricted by their superiors.[29]

Accordingly, the court held that the rapes and sexual assaults were a natural and foreseeable consequence of the JCE to destroy the Tutsi ethnicity.[30]

Crucially, the court noted that the accused may have lived a life that sheltered him from direct confrontation with the actual perpetration of killings, rapes, and sexual assaults, and was away from the country on official mission during part of the genocide.[31] However, it relied on two reasons to hold that the accused

27 *Édouard Karemera and Matthieu Ngirimpatse v The Prosecutor*, Case No. ICTR-98-44-T and Case No. ICTR-98-44-A.

28 *Karemera*, paras [1453]–[1456].

29 *Karemera*, para [1476].

30 *Karemera*, paras [1479]–[1489].

31 *Karemera*, para [1482].

was aware and accepted the risk of the rape and sexual assaults: (1) the accused's MRND[32] leadership would have given him access to information that would have revealed the commission of sexual crimes against the Tutsis, and (2) the fact that rapes and sexual assaults on Tutsi women and girls were vast in scope and conducted in an open and notorious manner over a long period of time.[33]

The reasons provided by the court for holding that the rapes and sexual assaults were foreseeable are significant as they show how the court had imputed subjective knowledge from the examination of the accused's leadership position and the obvious nature of the circumstances under which genocidal killings were committed (i.e. that it frequently involved rape and sexual assaults). In this respect, note that the court had not found evidentiary proof of the accused's actual knowledge of the rapes and sexual assaults, as would be required at the national level.[34] In fact it had found in the reverse. Lacking this direct subjective proof, the court used the accused's leadership position to assert that knowledge of the rapes and sexual assaults needed to be present. Moreover, the reference to the 'open and notorious manner' in which the rapes and sexual assaults were being committed evinces an attempt by the courts to replace the subjective foresight test with a determination of risk test which focuses on the historic or statistical coincidence in occurrence between the primary and secondary crimes.

As to the second divergence between the national and international jurisdictions, the ICC's broad definition of the JCE's common intention is well shown through the case of *Prosecutor v Milan Martic* ('*Martic*').[35] This prosecution alleged that the accused was a participant in the alleged JCE, the common intention widely defined as 'the forcible removal of a majority of the Croat, Muslim and other non-Serb population from approximately one-third of the territory of the Republic of Croatia and large parts of the Republic of Bosnia and Herzogovina.'[36] Phrased in encompassing fashion, the inferred common intention of the JCE enabled the court to hold the accused liable for almost any crime which would loosely relate to the illegal forcible removal. This scope could include killings, rape, and destruction of property, all of which can be said to link incidentally to the *forcible removal.*

32 *le Mouvement Révolutionnaire National pour le Développement*, later *le Mouvement Républicain National pour la Démocratie et le Développement.*

33 *Karemera*, para [1482].

34 *Rahman*, para [14] states: 'To accept this type of reasoning would be to fix an accessory with consequences of his acts which he did not foresee and did not desire or intend. The modern development of the criminal law has been away from such an approach and towards a greater emphasis on subjective tests of criminal guilt, as Sir Robin Cooke pointed out in *Chan Wing-Siu*: "Although the rule remains well entrenched that an intention to inflict grievous bodily harm qualifies as the *mens rea* of murder, it is not in my opinion necessary to apply it in such a way as to fix an accessory with liability for a consequence which he did not intend and which stems from an act which he did not have within his contemplation. I do not think that the state of the law compels me to reach such a conclusion, and it would not in my judgment accord with the public sense of what is just and fitting."'

35 *Prosecutor v Milan Martic*, Case No. IT-95-11-T.

36 *Martic (Trial)*, para [442].

On a similar point, in *Prosecutor v Kupreskic et al* the accused was charged with adhering to the common plan for the execution of the 'cleansing campaign in the village.'[37] On this basis the court held that there was a highly coordinated effort on part of the accused and the co-perpetrators towards the common intention and there was also full prior knowledge of the intended activities and subordination to a common plan of action.[38] Similarly to the case of *Martic* the court in defining the common intention broadly held that the infringement of the victim's freedom of movement, freedom to enjoy family life and property, killings and wounding were all foreseeable crimes under the common intention to perform the cleansing campaign.[39]

Thus, this trend of case law indicates a distinct and conscious expansion of the joint liability principles.[40] First, the courts have shown themselves willing to infer foresight by reference to the obviousness or apparent risk determined by a reasonable man, of the crime occurring under the JCE, thereby clearly departing from the subjective foresight requirement at the national level. Second, the wider interpretation of common intention clearly expands the precedents at the national level where joint liability can only arise in relation to a *specific* and not a broad range of crimes.

Problems with the courts' interpretation of foreseeability

The following observations do not canvass an overarching distortion of secondary liability proof which sees the objective determination of foreseeability as somehow substituting the need to find knowledge and agreement. Nor does this reasoning at this stage posit whether the requirement to establish common intention at the international level genuinely defers to subjective knowledge. We let these concerns pass for now because it might be argued there has developed a thinking in national jurisdictions that the proof of some consequential crime can be satisfied by findings of natural and foreseeable consequences. If time allowed, we would challenge the international criminal court's approach as not being aligned even with this development because in the national context it is still necessary to establish some subjective mental state among all members of the enterprise right up to the circumstances of the consequential crime.

That point taken into account, as alluded to at the beginning of this chapter, there are important implications from the divergences between the national and international approaches to foresight and foreseeability which we identified above. In employing a *risk analysis* for determining foresight (in many respects amounting to foreseeability), the court is in effect using a *categorical (and consequentialist)* method to settle whether the secondary crime was foreseeable. In *Karemera*, the court held that the nature of rape in genocidal killings was 'vast

37 *Prosecutor v Kupreskic et al*, Case No. IT-95-16, para [782].
38 *Kupreskic*, para [782].
39 *Kupreskic*, para [781].
40 As found at the national level.

in scope and conducted in an open and notorious manner over a long period of time.'[41] As such, by reason of ***historical association*** between genocidal killings and rape the court determined the latter to be undeniably foreseeable and, as such, to satisfy the knowledge requirement. This approach is categorical through automatically associating the commission of the secondary crime with the primary crime based solely on historical or statistical coincidence between the two, and as such is consequentialist arising out of these historical predispositions. So understood, the foreseeability analysis is equated to a determination of risk from an objective or and a situational perspective, encroaching on subjective knowledge. Therefore, the courts rely on the obvious nature of the circumstances and the accused's leadership position to infer that the accused had the requisite knowledge. In other words, faced with a similar case, the court would merely refer to genocidal killings as the main category under which other crimes like rape and destruction of property are foreseeable. Such a method of assessing foreseeability through the precedent of common knowledge and practice, and thereby satisfying the courts with some knowledge requirement, places too much weight on the obvious consequences that can be drawn from the commission of the primary crime without any deference to the proof of the accused's subjective mental states as the crime evolved. Again in *Karemera*, the court side-stepped the proof of subjective intention when they gave no weight to the fact that the accused was not directly exposed to the rapes and sexual assaults and thus would not have actual knowledge of their occurrence.[42] From this reasoning, the courts are willing to determine the accused's criminal responsibility based largely on the nature of association and the obviousness of the risk of secondary crimes in the most general and often removed situations of conduct.

Under the common law, judges are cautious not to over-extend the reach of foreseeability (for consequential crime) in any similar manner to that which is now the practice of international trial courts. In an effort to ensure a more predictable and principled approach at common law if secondary liability is established through natural and foreseeable appreciations, several safeguards have been created. One such qualification was briefly introduced at the start of the chapter – the consideration of fundamental departure from the common purpose.[43] In determining whether there was a fundamental departure, the national courts will compare the two mental states involved: that to commit the primary crime (essentially subjective) and the other to commit the secondary crime (from there natural and foreseeable). If the difference between the two mental states cannot constitute a fundamental departure from each other the accused is then liable for the secondary crime. In *R v Hyde* ('*Hyde*'),[44] an example was given to illustrate a situation where a secondary crime does not essentially depart from the common intention:

41 *Karemera*, para [1482].
42 Ibid.
43 *Yemoh*, para [140], *Powell* [1999], para 10B-D, 12A-B, 30B-D, *Rahman*, para [33].
44 *R v Hyde* [1991] 1 QB 134.

> If B *realises* (without agreeing to such conduct being used)[45] that A may kill or intentionally inflict serious injury, but nevertheless continues to participate with A in the venture, that will amount to a sufficient mental element for B to be guilty of the murder *if A, with the requisite intent, kills* in the course of the venture.[46]

As such, the intention to 'inflict serious injury' and the intention to 'kill' are not fundamentally distinct as the consequences of these acts are not remote from each other. Further, the infliction of serious injury on the victim naturally results in killing the victim. Hence, the intention for the primary crime (inflicting serious injury) satisfies that of the secondary (consequential) crime (the killing).

The consideration of any fundamental difference of intention guards against the overreach of judicial reasoning in that it requires the court to examine the mental state of the parties at all stages of the criminal conduct (original and consequential) and in addition, the court has to determine through comparison, the satisfactory similarities between the common intention and the intention required for the secondary crime.

Other different approaches to determining the foreseeability of a secondary crime out of the proofs of the primary crime in the international law context, so as to minimise a diversion from subjective considerations, are revealed in the seminal ICTY decision of *The Prosecutor v Dusko Tadic* ('*Tadic*').[47] Enunciating the principles relating foreseeability under JCE III situations, the Tadic trial and appeal chambers elaborated scenarios where there was a common, shared intention to forcibly remove members of one ethnicity from their town using weapons.[48] While murder may not have been explicitly acknowledged to be part of the common design, it was nevertheless foreseeable that the forcible removal of civilians *at gunpoint* might well *result in the deaths* of one or more of those civilians.[49] Another example given in *Tadic* involved a common plan to forcibly evict civilians by burning their houses; if some of the participants in the plan killed civilians through the ensuing conflagration, all the other participants would be jointly liable.[50]

With reference to the first example, the court had made specific mention of carrying guns which made the deaths of the civilians foreseeable.[51] Regarding civilian deaths resulting from the burning of their houses, these were also predictable.[52] Such extensions of responsibility through considering inevitable risk, tie in more closely with the concept of foreseeability as understood in the national jurisdictions because the secondary crime was not remote from the primary crime

45 Note here that 'realise' refers to a subjective mental state – knowledge.
46 *Hyde*, p. 139.
47 *Prosecutor v Dusko Tadic*, Case No. IT-94-1-A.
48 *Tadic (Appeal)*, para [204].
49 Ibid.
50 Ibid.
51 *Tadic (Appeal)*, para [204].
52 Ibid.

having regard to the specific conduct and intentions of the parties, and this spoke to the comparative similarities. The intention of carrying guns during the forcible removal would imply that the weapons would be used to harm or kill if resistance was shown. Further, the forcible removal by burning civilians' houses with occupants inside is not remote from the intention to cause their death by incineration.

The examples provided in *Hyde* and *Tadic* are distinct from a situation where the common intention was to kill the victim and instead, say, rape was committed. In such a scenario, the two crimes are fundamentally distinct as the original plan to kill could have been performed without the commission of the secondary crime, rape. The commission of the primary crime does not necessitate the commission of the secondary crime. Despite this apparent logic, as mentioned above, a different outcome was reached in the *Karemera* case where, as previously noted, the ICC held that the secondary crime of rape was foreseeable in relation to the primary crime of killing based solely on the leadership position of the accused and the historical or statistical coincidence between the occurrence of the primary and secondary crimes. The use of the risk-analysis approach thus moves the inquiry away from subjectively determining the mental state of the accused or whether it could be naturally and foreseeably inferred from the specific and similar facts at the time of the purpose being settled, over to the general prevailing circumstances of the case prior to any agreement, and linking these to the necessary proofs of the consequential crime.

The risk-analysis approach expands individual criminal liability allowing for judicial reasoning that draws inference from all aspects of the atrocity's evolution, whether or not there is *sufficient inferential proof of the accused's specific mental state* with respect to the particular crime in question. In *Joint Criminal Enterprise Liability: Result Oriented Justice*, Jordash highlights the ICC judges' use of modes of liability that could be impugned for attempting to prove guilt without evidence or proof of the substantive requirements of criminal mental state. He argues that the disposal by the courts of the need for a clearly defined criminal purpose and substantive requirements of JCE essentially pre-determines the guilt of the accused against the nature of the conduct and their connection to it.[53] Thus by doing away with the need to prove subjective foresight, or foreseeability which looks first at what the accused actually knew, the risk-analysis approach infringes on the presumption of innocence found in Article 66(1) of the Rome Statute which states: 'everyone shall be presumed innocent until proved guilty before the Court in accordance with the applicable law' (that being up until now the proof principles employed in the principle domestic traditions).[54] The reasoning developed by the ICC judges seems to suggest that the legal tests and requirements are to be applied flexibly to reach a desired outcome where the circumstances

53 Jordash, Wayne, "Joint Criminal Enterprise Liability: Result Oriented Justice," in William Schabas, Yvonne MacDermott and Niamh Hayes (eds), *The Ashgate Research Companion to International Criminal Law*, Ashgate: Aldershot, 2013, p. 160.

54 UN General Assembly, Rome Statute of the International Criminal Court (last amended 2010), 17 July 1998, Art 66(1).

of atrocity prosecutions are so persuasive, and in that respect are fast becoming unduly consequentialist and abstracted. A similar point is made by Ohlin that a result-oriented interpretation of responsibility for crimes under the Rome Statute was 'clever but regrettable' as it suggests that courts can work backwards from the proposition that the defendants must be punished for crime contexts so horrifying to the human conscience.[55] Ohlin notes that although it is clear the framers of the Rome Statute intended to impose criminal responsibility for perpetrators in various situations of involvement, this fact alone tells us little about which theory of proof they meant to apply in order to be satisfied that the prosecution case, and under what factual circumstances, addressed the required mental state, more than just establishing atrocious criminal conduct.[56] In other words, the ICC in the application of proofs which are in line with national court thinking should not be free to dispose of the substantive requirements of JCE such as the proof of subjective foresight, or foreseeability after knowledge has been tested even when it is convinced that the accused is somehow criminally responsible along a complex chain of criminal involvement. No such concerns would arise in the determination of tortious duty in aggregated or contributory settings.

The imposition of criminal liability without sufficient consideration of criminal mental state and an essential connection to personalized participation was warned against by Antonio Cassese:

> In International Criminal Law the general principle applies that no one may be held accountable for an act he has not performed or in the commission of which he has not in some way participated or for an omission that cannot be attributed to him.[57]

As seen in the *Karemera* case, the accused's subjective knowledge of the crime was imputed by reason of his MRND leadership without actual proof of any subjective foresight on his part, or foreseeability after his knowledge was first tested.[58] This result is precisely what the Trial Chamber in *Prosecutor v Milomir Stakic* ('*Stakic*') signaled.[59] In that case, the court emphasised that joint criminal enterprise cannot be established simply through membership in an organisation because to do so would constitute a new crime not foreseen under the Statute and therefore amount to a flagrant infringement of the principle *nullum crimen sine lege*.[60]

55 Ohlin, J. David, "Three Conceptual Problems with the Doctrine of Joint Criminal Enterprise," *Journal of International Criminal Justice*, 5 1, 2007, p. 72.

56 Ibid.

57 Sliedregt, Elies, *The Curious Case of International Criminal Liability*, Oxford University Press: Oxford, 2012, p. 1172.

58 *Édouard Karemera*, para [1482].

59 *Prosecutor v Milomir Stakic*, Case No. IT-97-24-T.

60 *Stakic*, para [433]. See Chapter 6 and the discussion of criminal associations to appreciate a further divergence from this position at the national level.

If the criticised approach to proofs amounts to law-making suiting the individual situation of each atrocity, rather than a tight ascription to consistent rationales irrespective of the circumstances in which the atrocity occurs, then certainty in the principle of precedent essential for common law decision-making is diminished. In the suggestions for transformation argued in Chapter 5 we link these problematic developments from the essentials of international criminal justice, through the peculiar elements of global crime, to the demands of proving responsibility in the most complex contexts of collective perpetration and mass victimisation. In so doing we move on from this critical commentary to suggest that the foundations of this trend are as inevitable as they are reducible through the application of proof technologies beyond the limitations of domestic criminal prosecution case confirmation.

The solution to the dilemma underlying juridical reasoning in JCE is not reached by ever-more widening the elements and definitions of crimes which are encompassed in the common intention of the JCE, to a state where almost any crime remotely connected with the consequential crime would fall within the JCE's scope. In this vein most secondary crimes can be positioned under the broad purpose which may well be drawn from the apparent nature of the circumstances of global atrocity crimes. For example, in *Prosecutor v Milan Martic* ('*Martic*') the common intention was the 'forcible removal of a majority of the Croat, Muslim and other non-Serb population' from a given area.[61] This generous definition allowed the courts the leeway to hold the accused liable for any crime conducted in furtherance of the common intention.[62]

It is perhaps for the above reasons that the common law courts have been cautious against imposing liability on an accused for merely having a broad common intention to 'behave criminally.'[63] Instead these courts require a common intention to commit the *precise* crimes alleged, or at least so that precision falls within what could be known at the time that the purpose was settled. In the international interpretation the reasoning is reversed. The obvious nature of the risk that the crime would occur, given its broad interpretation, then serves to establish purpose which the JCE members are imputed to possess. Having discussed the difficulties associated with the ICC's deviation from the national courts' interpretation and application of joint criminal liability principles, we can now speculate the reasons for this development of judicial reasoning.

Genocide killings are often perpetrated by large groups of individuals, harming multiple victims (individuals, communities and cultures). JCE members do not necessarily commit the crimes together or at the same time, or even in the same place. These are crimes that range over historical epochs, involving different arrangements of participation, in sequences of individual criminal conduct. Hence, it is unlikely that all the JCE members will know how other members behave in the immediate moments leading up to the commission of the offenses

61 *Martic (Trial)*, para [5].
62 *Martic (Trial)*, para [93].
63 *Rex v Vincent Banka & Anor* [1936] MLJ 53, per Huggard J.

constituting genocide, and by extension what secondary crimes were 'reasonably foreseeable.' By contrast, in national jurisdictions the JCE group usually commits the crime in the same place/time frame and each individual member can therefore be said to have foreseen/willingly accepted the other member's actions provided they form natural consequences from an earlier agreed purpose. Such profound differences in crime context may challenge proof frames and even the legal device of JCE when it is translated to the international context (discussed in Chapter 4).

Another proof paradigm which shows the strained application of JCE principles in international criminal law relates to how JCE members can potentially *be responsible for non-JCE members' crimes*. The common intention in JCE forms the basis for the imposition of joint liability on the accused, along with the nature of knowledge about what is intended. However, the international courts have modified the concept of secondary liability by holding the accused responsible for secondary crimes committed by individuals who do not strictly form part of the JCE group. In this respect, not only is the concept of foresight given greater scope in the international model but so are the nature of the enterprise and the commonality of purpose. Responsibility for crimes committed by non-JCE members is deemed possible with indicating *sufficient links* (again contextual and consequential) between those who carry out the *actus reus* and the members of the JCE. An examination of case law suggests that a *sufficient link* is present under the following situations:

1 when the accused forms part of the leadership of an organisation to which the principle perpetrator belongs outside the JCE, and
2 when the accused operates in the same JCE group as an individual who is the leader of the organisation to which the principle perpetrator belongs outside the JCE.

In *Tadic*, the appeal chambers expounded on the 'objective elements' of JCE in these terms:

> There is no necessity for this plan, design or purpose to have been previously arranged or formulated. The common plan or purpose may materialise extemporaneously and be inferred from the fact that a *plurality of persons* acts in unison to put into effect a joint criminal enterprise.[64]

Plurality of persons is a worryingly expansive parameter for perpetration and its subjective appreciation. It implies that the collaboration once required through agreement could be deemed to prevail across the loosest of associations even outside the specific enterprise at the heart of a JCE. Additionally, the *Tadic* requirements so expressed should not do away with the need for the common purpose

64 *Prosecutor v Dusko Tadic*, Case No. IT-94-1-A, para [227].

or design to be shared, despite the constituency of this sharing having expanded beyond nation-state law recognition. Instead, the *Tadic* provision concerns the *timing* at which this intention is formed. Spreading the temporal range of the enterprise enables a much more expansive and inclusive application of common purpose (similar to the extension of interpretations of coincidence where the criminal conduct is seen as a series of interconnected events). By expressly referring to the connection between the 'common plan or purpose' as the criminal mental state, and the 'unison to put into effect a joint criminal enterprise' being the criminal conduct, the requirement of mental state shared between all the participants of the JCE is emphasised, even if its distillation through membership of a criminal enterprise has slipped away.[65] Essentially linked to the enterprise as it may be seen, the judgment in *Tadic* has been distinguished by the courts in subsequent cases to hold JCE members liable for non-JCE members' crimes. This line of authority has led to a new head of liability (but perhaps the logical extension of 'plurality of persons') under which a JCE member can be held liable for a non-JCE member's crime, resulting in a confusing state of law in secondary participation situations.

The first case in point is *Prosecutor v Nikola Sainovic* ('*Sainovic*'),[66] where the accused Ojdanic was the Chief of the General Staff and exercised command and control over all units and organs of the Army of Yugoslavia (VJ). He worked closely with the then President of Federal Republic of Yugoslavia (FRY) before and during the NATO air campaign, and exercised *de facto*, as well as *de jure*, authority over the VJ. The accused was found to be aware of VJ involvement in the arming of the non-Albanian civilian population in Kosovo. He also supported the appointment of VJ personnel to high-level posts who either assisted the activities of the VJ in Kosovo, such as the accused Pavković, or else simply raised no objection thereto, and was aware of the removal of high-level VJ officers who objected to the use of the VJ troops in Kosovo. Ojdanić issued orders for the VJ to carry out operations throughout Kosovo. He also mobilised extra VJ units for deployment in Kosovo during the time-period when the majority of crimes found by the Chamber to have been committed took place.

In the trial proceedings, the accused sought to challenge the ICTY's jurisdiction to prosecute him under the form of responsibility deemed 'indirect co-perpetration,' as there was argued to be no basis for this form of responsibility either in the Statute of the Tribunal or under customary international law. During the examination of this issue, the court made a determination on whether joint responsibility for participation in a JCE can arise where the physical perpetrator is not a participant in the JCE.[67] On this point the Trial Chamber concluded that it is not inconsistent with the jurisprudence of the Tribunal for a participant in a

65 Decision on Ojdanic's Motion Challenging Jurisdiction: Indirect Co-Perpetration, Case No. IT-05-87-PT. See: Separate judgment of Judge Iain Bonomy, paras [7]–[8] on *Tadic*.

66 *Prosecutor v Nikola Sainovic*, Case No. IT-05-87-A.

67 Decision on Ojdanic's Motion Challenging Jurisdiction: Indirect Co-Perpetration, Case No. IT-05-87-PT. See: Separate judgment of Judge Iain Bonomy, para [18].

JCE to be found guilty of commission where the crime is perpetrated by a person or persons who simply act as an instrument of the JCE, and who are not shown to be participants in the JCE.[68]

Having explicitly recognised that *Tadic* did not dispose of the requirement that the principle perpetrator share the common intention of the JCE group, the tribunal in *Sainovic* sought to distinguish the case on grounds of factual differences and considerations of 'justice and common sense.'[69] To this end, the tribunal held that:

> In any consideration of *Tadic* it is important to bear the *specific facts of the case in mind. The JCE comprised a small group of active participants.* The sort of situation envisaged in the present Indictment, and indeed in the factual scenario detailed above in paragraph 4, are far removed from the circumstances in *Tadic* . . . Although many subsequent judgements have employed the *Tadic* language in setting out the elements of JCE, and therefore appear to restrict JCE liability —at least in the third category—*to crimes physically perpetrated by JCE participants in almost all of these Judgements the JCE was, like the enterprise in Tadic, relatively small.* The fact that some of the physical perpetrators may not have been JCE participants does not appear to have been much of an issue. That is understandable, since *considerations of both justice and common sense would suggest that concentration should be upon the responsibility of the JCE participants, and that such a requirement is superfluous.* Accordingly . . . these cases do not give decisive guidance as to whether the Tribunal's jurisprudence requires that the physical perpetrator be a participant in the JCE.
>
> (emphasis added)[70]

In distinguishing *Tadic*, the court highlighted the 'broader and more complex factual situations that arose' in the case of *Sainovic*. In other words, implying the requirement that the principle perpetrator share the common intention was too restrictive to accommodate the collective, multi-actor nature of the crime at hand. As such, the solution was to hold that an overly restrictive requirement did not apply relative to the factual scenario at hand having regard to the interests of justice in the case.

Another expressive decision on this point is *Prosecutor v Radoslav Brdanin* ('*Brdanin*'),[71] where the issue of JCE was dismissed on a procedural question. In the trial the prosecution had initially proceeded on the basis that the JCE in such a context must include the physical perpetrators.[72] However, on appeal,

68 *Ojdanic*, para [13].
69 *Ojdanic*, para [8].
70 Ibid.
71 *Prosecutor v Radoslav Brdanin*, Case No. IT-99-36-T and *Prosecutor v Radoslav Brdanin*, Case No. IT-99-36-A.
72 *Brdanin (Trial)*, para [366].

the prosecution altered its stance to continue the case on the basis that the principle perpetrators *need not* be JCE members.[73] The Appeals Chamber held that it would be unfair to the accused for the prosecution to enter new charges. However, the court clarified that it agreed with the prosecution's stance that a JCE member could be jointly liable for crimes committed by a non-JCE member, provided that the common design involves the perpetration of crimes covered in the statute. In support of its conclusion, the tribunal in *Brdanin* relied on the case of *Sainovic* to distinguish *Tadic*. In this regard the following was decided:

> The factual scenario in *Tadic*, contrary to the one in the case at hand, involved a small group of participants operating in one municipality, and that the principal perpetrators were clearly participants in the JCE. It is therefore not surprising that the Appeals Chamber in that case essentially focused on post-World War II cases where this was also the case, even though not every case cited by *Tadic* required participation of the principal perpetrator in the JCE as the *sine qua non* for ascribing of liability to the accused. In light of the above, the Appeals Chamber judgment in *Tadic* . . . [is not] . . . conclusive as to whether principal perpetrators must be members of the JCE.[74]

Further, the court in *Brdanin* relied on two cases – *Prosecutor v Radislav Krstic* ('*Krstic*') and *Prosecutor v Blagoje Simic* ('*Simic*') – in ruling that the principle perpetrator need not share the common intention.[75] In *Krstic*, the Trial Chamber did not explicitly require principal perpetrators to be members of the JCE. The Chamber found that there existed two JCEs, one with the objective of 'forcibly transferring the Bosnian Muslim women, children and elderly from Potoari on 12 and 13 July' and 'creating a humanitarian crisis in support of this endeavor,' the other with the objective of 'killing the military-aged Bosnian Muslim men of Srebrenica.'[76] It accordingly found the accused guilty of inhumane acts and persecution as crimes against humanity for his participation in the first JCE and genocide for his participation in the second JCE. The members of these JCEs included only high-ranking Bosnian Serb political and military leaders, not the principal perpetrators.[77] The principal perpetrators, though not mentioned explicitly, were probably low-ranking members of the Drina Corps of the VRS.[78]

In *Stakic*,[79] the Appeals Chamber, relying on the Trial Chamber's findings, treated a JCE operating in the municipality of Prijedor in 1992 as composed

73 *Brdanin (Trial)*, paras [345]–[356]. See also, *Prosecutor v Radoslav Brdanin*, Case No. IT-99-36-A, paras [361]–[362] and [410].

74 *Brdanin (Appeal)*, para [406].

75 *Prosecutor v Radislav Krstic*, Case No. IT-98-33-T, paras [601], [611], [613]. See also: *Prosecutor v Blagoje Simic*, Case No. IT-95-9-T, paras [156]–[160].

76 *Brdanin (Appeal)*, paras [407]–[408].

77 Ibid.

78 Ibid.

79 *Brdanin (Appeal)*, para [409].

only of the leaders of political bodies, the military and the police. Its common purpose was however clearly carried out by a larger number of individuals (some unknown) including the Bosnian Serb police, military, and paramilitary forces.[80] It is particularly noteworthy that Stakic was convicted of certain crimes (murder and extermination) committed by non-members under the third JCE category.[81]

Reasons for the court's wide interpretation of nation-state principle

Having distinguished *Tadic* and relying on the cases of *Krstic* and *Simic* the court in *Stakic* was able to hold that nothing prevented it from imposing liability on the accused, despite the perpetrator not sharing the common intention. The court then added the essential proof that the accused or any other member of the JCE *closely cooperated* with the principal perpetrator in order to further the common criminal purpose. This requirement suggests that joint liability can be imposed as long as there is a *sufficient participatory link* between the accused and the principle perpetrator. Therefore, although the Bosnian Serb leadership including the accused had shared the common intention, particularly for the deportation and the forcible transfer of non-Serbs, they were held responsible for the crimes committed by non-JCE members such as the army, the Bosnian Serb police, Serb paramilitary groups, Bosnian Serb armed civilians and even unidentified individuals.

Further, in the case of *Martic*, the court confirmed Milan Martic's responsibility as a JCE member for crimes that were carried out by non-JCE members who belonged to hierarchical organisations, such as the police or the military.[82] The court based its reasoning on the fact that perpetrators of the crimes (the JNA, the TO and the *Milicija Krajine*)[83] were '*under the control of the other members of the JCE*,'[84] thus emphasising the essential requirement of a sufficient link between the accused and the principle perpetrator. By referring to *control* there is the risk of collapsing JCE into less constrained notions of secondary participation which require no shared action beyond some mutual agreement (such as conspiracy).

The court also cited evidence that prior to their deaths the victims were intimidated by individuals who referred to themselves as 'Martic's men' or 'Martic's Militia.'[85] Although the court did not explicitly explain the relevance of this evidence, it can be inferred that the aforementioned facts went towards proving the *control* element by the JCE members over the perpetrators. The reliance of the court on Martic's control over the police and TO in general does not clarify Martic's engagement with these forces, in order to ascertain whether these

80 Ibid.
81 Ibid.
82 *Martic*, Case No. IT-95-11-A, paras [187]–[188] and [438].
83 Yugoslav People's Army ('JNA'), Territorial Defence ('TO') and Special Purpose Police Units ('*Milicija Krajine*').
84 *Martic (Appeal)*, para [166].
85 *Martic (Appeal)*, para [186].

groups had been used by him in furtherance of the common purpose. Rather, merely inferring by reason of his control, all subsequent crimes committed by the police and TO were his responsibility, was the tenor of this reasoning.[86] The case, therefore, suggests that as long as there is a sufficient link between the primary perpetrator (who may be outside the JCE) of the crime and the JCE member, individual liability can be imposed on JCE members no matter what their connection to the consequent criminal conduct.

From the above examples, one could infer that the notion of sufficient link is generously determined in that the parties involved need not know of each other's existence, be aware of the other's mental state towards the commission of the crime or even the details leading up to the crime.

Problems with holding a JCE member liable for non-JCE members' crimes

The main difficulty with the decisions of *Sainovic*, *Brdanin* and *Martic* is the illogicality of asserting JCE and non-JCE members can share a common purpose which is sufficiently specific to the crime or its reasonable foreseeability. What the courts seem to be doing is transposing some broad common purpose as if it could be said to cover many things, including the crime in question committed by some members of that all-encompassing common purpose. The imposition of joint liability under these circumstances is intuitively distorting the notions of enterprise, agreement and purpose, as there is no basis for holding that the JCE member and the principle perpetrator are *joint* in the commission of the offense, beyond the vaguest meeting of minds through association which may have been formed without the specific criminal enterprise which forms the offense, in contemplation directly at any stage.

In terms of strict legal principles, the aforementioned cases have opened up new ground for criminal liability where there is a lack of coincidence between the *mens rea* and the *actus reus* of the offense committed, unless the criminal conduct is so extended as to commence when associations were made before the particular criminal enterprise was formulated, no matter how remote that eventuated in fact. This differs starkly from the position taken in the national jurisdictions (e.g. common law) where a fundamental principle of criminal law is that a person can only be liable for harm caused by his own conduct and not by others.[87] To ensure that liability is not unfairly imposed on the accused, the requirement of coincidence between his *actus reus* and *mens rea* is deemed an essential proof requirement necessitating coincidence and causation. Under common law, where qualifications to the principle of coincidence have been developed such as seeing the conduct as a series of acts with which the mental state can coincide at some

86 Jordash, 2013, p. 154.

87 Sayre, Francis, "Criminal Responsibility for the Acts of Another," *Harvard Law Review*, 43 5, 1930, pp. 689–723.

stage, the courts have been clear to hold that the required mental state should be sufficiently spontaneously formed before the commission of the conduct only where there is a specific link between the initiation of conduct and the commission of the offense. Further, cases such as *Thabo Meli and Others Appellants v The Queen* suggest that an accused can be liable for an offense so long as the *mens rea* was developed at anytime during the commission of the *actus reus*.[88] Even so this series of events approach is curtailed by instances which necessarily link together to produce the particular criminal conduct. Although the precise point of coincidence between the *actus reus* and *mens rea* may be subjectively unknown to the accused, there must have been an objective fulfillment of the two proof conditions in substance through the requirement that the series of events making up the *actus reus* in total. There is no suggestion that coincidence with outside events so linked would comprise a sufficient proof of causation and mental state. Even with JCE in domestic principle the causation and coincidence requirements are mediated by the strict adherence to agreement, subjective intent, and knowledge. With consequent crime the accused must have purposefully linked with the perpetrator to advance the initial crime, and through his acceptance of risk participated naturally and foreseeably in the consequent criminal conduct so as to have sufficiently shared in its coincidence and causation.

However, in the international crime cases mentioned above there is no identifiable point at which the *actus reus* committed by the principle perpetrator and the *mens rea* possessed by the accused meet. In fact the two parties themselves may have never met in any personal sense. Indeed, the missing link between them is the lack of common intention to commit any element of the crime in question, as the principle perpetrator does not form part of the JCE. The Trial Chamber in *Brdanin* (holding a different view from that later determined by the Appeals Chamber) ruled that for joint liability to be imposed the strict legal requirement that the accused had entered into an agreement with the relevant principle perpetrators to commit a crime must be satisfied. Interestingly, it noted that the evidence in *Brdanin* allowed for other reasonable inferences to be drawn.[89] For example, one such inference would be that both the accused and the relevant physical perpetrators, all holding the requisite *mens rea* for a particular crime and driven by the same motive to implement the *strategic plan*, furthered the commission of the same crime, without, however, entering into an agreement between them to commit that crime. Yet another reasonable inference to be drawn would be that the *relevant physical perpetrators* committed the crimes in question in execution of orders and instructions received from their military or paramilitary superiors who intended to implement the *strategic plan*, whereby the relevant physical perpetrators did not have to enter into an agreement with the accused to commit these crimes. However, the final conclusion on the issue was that JCE on those facts was not an appropriate mode to describe the individual

88 *Thabo Meli and Others Appellants v The Queen* [1954] 1 W.L.R. 228, para [230].
89 *Brdanin (Trial)*, para [354].

criminal responsibility of the accused.[90] Arguably, retaining a consistent ascription to domestic principle (which we do not say in Chapter 5 is preferred) is a desirable outcome as it is compatible with even the more rigid proofs for JCE at the national level. To allow the courts to infer the required *mens rea* from speculation of the accused and principle perpetrator's motives in engaging in the crime would be to overturn the well-established criminal proof distinction between intention and motive by somehow extracting the former from the latter. Further, if through judicial reasoning new legal tests for proof are created on a case-by-case basis and are said to respect pre-existing principle, when the nature of their elements genuinely confound such an interpretation, then uncertainty at the expense of creativity is the result. The consequence of so doing undermines the integrity of established principle even in the context of legal harmonisation and avoids confronting the need to develop a jurisprudence more applicable to the nature of the offenses prosecuted and the interpretation of the judicial mission in their punishment. It is the latter concession which we both oppose and remedy in Chapter 5, as more undermining of ICJ than the failure to produce the utopia of harmonisation in ICL proofs.

It is important here to re-iterate that our argument is not for the unshakeable pre-eminence of the national courts' approaches to participation and secondary liability. Indeed, as we have detailed above, the common law position particularly on natural and foreseeable consequences is already in many applications taking proofs too far from the requirement of a high degree mental state the further the accused is from the crime. What we are suggesting is that in recognising these deficiencies as well as the new challenges that global crimes present for proof, the answer is not further convolution in proof principles and technologies (see Chapters 4 and 5).

Having identified the potential weaknesses relating to the ICC's use of *sufficient link* to establish legal connections between non-JCE and JCE members, it is now left to explain why the court embarked on such a precarious route.

Why hold JCE members liable for non-JCE members' crimes?

There are several reasons which could account for the ICC's decision to hold a JCE member liable for a non-JCE member's crime. The initial reason is the perceived need to produce just outcomes, the next is related to evidentiary or proof issues, and finally there is the deference to the collective multi-actor nature of JCE crimes consistent with the unique characteristics of atrocities.

The *just outcomes* rationale features prominently in the *Brdanin* Appeals Chamber decision where the court held that in order to *fulfill the object and purpose of international criminal law*,[91] it is necessary to prosecute and punish those

90 *Brdanin (Trial)*, para [355].

91 Such a holistic justification for judicial decision-making at the international level accords with our recurrent assertion of object-oriented justice, but more particularly reveals a higher order rationale for moving beyond the limits of nation-state proof technologies.

who commit international crimes as leaders and not only their subordinates. The court then cited a 'common sense' notion that would be offended if high-level individuals directing the execution of crimes that have a more significant degree of responsibility than the individuals who physically perpetrate the crimes go unpunished.[92] The court avoided explaining what it meant by its 'common sense' approach. This lack of precision when applying some form of customary position adds to the confusion of what influences proof. It is one thing to say that the accused, having directed the perpetration of certain offenses, should be somehow liable for their commission. It is quite another to assert that 'common sense' would require the accused to be punished for every offense committed by his subordinates regardless of how foreseeable the crimes were or whether the accused and the perpetrator had shared a common intention to commit the crime.

Another reason for allowing joint liability to extend to situations where the primary perpetrator was not a participant in the JCE is found in the *Sainovic*.[93] There the prosecution gave an example of what it considered would be the 'absurd result' if the Trial Chamber were to limit JCE liability to instances in which the physical perpetrator is a participant in the JCE:

> where X and Y come to an agreement to kill all the inhabitants of a village, and Y uses a weapon of mass destruction to destroy the village, then X would bear responsibility, but where Y orders troops under his command to do the killings, then X can at the most be an aider and abettor.[94]

Yet again there is reliance placed on a 'common sense' notion for the purposes of proof, and as such, normative projections on surrounding just outcomes (or their inconsistency) replace more forensic considerations of what is reasonable in terms of foreseeability. The necessity for convictions on the basis of non-JCE participation is a perfect invitation to consider tortious applications of contribution and aggregation.

If the ICC judges are falling back on their sense of justice and fairness in circumstances where the traditional legal mechanisms do not provide sufficient flexibility in interpretation, is this 'common sense'? As seen previously in the cases of *Sainovic* and *Brdanin* the courts referred to the 'broad and complex' factual matrix in the aforementioned cases to distinguish *Tadic* and expand JCE liability to hold a JCE member liable for a crime despite the principle perpetrator falling outside the JCE. Here we see another judicial reasoning technique beyond expanding the proof parameters, that is, to distinguish authorities reliant on principles which do not support the intended outcome of the latter case. On the facts of both cases, the primary perpetrators could not be identified, thus posing an evidentiary problem in holding the accused responsible for JCE through association

92 *Brdanin (Appeal)*, para [370].

93 Decision on Ojdanic's Motion Challenging Jurisdiction: Indirect Co-Perpetration, Case No. IT-05-87-PT, para [21].

94 Ibid.

and agreement, as under the *Tadic* approaches. Had the courts refused to expand the scope of JCE liability as they did, the *intellectual perpetrators* of the crime at the leadership level would avoid responsibility despite contributing to the commission of the crime.[95] Indeed former ICTY judge Antonio Cassese noted that the collective criminal nature of international crimes makes it extremely difficult to pinpoint the specific contribution made by each individual participant to the crime, for not all participants will have acted in the same manner but each of them may have played a different and no-less definitive role in the criminal conduct. Further, the evidence relating to each individual's conduct could prove difficult or impossible to find as the conflict may have occurred under the spontaneous and conflagratory conditions of war. Yet Cassese stressed that it would nevertheless be immoral and contrary to the general purpose of criminal law relating to the presumption of innocence, to instead prioritise community protection from deviant behavior and its consequential damage, driven by a desire not to let those actions go unpunished.[96] Heavily influenced by the protectionist imperatives of the Rome Statute Preamble, the courts have shown great resistance against allowing the accused to avoid individual criminal liability for the mere lack of evidentiary proofs as determined through national jurisdiction requirements. Implicit in this resistance is the need for justice to be served on individuals who have engaged in the most heinous crimes against humanity. A driving fear is from the damage caused to the court's reputation if the leaders go unpunished and the legitimacy of the ICC dwindles in the eyes of the victims it is meant to protect.[97]

On another level, if judges are allowed to disregard even the loose limits of established criminal law principles at the national level to administer what is essentially damages-driven justice, then the defense will be unable to put the prosecution to proof against pre-existing principle. Wedged somewhere between insufficiently flexible proof requirements and the horror of atrocity, ICC judicial reasoning seems compelled to undermine certainty of proof requirements, to achieve a more victim-centered notion of justice. This is a regrettable if totally understandable compromise and one which needs a rational remedy.

As canvassed in Chapter 1, the ICC judges under the Rome Statute owe an obligation to promote victims' justice for the broader purposes of protection and peace-making. The focus on victims' justice is consistent with the trend in the ICC case law which evinces the relaxation or disposal of traditional JCE principles to pursue judicial creativity in molding individual criminal liability toward considerations of more inclusive responsibility in a contributory fashion.

Another reason for excluding the requirement of membership in the JCE group for liability to be imposed is the collective, multi-actor nature of the crimes committed (see Chapter 4). International crimes such as genocide are

95 Sliedregt, 2012, p. 1174.

96 Cassese, Antonio, "Proper Limits of Individual Responsibility Under the Doctrine of Joint Criminal Enterprise," *Journal of International Criminal Justice*, 5 1, 2007, p. 110.

97 Rome Statute, Preamble.

often committed by one group of aggressors against a specific victim group in society. Within the aggressor group, there is an unspoken mutual or general understanding that the destruction of the victim group is desirable. In this regard, the aggressors, having not discussed their common intention and who might each have different purposes for the commission of the crime all act under a common motive or broad understanding. Against such 'common sense' it is apposite to consider the relationship between individuals within the aggressor group in genocide situations shown by these two examples (and elaborated in Chapter 4):

1 JCE members discuss their common intention to commit killings amounting to genocide, and a JCE member requests help from his brother to kill individuals of a particular group. In such a situation, there is no need to explain the common intention because of the social ties between the parties, and the brother might act upon certain understandings between himself and the JCE member which do not relate to the detailed plans of the group.
2 JCE members who represent the leaders of the aggressor group discuss their common intention to commit killings amounting to genocide, and one JCE member proceeds to initiate the common purpose through ordering part of his military forces to start the killings. Over an extended period of time, new members join the military forces and other individuals from the aggressor group community join in the killings as their nature and scope become more widespread. These late-comers do not share the common intention of the original JCE members and do not form part of the JCE but they share a common motive or understanding between them that the killings be performed.

As mentioned above in the section concerning the expansion of the foreseeability and common intention requirements, the link between the needs of victims' justice on one hand and the equally resilient tug in the direction of fairness to the accused as well as recognition of the procedural and substantive legitimacy of the ICC's proceedings on the other, entangles into a Gordian knot of proof perplexity. One way to cut the knot is by severing the rigid obligations the international courts have to national jurisdictional principles, and this is indeed just what the international judges have been attempting through re-interpretation and distinction, case by case. The JCE examples presented above have shown that the tests at the national level for JCE crimes are not well suited to deal with the complexities of international crimes. Hence, to give weight to the concern for legitimacy and the need for just outcomes, the tort/crime hybrid which is flexible in its application through incorporating concepts such as vicarious liability, will be argued in Chapter 5 as a better way forward. Indeed, to retire to tort proof technologies is in keeping with the spirit of harmonisation, and as was proposed in Chapter 2 is a manifestation of hybridisation across the influence of domestic jurisdiction, again consistent with the sources of international criminal jurisprudence as currently conceived.

To give further weight to our concerns regarding the manner in which national criminal procedural traditions are being strained at the international level in order to achieve a more outcome-oriented notion of justice, the next section interrogates the ICC and the international tribunal approaches to proving participation. This exposition will also lay foundations in furthering the argument for a tort/ crime hybrid approach in proving secondary responsibility for global crimes.

Aiding and abetting

Introducing the second major area of contributory responsibility, it is instructive to reflect briefly on the common law and Continental civil law positions regarding aiding and abetting.

Although often used conjunctively, the terms 'aiding' and 'abetting' can be explained independently. Under common law systems, abetting broadly involves encouraging the principal to commit the offense and this usually accompanies or is implicit in an act of aiding.[98] Aid may be given by supplying an instrument to the principal, keeping a look-out while the offense is committed, doing preparatory acts and many other forms of assistance given prior to or after the offense. So long as it has been shown that the accomplice's conduct helped or might have helped the principal offender in some way it does not have to be established that the accomplice caused the substantive offense.[99] Here it is crucial to note that the exact elements leading to liability under aiding and abetting at the national level are often governed by statute.[100]

Under the Continental civil law system in Germany for example, the requirements to find similar forms of contributory liability are located in the Criminal Code, Sections 26 and 27. Therein an abettor is any person who intentionally induces another to intentionally commit an unlawful act,[101] while an aider is any person who intentionally assists another in the intentional commission of an unlawful act.[102] By contrast, Articles 121–7 of the French Penal Code cover liability for complicity. In this situation, complicity can consist of helping or assisting the commission of the principle offense or instigating its commission, and the act or omission which represents assistance must have encouraged the perpetration of the crime.[103] Complicity by instigation can take the form of either provocation or the giving of instructions and must have been committed prior to or at the time of the principal offense. Accomplices must knowingly participate in the

98 Ashworth, 1991, p. 407.

99 Ibid.

100 See for example: England and Wales, Accessories and Abettors Act 1861 Art 8, Australian Federal Crimes Act 1958 Sect 181). Note in some jurisdictions like Canada, the Criminal Code is not conclusive on what defines aiding and abetting.

101 German Criminal Code 1998, Section 26.

102 German Criminal Code, Section 27.

103 Elliot, Catherine, "The French Law of Intent and Its Influence on the Development of International Criminal Law," *Criminal Law Forum*, 11 1, 2000, pp. 35–46.

substantive offense but need not share the criminal intention of the principal offender.[104] Where these approaches deviate from common law is in their particularity of contribution, while being similar in the mental states required and the requirement of cause and effect.

As Catherine Elliott points out both the French and English law positions toward accomplices require the existence of a substantive offense but not a conviction of a perpetrator for that offense. Further, both systems essentially cover help or encouragement provided before or at the time of the substantive offense.[105]

International criminal law approach to aiding and abetting

In examining aiding and abetting as a technology of proof for secondary or accessorial liability at the international level we will examine in particular the distortions of *specific direction* and *substantial contribution*.

Tadic broadly defined an aider and abettor as an individual who carries out acts specifically directed to assist, encourage or lend moral support to the perpetration of a certain designated crime (murder, extermination, rape, torture, wanton destruction of civilian property, etc.) and this support has a substantial effect upon the perpetration of the crime.[106] Additionally, the appeal judgment of *Simic* laid out the *actus reus* and *mens rea* requirements of aiding and abetting.[107] There the Chamber held that it is not required that a cause–effect relationship between the conduct of the aider and abettor and the commission of the crime be shown, or that such conduct served as a condition precedent to the commission of the crime. The *actus reus* of aiding and abetting a crime may occur before, during, or after the principal crime has been perpetrated, and the location at which the *criminal conduct* takes place may be removed from the location of the principal crime. The requisite *criminal mental state* for aiding and abetting is knowledge that the acts performed by the aider and abettor assist in the commission of the specific crime of the principal perpetrator. The aider and abettor must be aware of the essential elements of the crime that was ultimately committed by the principal. In relation to the crime of *persecution*, an offense with a specific intent,[108] he must thus contemplate not only the crime, the perpetration of which he is facilitating, but also the direct intent of the perpetrators of that crime. He need not share the intent but he must be cognisant of the discriminatory context in which the crime is to be committed and know that his support or encouragement has a substantial effect on its perpetration. However, it is not necessary that the aider and abettor knows either the precise crime that was intended or the one that was, in the event, committed. If he is aware that one of a number of crimes will probably be committed,

104 Ibid.

105 Ibid.

106 *Tadic (Appeal)*, para [229].

107 *Prosecutor v Blagoje Simic*, Case No. IT-95-9-A, para [86].

108 The highest level of subjective intention which goes to the criminal conduct and to consequences.

and one of those crimes is in fact committed, he has intended to facilitate the commission of that crime, and is guilty as an aider and abettor.

Significantly, the difference between aiding and abetting and JCE crimes was also canvassed in the *Tadic* Appeal Judgment.[109] The Appeals Chamber underscored that, while the *actus reus* of JCE requires only 'acts that in some way are directed to the furthering of the common plan or purpose,' the *actus reus* of aiding and abetting requires a closer link between the assistance provided and particular criminal activities: assistance must be 'specifically' – rather than 'in some way' – directed towards relevant crimes.[110] The court also laid down the following observations in relation to aiding and abetting:

1 The aider and abettor is always an accessory to a crime perpetrated by another person, the principal.
2 In the case of aiding and abetting no proof is required of the existence of a common concerted plan, let alone of the pre-existence of such a plan. No plan or agreement is required: indeed, the principal may not even know about the accomplice's contribution.
3 The aider and abettor carries out acts specifically directed to assist, encourage or lend moral support to the perpetration of a certain crime, and this support has a substantial effect upon the perpetration of the crime. By contrast, in the case of acting in pursuance of a common purpose or design, it is sufficient for the participant to perform acts that in some way are directed to the furthering of the common plan or purpose.
4 In the case of aiding and abetting, the requisite mental element is knowledge that the acts performed by the aider and abettor assist the commission of a *specific crime by the principal.* By contrast, in the case of common purpose or design more is required (i.e., either intent to perpetrate the crime or intent to pursue the common criminal design plus foresight that those crimes outside the criminal common purpose were likely to be committed), as stated above.

One of the crucial requirements of aiding and abetting at the international level seems to be 'specific direction.' While certain appeal judgments rendered after the *Tadic* appeal made no explicit reference to specific direction, several of these invocations employed alternative but equivalent formulations. In particular, the *Simic* appeal judgment defined the *actus reus* of aiding and abetting as 'acts directed to assist, encourage or lend moral support to the perpetration of a certain specific crime.'[111] Similarly, the *Prosecutor v Naser Ori* appeal judgment, discussing aiding and abetting in the context of omission liability, explained that the 'omission must be directed to assist, encourage or lend moral support to the perpetration of a crime and have a substantial effect upon the perpetration of

109 *Tadic (Appeal)*, para [229].
110 *Prosecutor v Momcilo Perisic*, Case No. IT-04-81-A, para [27].
111 *Simic (Appeal)*, para [85].

the crime.'[112] Finally, the ICTR's *Francois Karera v The Prosecutor* appeal judgment stated that the '*actus reus* of aiding and abetting is constituted by acts or omissions that assist, further, or lend moral support to the perpetration of a specific crime.'[113] Despite the direct and thematic references to 'specific direction,' much confusion surrounds its proof requirement, with preceding cases qualifying the instances when specific direction is relevant and others excluding the requirement altogether. The foregoing evaluation will be primarily focused on the controversial case of *Prosecutor v Momcilo Perisic* ('*Perisic*') and the majority's interpretation and application of the 'specific direction requirement.'

The case of *Perisic* concerned Momčilo Perišič who was the top military officer of the Yugoslav Army. Perisic was charged with aiding and abetting the crimes of murder, inhumane acts and attacks on civilians in Sarajevo by providing substantial assistance to the VRS. That assistance allegedly involved provisioning considerable quantities of weaponry, as well as salaries and other benefits to the top officers of the VRS, including General Ratko Mladić, the VRS Commander. Further, it was alleged that Perisic had offered logistic and personnel assistance and thus aided and abetted the crimes perpetrated by the VRS during its takeover of Srebrenica in 1995.[114]

The Appeals Chamber held that 'specific direction' was a requirement for finding an accused liable for aiding and abetting.[115] In reaching its decision, the Chamber noted that the lack of the application of 'specific direction' in preceding Appeals Chamber cases was attributed to the fact that prior convictions for aiding and abetting entered or affirmed involved relevant acts geographically or otherwise proximate to, and thus not remote from, the crimes of the principal perpetrators.[116] The court asserted that where such proximity is present, specific direction may be demonstrated implicitly through discussion of other elements of aiding and abetting liability, such as 'substantial contribution.'[117] In these contexts the specific direction is therefore self-evident. By extension where the accused aider and abettor is remote from relevant crimes, evidence proving other elements of aiding and abetting may not be sufficient to establish specific direction. On the facts Perisic was removed from the crimes committed and hence explicit consideration of specific direction was required.[118] This qualification of the 'specific direction' test to apply only where the accused is distant from perpetration is one of the peculiar outcomes of the case.

The second proof peculiarity is found in the Appeal Chamber's application of the 'specific direction' requirement. As the court saw it, the question if there was

112 *Prosecutor v Naser Ori*, Case No. IT-03-68-A, para [43].
113 *Francois Karera v The Prosecutor*, Case No. ICTR 04-71-A, para [321].
114 *Perisic (Appeal)*, para [126].
115 *Perisic (Appeal)*, paras [37]–[40].
116 *Perisic (Appeal)*, paras [37]–[40].
117 Ibid.
118 *Perisic (Appeal)*, para [39].

specific direction turned on whether the policy Perisic implemented through the VJ involved providing assistance specifically linked to VRS crimes; whether he sponsored a policy meant to aid the general VRS war effort in a manner that specifically directed that assistance towards the VRS-perpetrated crimes; or, whether acting outside the scope of the SDC's official policy, he gave aid and comfort specifically directed towards VRS crimes.[119] The following questions arose as a result. Was the VRS an organisation whose sole and exclusive purpose focused on the commission of crimes like those in question? Such a finding would suggest that assistance by the VJ to the VRS was specifically directed towards such VRS crimes, including those in Sarajevo and Srebrenica.[120] The additional question determined whether the SDC endorsed a policy of assisting VRS crimes; such a finding would again suggest that the assistance from the VRS was specifically directed towards the VRS crimes in Sarajevo and Srebrenica.[121]

Concluding on these issues, the Appeals Chamber found that the VRS was not an organisation whose actions were criminal per se; instead, it was an army fighting a war.[122] The Appeals Chamber noted the Trial Chamber's finding that the VRS's strategy was 'inextricably linked to' crimes against civilians.[123] However, it did not find that *all* VRS activities in Sarajevo or Srebrenica were criminal in nature and hence the 'specific direction' requirement was not satisfied.[124] Turning to the other proof question, the Appeals Chamber noted that there was Supreme Defence Council (SDC) approval of measures to secure financing for the VRS and aid was given in the transfer of equipment and supplies. However, the Appeals Chamber observed that the volume of assistance did not necessarily demonstrate specific direction, and thus such evidence did not automatically establish a sufficient link between aid provided by an accused aider and abettor and the commission of crimes by principal perpetrators. The Appeals Chamber held that the VRS was participating in lawful combat activities and was not a purely criminal organisation and hence there was no specific direction providing aid to the crimes.[125] As such, the aiding and abetting charge was unsubstantiated.

The application of the 'specific direction' test in *Perisic* is questionable, as although the nature of the VRS was not essentially criminal and the body had engaged in legitimate combat activities, it was *simultaneously* responsible for terrible crimes against civilians. The question of whether the VRS engaged in legitimate combat activities does not answer the main issue of whether Perisic had aided and abetted the crimes which were committed during the same time frame by the agency he helped. It has long been established in preceding judicial decisions that it is irrelevant whether the assistance could have contributed to

119 *Perisic (Appeal)*, para [51].
120 *Perisic (Appeal)*, para [52].
121 *Perisic (Appeal)*, para [52].
122 *Perisic (Appeal)*, para [57].
123 *Perisic (Appeal)*, para [53].
124 *Perisic (Appeal)*, para [57].
125 *Perisic (Appeal)*, para [57].

or facilitated lawful activities so long as it had actually substantially contributed to the crime committed.[126] Hence, by focusing on whether the VRS was lawful in nature did not address the issue of whether Perisic had aided and abetted crimes perpetrated by the military. One should not evade criminal responsibility by claiming that the resources he supplied could have been used for lawful purposes as the organisation had a predominantly lawful purpose even though the resources were also directed towards criminal ends.

To add to the confusion, other cases such as *Prosecutor v Vidoje Blagojevic and Dragan Jokic* ('*Blagojevic and Dragan Jokic*') have adopted an alternative line of reasoning to exclude the 'specific direction' requirement altogether. In this regard, the Appeals Chamber held that 'specific direction' would often be implicit in the finding that the accused had provided practical assistance to the principal perpetrator thereby substantially facilitating the commission of the crime.[127]

Problems with the 'specific direction' and 'substantial contribution' requirements

It appears that as part of the proof process at the international level, these terms have been used interchangeably, leaving much conjecture as to the correct application of the specific direction requirement. Here, the two distinct requirements of 'specific direction' and 'substantial effect' are used as mutually contingent. Arguably, the appeal chambers had in substance applied the former test of 'substantial effect' in determining whether Jokic had aided and abetted the crimes. It was held that Jokic's acts of assistance were found to include coordinating, sending, and monitoring the deployment of Zvornik Brigade's resources and equipment to the mass execution sites.[128] More importantly, without mentioning whether the assistance was 'specifically directed' the Appeal Chamber concluded that the assistance Jokic provided in his capacity as Chief of Engineering in deploying engineering machinery and personnel for the burial operations at Orahovac, Pilica/Branjevo Military Farm, and Kozluk, had *a substantial effect* on the commission of the mass executions at these three sites.[129]

In contrast Farrell in 'Attributing Criminal Liability to Corporate Actors'[130] points out conduct that substantially contributes to a crime may not necessarily be direct in terms of the causal chain and hence 'specific direction' does not equal substantial contribution.[131] Farrell further contends that there is no need that the act of assistance serve as a condition precedent for the commission of the crime nor must the assistance have caused the act of the principal offender (as seems to

126 *Prosecutor v Vidoje Blagojevic and Dragan Jokic*, Case No. IT-02-60-A.

127 *Jokic (Appeal)*, para [202].

128 *Jokic (Appeal)*, para [180].

129 *Jokic (Appeal)*, para [196].

130 Farrell, Norman, "Attributing Criminal Liability to Corporate Actors: Some Lessons from the International Tribunals," *Journal of International Criminal Justice*, 8 3, 2010, pp. 873–894.

131 Farrell (2010), p. 890.

be the case where 'specific direction' is concerned in *Perisic*).[132] In other words, there is no requirement that the contribution must be direct, the provision of the resources can amount to aiding and abetting as long as the acts have a substantial effect on the commission of the crime.

Having established that the meaning of the specific direction requirement has been conflated with that of substantial contribution, *Perisic*'s problematic application of the 'specific direction' requirement adds to contested principle and uncertain precedent by ignoring essential requirements for aiding and abetting. As mentioned above, the Appeals Chamber in determining whether Perisic had specifically directed resources to the crimes said to be assisted, confined its determination to whether the VRS was an organisation whose sole and exclusive purpose was the commission of crimes and whether the SDC endorsed a policy of assisting VRS crimes. It has been suggested above that this approach misses the issue of whether there was sufficient and substantial involvement or contribution by Perisic towards the crimes committed by the VRS as the essence of aiding and abetting.

More crucially, the decision of the *Perisic* Appeals Chamber that specific direction can be presumed or implied for those aiders and abettors who are proximate to the crime (geographically or otherwise) has been resisted and criticised by academics and legal professionals in subsequent cases. The prosecutor's arguments in the case of *Sainovic* challenging this approach had been summarised by Coco and Gal.[133] The prosecution submitted that the differential application of specific direction depending on the remoteness of the accused had no basis in the ICTY Statute or in its jurisprudence. The prosecution then countered that it would create an unjustified difference in treatment based on the location of the accused at the time when the assistance was given and the crime perpetrated. Additionally, it was posited that proximity or remoteness should, in theory, have no influence on the substantial effect of the accused's conduct, nor on his criminal mental state. As remarked by the prosecution, a 'remote' aider and abettor might even be able to provide more effective assistance than a 'proximate' aider and abettor and have more extensive knowledge of the circumstances of the crimes, especially if he/she is a high-ranking official of an army involved in a conflict. Finally, the exact meaning of proximity or remoteness has been left undefined by the *Perisic* appeal judgment, which only referred to an assessment to be conducted on a case-by-case basis.

In this brief analysis of problematic proof perspectives regarding secondary responsibility and participation it remains to speculate on why the remoteness of the accused from the scene of crime should influence substantial effect or specific direction. In many of the cases referred to above, the context in which the JCE crimes were committed involved groups or parties which were geographically remote from one another and operated on different time lines. Alternatively, the

132 Farrell, 2010, p. 891.

133 CoCo, Antonio, and Gal, Tom, "Losing Direction," *Journal of International Criminal Justice*, 12 2, 2014, p. 359.

substantive JCE requirements at the national level are usually more related to small-scale group crimes committed at the same place and time. As already noted on several occasions, such contextual differences suggest the inadequacy of domestic proof requirements to accommodate the realities of crimes at the international level. The same understanding can be found in the *Perisic* appeal judgment which acknowledged the difficulties of proving crimes occurring in the international context due to the remoteness of the accused from the scene of crime.[134] Essentially, the Appeals Chamber observed that prior convictions for aiding and abetting entered or affirmed by it involved relevant acts geographically or otherwise proximate to, and thus not remote from, the crimes of principal perpetrators.[135] Reiterating, where such proximity is present, specific direction may be demonstrated implicitly through discussion of other elements of aiding and abetting liability, such as substantial contribution. For example, an individual accused of aiding and abetting may have been physically present during the preparation or commission of crimes by principal perpetrators and could have made a concurrent substantial contribution, or in turn deterred the crime. In such a case, the existence of specific direction, which demonstrates the culpable link between the accused aider and abettor's assistance and the crimes of principal perpetrators, will be, in the court's reasoning, self-evident.

However, in the converse situation where the accused is far removed from the crime, the court seemed to suggest that a higher threshold would need to be passed if aiding and abetting were to be imposed. This is based on the court's practical understanding of international crimes. For example, significant temporal distance between the actions of an accused individual and the crime he or she allegedly assisted decreases the likelihood of connecting that crime to the assistance offered, and thereby the culpability of the accused individual's actions will equally diminish. As such, there would be a more exacting 'specific direction' requirement to prevent the accused from incurring liability where there should be none.

Harking back to the international judicial reasoning in JCE proof situations, the commonsense pathway to arrive at legal tests and conclusions, which are tailored to the specific context of international crimes, is circumspect. The shortcomings of this approach are evident from the specific direction requirement where courts in an attempt to formulate practical tests to accommodate the unique proof challenges of international crimes leave a trail of uncertainty in their wake and sometimes confound the influence of prevailing domestic legal authority altogether.

A new way forward?

As a broad alternative to the strained reasoning discussed throughout this brief overview, we propose the tort/crime hybrid for better resolving till-now contentious issues of proof facing international criminal prosecutions and judicial determinations. Through this hybrid proof technology (elaborated on in Chapter 5) the

134 *Perisic (Appeal)*, para [38].
135 Ibid.

problematic reasoning associated with specific direction and sufficiency would largely be avoided by engaging the tortious principles of contribution and aggregation. For instance, the introduction of aggregation would refocus the legal question central to the proof of aiding and abetting, that being whether the accused's support had a *substantial effect* upon the perpetration of the crime. It will be argued in Chapter 5 that substantial effect can be equated to material contribution, and responsibility derived from the aforementioned contribution can be aggregated according to the estimated significance of the accused's support relative to other individuals involved in the stages of commission. This approach has these benefits: it does away with the concerns arising from the specific direction-substantial contribution divide; it addresses the problems that surface when an accused is remote from the crime; and it gives a more nuanced picture of criminal responsibility relative to the actual circumstances of global criminal conduct.

This proposed approach – although novel – is not completely unsupported by legal reasoning rooted in harmonisation and hybridity (as we speculate in Chapters 2 and 4). In this regard, Chapter 6 will recall the recent developments in corporate criminal liability and crimes of association. In the common law authority of *Lennard's Carrying Co Ltd v Asiatic Petroleum Co Ltd*[136] the reasoning saw a corporation as an 'abstraction . . . its active mind and directing will therefore must consequently be sought in the person . . . who is really . . . the very ego and centre of the personality of the corporation.'[137] This tortured legal fiction cried out for the introduction of a more realistic (and contributory) appreciation of the culture of the body corporate. The identification principle represented the limit of strained proof reasoning based on the mind of the fictional individual driving the actions of the fictional corporate personality. In actual commercial practice corporations are controlled collectively. The Australian 'corporate culture' analysis, which seeks to aggregate liability amongst the individuals in the corporation for their contribution to the crime, presents a much more grounded understanding of contributory responsibility (developed in Chapter 6).[138] Corporate culture is briefly defined as:

> an attitude, policy, rule, course of conduct or practice existing within the body corporate generally or in the part of the body corporate in which the relevant activities take place.[139]

Under this approach the corporation may be found to have the requisite fault element even though no one individual could be proved sufficiently to possess that fault element, by viewing the conduct of the corporation 'as a whole.'

136 *Lennard's Carrying Co Ltd v Asiatic Petroleum Co Ltd* [1915] AC 705.

137 Ibid., per Lord Viscount Haldane.

138 Robinson, Allens Arthur, "Corporate Culture as a Basis for the Criminal Liability of Corporations," United Nations Special Representative of the Secretary-General on Human Rights and Business February 2008, p. 16.

139 Ibid.

This aggregation of responsibility approach to proof could also influence the application of contributory involvement within the context of aiding and abetting via association, as criminal organisations at the international level in many ways resemble corporations and organisations that commit crimes.[140] We will argue more convincingly in Chapters 5 and 6 that the tort/crime hybrid and its application in the corporate culture analysis has the potential to guide the transformation of aiding and abetting at the international level and is the link to ICL growing from domestic jurisdictional harmonisation.

Conclusion

Having selectively surveyed the ICC and international criminal tribunal judgments on secondary liability and participation, addressing specifically the trends in proof for JCE and aiding and abetting, a disturbing pattern emerges, when reflecting on the development of a predictable and principled approach to the proof process demonstrated through:

- the broad definition of JCE common intention;
- the expansive interpretation of JCE 'foreseeability' employing very open objective standards;
- the satisfaction that non-JCE members can still be causally linked to the perpetration of the offense even despite the uncertainty of coinciding mental states; and
- the remoteness-dependent 'specific direction' requirement for aiding and abetting seeming to replace the need for a strict interpretation of knowledge and actual assistance.

These features of judicial reasoning demonstrate an over emphasis on the significance of criminal conduct when compared with criminal mental state, and the desire not to have those responsible through some insufficiency of contribution, escape conviction. Add to this a worrying diminution of authorities which do not favor the prosecution case and the perception of results-oriented justice delivery is inescapable through:

- re-interpreting legal authority to suit the proof requirements of the case at hand as the juridical personality sees them; or
- distinguishing the authority as not having force or application to the case at hand.

As emphasised throughout this chapter, the collective nature of international crimes committed by multiple actors across a vast terrain of the temporal and

140 Both criminal organisations and corporations are collective in nature and usually organised in hierarchical order; the leaders or masterminds at the top of the chain might not have physically participated in the crimes but have contributed to its commission.

spatial generates peculiar difficulties in meeting the proof requirements of JCE and aiding and abetting as they exist at the national level. Add to the unique nature (concerning perpetration and victimisation) of global crimes prosecuted in international criminal courts and tribunals, the need to obtain practical justice in the interests of victims under the Rome Statute, and it seems inevitable the developing judicial reasoning consistent with this demand has fabricated very problematic areas of proof revealing radical manipulation of the substantive requirements of the national tests. Our answer is to move away from crime proofs as the sole terrain for hybridity, and consequent harmonisation.

This analysis has set out the issues associated with straining inappropriate nation-state proof principle and, in doing so, suggests the opportunities for a tort/crime proof process to replace the tenuous twisting of national crime proof requirements, with more rational reasoning of proof technologies. This notion of a tort/crime hybrid, that is a merging of common proof requirements for a better fit with collective perpetration and the communal damage it causes, is aimed at resolving the evidential difficulties associated with establishing individual criminal responsibility in global crime contexts (see Chapter 4).

This chapter primarily establishes the case for change. The prospect of a tort/crime hybrid will be explored in further detail in Chapter 5, returning again to the unique collective and participatory features of global crime (expanded in Chapter 4). Chapter 6 will elaborate on the ideas offered in our sketch of corporate criminal liability and criminal association reform, in seeking to chart the future for international criminal procedure within the frame of determining individual and collective responsibility set free of domestic crime proof technologies.

4 Contextualising global crimes

Introduction

In other parts of this text (see Chapters 1 and 3) we have suggested through the expansionism of judicial reasoning and the case-law narrative which follows, there is developing a jurisprudence, the boundaries of which seem to sacrifice rationality and predictability in favor of outcome-driven decision-making. The book's concluding chapter will exemplify how, when *new* crime contexts (such as corporate criminal liability, and criminal organisations) gain notoriety and promote political concern, prior to legislative reform, judicial reasoning pushes proof technologies. For instance, to compensate for the limitations of law and practice designed before the corporate personality or complex organisations became a locus for crime, tortious notions of contribution and aggregation have been toyed with. For understanding and explaining this phenomenon, beyond some shallow critique of judicial discretion and procedural immaturity, and to connect the experience of domestic jurisdictions to the international frame, this chapter has two purposes, one simpler than the other:

- To selectively test the current proof technologies employed in the determination of international criminal trials, against the evidentiary elements of the global crimes being prosecuted and judged, so that, with particular reference to the proof of individual responsibility and the recognition of legitimate victim interests, there is an empirical appreciation of *miss-fit*.[1] From this position it is possible to reveal that the nature of global crime (in terms of perpetration and victimisation) is profoundly different to crimes that are prosecuted in the courts of nation-states. Consequently, the utilisation of proof technologies designed for the evidentiary requirements of nation-state crimes will be ill-suited to the task of adjudicating global crimes. As Chapter 2 discusses, with international criminal law, and its rules and procedures intended to evolve as some harmonisation of the dominant criminal justice traditions,

1 By 'miss-fit' we refer to the incompatibility of proof procedures drawn from nation-state traditions and therein developed for very different crime contexts, being applied to the unique collective constituents of global crime.

and a hybridisation of competing principles, it is logical to expect that juridical analysis and decision-making in the international criminal jurisdiction will require the type of expansionism which is elaborated on in Chapter 3 so that old proof technologies can be applied to new crimes. However, leaving this uncomfortable reconciliation to prosecutorial and judicial creativity is producing the problematic interpretations we target in the empirical component to follow.

- To recognise that this process is not much assisted by distinguishing different types of expansionism (see Chapter 1) but rather having established the manipulation of the limitations of state-based principles, there is another significant force at work which fuels such problematic interventionism. In Chapter 1 we set out a case for constituting a new notion of justice being delivered through international criminal trials. The wider aims and obligations inherent within this new notion (relative to that which applies in state-based jurisdictions) pressures prosecutors and judges to interpret proof requirements as flexibly as possible in order that the end to impunity will apply to each and every sufficient perpetrator brought before the courts. In such circumstances, critical analysis needs to make judges and prosecutors more aware of the contradictions punctuating ICJ, and in so doing to be assisted beyond distortion in developing a jurisprudence better suited for the demands of proof (Chapter 5) and the requirements of justice (Chapter 1). We encapsulate this understanding as the foundation of a new vision for the juridical project when adjudicating global crimes (expanded on in Chapter 6).

This chapter in basic thematic mode, deconstructs the crimes of ICC jurisdiction, concentrating particularly on the prosecution of genocide, so that the importance of the atrocity context can further explain how proofs engage with collective perpetration and victimisation. The uniquely collective contextual features of global crime (perpetration and victimisation), the chapter argues, need to be accorded significance in the determination of individual responsibility at the international level. Global crimes not only represent armies, organisations and tribes victimising communities, but aligned with the wider aims of ICJ, require more than the determination of the blameworthy individual. The end to impunity should be directed against everyone responsible for the mass harms that ICJ wants to avoid as much as punish (Chapter 1). If this is to be achieved through prosecutions and trials, judicial reasoning must be assisted by more than abstractions of national jurisdictional legal fictions, and creative outcome-driven reasoning (Chapter 6).

Here we are not proposing some functionalist/reductionist argument either that new crimes produce new judicial reasoning, or that wider aims for criminal justice expiate expansionist decision-making. Both the enormity of atrocity crimes and the broad field of justice which their adjudication now demands, is creating in prosecutors and judges a cultural revolution – one that, as a result of new crimes and new justice, is inevitable (see Chapter 6). It is an ethos beyond determining the blameworthiness of the individual and it is also not to be belittled as some adventure in social necessity. Unfortunately, in its present stage this new culture is overly driven by expedience and not assisted by purpose-designed proof technologies. This chapter will conclude that if a new jurisprudence for international criminal law is possible through a deductive reasoning by judges which is not recklessly consequentialist, but complemented by new and amenable proof technologies, the function of the juridical personality in achieving new justice for new crimes will be indispensable in the formulation of this jurisprudence, and more so than through adding principle to opinion juris. A juridical cultural revolution in the delivery of ICJ will grow from understanding the unique justice enunciated in the Preamble and applying it to the proof of individual responsibility for new crime, with the assistance of dynamic frames of principle which align in a more reasoned form than what is currently hamstringing such developments.

A new international criminal jurisprudence: outcome-driven in addressing atrocity?

The wider aims and obligations motivating what we argue should be a new approach to international criminal jurisprudence (relative to that which applies in state-based jurisdictions) are at one level justifying the pressures experienced by prosecutors and judges to interpret proof requirements as flexibly as possible (see Chapter 3).[2] Central to this justification is the recurrent echo of the end to the impunity around uniquely particular perpetrators brought before the courts to answer for uniquely expansive and harmful crimes against humanity, and violating the conscience of the global community.[3] So cast, the emergent juridical culture is beyond determining the blameworthiness of the individual (discussed in Chapter 5). Rather throughout this chapter, we intend to show that there pre-exists and prevails for juridical reasoning a need to confront and apply a *continuum of responsibility* peculiar to the atrocity context that is enunciated within international criminal justice narratives. Doubtless, it may be difficult to pinpoint the two extremes of this continuum, but this transitional dynamic

2 Borda, Aldo, "Appraisal-Based and Flexible Approaches to External Precedent in International Criminal Law," *Leiden Journal of International Law*, 28 3, 2015, pp. 643–664. See also: Birmingham, Peg, "Hannah Arendt's Philosophy of Law Approach to International Criminal Law," Georgetown Public Law and Legal Theory Research Paper No. 11–30; Findlay, Mark, and Henham, Ralph, *Beyond Punishment: Achieving International Criminal Justice*, Palgrave Macmillan: Basingstoke, 2010; Garbett, Claire, "The Truth and the Trial: Victim Participation, Restorative Justice, and the International Criminal Court," *Contemporary Justice Review*, 16 2, 2013, pp. 193–213; Tibori-Szabo, Kinga, and Hirst, Megan, *Victim Participation in International Criminal Justice: Practitioner's Guide*, T.M.C. Asser Press: Heidelberg, 2017; Glasius, Marlies, "What is Global Justice and Who Decides?: Civil Society and Victim Responses to the International Criminal Court's First Investigations," *Human Rights Quarterly*, 31 2, 2009, pp. 496–520.

3 Rauschenbach, Mina, Staerkle, Christian, and Scalia, Damien, "Accused for Involvement in Collective Violence: The Discursive Reconstruction of Agency and Identity by Perpetrators of International Crimes," *Political Psychology*, 37 2, 2016; Werle, Gerhard, "Individual Criminal Responsibility in Article 25 ICC Statute," *Journal of International Criminal Justice*, 5 4, 2007, pp. 953–954.

usefully describes how adjacent roles (global crime perpetrators and mass victims) are connected by prevailing responsibilities and obligations across the four crimes that are the jurisdiction of the ICC. Perpetrators and victims are enmeshed by the enormity of the evolving crime, and as Chapters 3 and 5 will argue, this makes inseparable accountabilities to repair damage along with facing and facilitating retributive punishment. The collective nature of global crime and victimisation, and the historical dynamics of crimes unlimited by time and space invite an interpretation of the perpetrator/victim encounter which is vibrant, ongoing and for that, almost unimaginable in any domestic crime context.[4]

Assuming such to be the case, a more nuanced critical analysis of the proof requirements for global crimes and the justice that their prosecution seeks to achieve, will make judges and prosecutors more aware of the contradictions punctuating the processes of international criminal trials as they are currently playing out.[5] Furthermore, the options presented by a continuum of responsibility discourage any simple or direct assigning fault for global crimes as if it is the province of an individual perpetrator on a single occasion against an individual victim (the domestic criminal law liability scenario). At the global level, the criminal law that judges operate within understands very different realities of responsibility not accommodated by an overly individualist and sectoral representation.[6] The case-study of genocide that we interrogate later in this chapter commonly involves a cast of perpetrators joined in their destructive enterprise for purposes ranging from personal greed and intolerance to histories of cultural or racial antipathy. They carry responsibility for harm encompassing assaulting individuals and exterminating societies and ways of life. In response, juridical professionals functioning in global criminal trials recognise through inevitable compromise, even if only to the extent of the inadequacies of the laws and the procedures at their disposal, the need to bridge their current hybrid proof technologies with novel and purpose-designed interpretations of rules and procedures to achieve outcomes covering retributive sanctioning on to a new justice vision (elaborated in Chapters 5 and 6).

Global crimes take place because of political, economic, and social forces often linking superiors and subordinates in a command structure, families and civilian communities who further the common design, the *silent majority* that turns a blind eye to the crimes around them, a racialised majority that propagates ethnic hate propaganda, and the actions (or inactions) of the international community. In such an interconnected context, responsibility cannot be artificially attributed to an individual perpetration, or otherwise some small collective with

4 Werle, 2007, pp. 953–954; Scheffer, David, "The Complex Crime of Aggression under the Rome Statute," *Leiden Journal of International Law*, 23 4, 2010, pp. 897–904.

5 Heath, J. Benton, "Human Dignity at Trial: Hard Cases and Broad Concepts in International Criminal Law," *The George Washington International Law Review*, 44 2, 2012; Murphy, John, *The Evolving Dimensions of International Law: Hard Choices for the World Community*, Cambridge University Press: Cambridge, 2010.

6 Guilfoyle, Douglas, "Responsibility for Collective Atrocities: Fair Labelling and Approaches to Commission in International Criminal Law," *Current Legal Problems*, 64 1, 2011, pp. 255–286.

an espoused common purpose and shared, agreed knowledge concerning the nature of the victimisation they intend to inflict. The approach where a handful of people are blamed and held culpable for the mass murder of hundreds of thousands is certainly no realistic appraisal of the dynamics of responsibility and consequent harm within societies engulfed by genocide. Via the empirical core of this chapter, through confronting impunity, and thereby addressing in any convincing way the justice aspirations set out in the Preamble (see Chapter 1) there is a need to recognise the inherent tensions in translating directly, or indirectly, the individualised justice-rooted proof technologies of nation-state criminal law into profoundly different contexts of criminalisation and victimisation. Within any massive crime causing massive harm, there are involved people of varying degrees of culpability, who contribute in different ways, who are independent or overborne in different situations, and can therefore be complicit in the overall blameworthiness of the conduct relative to an assessable but qualified subjectivity of their perpetration. Only an awareness and recognition of such determinants, and the broader identification of the actor's personal involvement in, and contribution into the collective, can responsibility be adjudicated in a manner that will genuinely impact on future behavior (if the other conditions for deterrence such as rational choice prevail). It is essential, we argue, to influence the behavior of present and future perpetrators, taking some degree of rational choice as a given, that responsibility is situated somewhere along a continuum which represents the collective and dynamic nature of a global crime. Such an understanding will enable the development of remedies and solutions that effectively stigmatise involvement in mass atrocity and cut across this continuum of responsibility otherwise overlooked through models of proof that simplify responsibility back to contestable notions of individual liability based on the temporally and spatially bound coincidence of conduct and mental state. Narrower approaches may suit criminal justice systems finding their roots in retribution-driven nation-state law. However, as we have shown (see Chapter 1), it is clear from an examination of the intentions for global criminal justice and the nature of global crimes that the prosecution project covers more complex responsibility deliberations than retribution alone.[7] The Preamble stipulates that the aims of the international criminal trial are as much to prevent as to punish the consequences of responsibility.[8] Considering responsibility along a continuum of contribution and culpability (which comprises responsibility) means that a wider range of actors can be more convincingly drawn into the court's determination, and thereby the apportionment of responsibility in a more personally *and* collectively subjective fashion

7 Regarding the wider limitations associated with a retributive focus for international criminal justice, see: Findlay, Mark, "Harmonising Global Criminal Justice for Peacebuilding," in Kerry Clamp (ed.) *Restorative Justice in Transitional Settings*, Routledge: London, 2016, pp. 152–172.

8 UN General Assembly, Rome Statute of the International Criminal Court (last amended 2010), 17 July 1998, Preamble states: 'The States Parties to this Statute, . . . determined to put an end to impunity for the perpetrators of these crimes and thus to contribute to the prevention of such crimes.'

will better ensure the development of remedies where the punishment can be calibrated to fit the actualities of global crime.

Limitations of nation-state law as the foundation for proving responsibility in global crimes – the myth of mental state

As revealed in the earlier chapters, there is a jurisprudence developing for international criminal law which seems to sacrifice rationality and predictability in favor of outcome-driven decision-making.[9] One salient feature of this trend is the incompatibility of proving the unique elements of the four global crimes, employing a substantive and procedural framework with its roots originally in determining the liability of a single (or rarely several perpetrators) causing harm to an individual victim. Atrocity trials do not present this causation dynamic. To understand and explain this miss-fit, the chapter will first selectively confront the current proof technologies employed in the determination of international criminal trials such as subjective mental states, against some of the discretionary proof interpretations of the global crimes being prosecuted and judged. By particularising the proof of individual responsibility, and the recognition of legitimate victim interests, we progress to empirically appreciating the inadequacies and incapacities of current proof technologies contrasted with the constituents and nature of global crimes, particularly genocide. The empirical core of this chapter is an examination of the difficulties encountered in prosecuting genocide under the current individualised and subjective proof requirements. Employing this example, we will engage commentators proposing solutions that not surprisingly resonate with the hybrid strategy advanced in Chapter 5, yet still remain confined within the thinking of individualised liability.

The straightjacket of individual subjectivity

At this point it is necessary to clarify that nothing we say concerning our continuum methodology digresses from the Rome Statute's focus on the responsibility of the natural person.[10] We accept this radical departure in the application of public international law,[11] while at the same time rejecting that the only

9 Tallgren, Immi, "The Sensibility and Sense of International Criminal Law," *EJIL*, 13 3, 2002, pp. 561–595.

10 Rome Statute, Article 25 states: (1) The Court shall have jurisdiction over natural persons pursuant to this Statute; Damgaard, Ciara, *Individual Criminal Responsibility for Core International Crimes*, Springer-Verlag: Berlin, Heidelberg, 2008; Jackson, Miles, "Individual Criminal Responsibility," in Miles Jackson, *Complicity in International Law*, Oxford University Press: Oxford, 2015, Chapter 3.

11 Although some academics have also sought to challenge the 'natural persons' notion under the Rome Statute further by proposing to include or recognise corporate liability through the corporate personality, for a detailed analysis on this issue see: Kyriakakis, Joanna, "Corporate Criminal Liability and the ICC Statute: The Comparative Law Challenge," *Netherlands International Law Review*, 56 3, 2009, pp. 333–366; Van Der Wilt, Harmen, "Corporate Criminal Responsibility for International Crimes: Exploring the Possibilities," *Chinese Journal of International Law*, 12 1, 2013, pp. 43–77.

interpretation of this responsibility frame is some mirror of what constitutes conventional criminal liability. It is true that ICL requires a person to be proved responsible for criminal conduct with the requisite mental state, but as we propose in Chapter 5 both elements and their coincidence and causation should be established through different means, not least because global crime is a unique dynamic of responsibility and obligation.

Nation-state criminal law and proof procedures are primarily designed to prosecute the individual for an offense against an individual victim in a specific time and place. Within nation-state criminal law, the subjective guilt of a person depends on the determination that he or she intended to commit the crime (or was reckless that it would be committed), based on two elements familiar to most – the unlawful act (*actus reus*) and proof of a guilty state of mind (*mens rea*).[12] These two elements comprise the accepted foundation for most criminal liability in common law traditions, and are equally significant in establishing legal guilt in Continental civil law frames[13] and now in international criminal law.[14]

Global crimes are similarly built upon the accepted understanding that the perpetrator must be subjectively connected to the purpose of the offense.[15] This approach is consistent with a basic proof maxim that the more serious the crime, and in some situations, the more removed the accused from its actual perpetration, the more subjective should be the proof of mental state.[16]

Distinct differences at the international level emerge regarding the way subjective mental states will be satisfactorily proved. We argue that this is an inevitable consequence of how people come together at different levels of an organisation and different stages in a collective perpetration, to exhibit this required mental state (see Chapter 6). For instance, with genocide, in the *Akayesu* judgment,[17] the elements of the crime of genocide were elaborated upon, and of interest to this analysis is the interpretation of the *mens rea* of the crime beyond a stringent forensic interrogation of the mind of one perpetrator.

12 Marchuk, Iryna, *The Fundamental Concept of Crime in International Criminal Law*, Springer: Berlin, 2013, Chapters 2 and 3; Mannheim, Hermann, "Mens Rea in German and English Law – II," *Journal of Comparative Legislation and International Law*, 17 4, 1935, pp. 236–250.

13 Criminal Code in the version promulgated on 13 November 1998, Federal Law Gazette [Bundesgesetzblatt] I, p. 3322, last amended by Article 1 of the Law of 24 September 2013, Federal Law Gazette I p. 3671 and with the text of Article 6 (18) of the Law of 10 October 2013, Federal Law Gazette, pp. 3799; Criminal Code of the French Republic (as of 2016).

14 Marchuk, 2013; Safferling, Christoph, *Towards an International Criminal Procedure*, 1st edition, Oxford University Press: Oxford, 2003, Preface.

15 Ochi, Megimi, "The Concept of *Mens Rea* in International Criminal Law: The Case for a Unified Approach," *Journal of International Criminal Justice*, 11 4, 2013, pp. 933–936; Knoops, Geert-Jan Alexander, *Mens Rea at the International Criminal Court*, Volume 10 of International Criminal Law Series, BRILL: Nijhoff, 2016.

16 See the higher need for proof of subjective mental state for liability under Joint Criminal Enterprise: Elliott, Catherine, "The *Mens Rea* Required of Secondary Parties," *Journal of Criminal Law*, 64 6, 2000, pp. 581–581; Krebs, Beatrice, "Joint Criminal Enterprise," *Modern Law Review*, 73 4, 2010, pp. 578–604.

17 *Prosecutor v Jean Paul Akayesu*, Case No. ICTR-96-4-T, Section 6.3.1.

In the context of mass atrocity, acting intentionally can be and has been interpreted in different ways. For instance, the ICTR eventually indicted Akayesu by:

> [deducing] the genocidal intent inherent in a particular act charged from the general context of the perpetration of other culpable acts systematically directed against that same group.[18]

Furthermore, the court stated that it is possible to infer genocidal intent from:

> other factors, such as the scale of atrocities committed, their general nature, in a region or a country, or the fact of deliberately and systematically targeting victims on account of their membership of a particular group.[19]

Beyond constructing such an essentially subjective mental state in nation-state traditions, the international judicial reasoning exhibits the necessity to twist even the most basic proofs of an accused's intention and purpose to fit the idiosyncrasies of atrocity crimes in the field. More than this, however, the mental states which combine to condone, assist, support, transact, commit and conceal a global crime are of their very nature a collective phenomenon. The Rome Statute recognises this paradox – some individual mental state proved by shared and progressive intentions and degrees of recklessness.

> As far as the forms of criminal participation are concerned, leadership, organization, instigation, and complicity in the formulation or execution of a common plan or conspiracy to commit any of those crimes entailed individual criminal responsibility 'for all acts performed by any persons in execution of such plan.'[20]

18 *Akayesu (Trial)*, para [477] states: In which the Trial Chamber declared that genocidal intent could be inferred from the physical acts and specifically 'their massive and/or systematic nature of their atrocity.' It held that 'in the absence of a confession from the accused, his intent can be inferred from a certain number of presumptions of fact.' The Trial Chamber considered 'that it is possible to deduce the genocidal intent inherent in a particular act charged from the general context of the perpetration of other culpable acts systematically directed against that same group, whether these acts were committed by the same offender or by others. Other factors, such as the scale of atrocities committed, their general nature, in a region or a country, or furthermore, the fact of deliberately and systematically targeting victims on account of their membership of a particular group, while excluding the members of other groups, can enable the Chamber to infer the genocidal intent of a particular act.' The Trial Chamber expressed 'the opinion that it is possible to infer the genocidal intention that presided over the commission of a particular act, *inter alia*, from all acts or utterances of the accused, or from the general context in which other culpable acts were perpetrated systematically against the same group, regardless of whether such other acts were committed by the same perpetrator or even by other perpetrators.'

19 Ibid.

20 Raimondo, Fabian, *General Principles of Law in the Decisions of International Criminal Courts and Tribunals*, BRILL: Leiden, 2016, p. 76.

However, there are various inherent difficulties in conceptualising roles of individual agency and responsibility from collective wrongdoing, and the Chamber's judgment in this case reflects this inherent challenge in its vague and expansive language. Such judicial reasoning is not unreasonable, considering the facts with which the judges were faced, and the necessity to respond to punitive and restorative imperatives for ICJ. The tribunal considered 'intent [to be] a mental factor which is difficult, even impossible to determine.' The judges enunciated one of the fundamental paradoxes in criminal proofs; that we require the establishment of the accused's mind at the time of committing the crime, and we reject inferential proofs, but in fact mental state is concluded not often from the admission of the accused, but rather out of the acceptance that other inference could be drawn from unequivocal conduct.[21]

The nature of mass atrocities and the difficulties with causation and contribution

As already observed, mass atrocity is not the product of random or spontaneous behavior, nor is it planned, deliberated, and orchestrated by one person against one person, at one time, in one place. Perpetrators often participate because they agree with and desire the outcome, or because it is rational for them to do so at the time, or they may not comply without pressure, or they experience situations where they never even think the act matters. For example, subordinates stand to gain when they follow the orders of their superiors. The reality is that 'a large number of people . . . find war and a barracks existence a step up rather than a step down' from their otherwise wretched lives.[22] Along with such oppressed perpetrators, there are the myriad that act anywhere from fear to the satisfaction of deep-seateded racist predispositions.

Furthermore, the offense contexts of global crimes are very likely prolonged spatially and temporally. For instance, the Democratic Republic of Congo has faced ongoing insurgent and race-based conflict since 1996, in the wake of the 1994 Rwandan genocide.[23] In 1996 Rwanda and Uganda invaded the eastern districts of the DRC ostensibly to root out the remaining perpetrators of the Rwanda genocide. However, the peace process in eastern Congo continues to be fragile with multiple armed groups operating throughout the region.[24]

In these endless cycles of insurgent conflict, both culpability and contribution are contingent on command structures and superior orders largely denied

21 *Akayesu (Trial)*, Para [523].

22 Kaplan, Robert, "The Coming Anarchy," *The Atlantic Monthly,* 1994, p. 72.

23 Odom, Thomas, and Reimer, Dennis, *Journey into Darkness: Genocide in Rwanda*, Texas A&M University Press: College Station, 2005, Chapter 1.

24 Human Rights Watch, "'You Will Be Punished' – Attacks on Civilians in Eastern Congo," Report, 2009; Human Rights Watch, "The War Within the War – Sexual Violence Against Women and Girls in Eastern Congo," 2002; Ventures Africa, "How Armed Militia Groups are Fueling Genocide in the Democratic Republic of Congo," November 2016.

as factors in culpability within conventional proofs of criminal liability.[25] Until the Second World War, superior orders routinely excluded the culpability of the subordinate who acted under those orders; only the superior was criminally responsible. However, in Article 8 of the Statute as confirmed by the International Military Tribunal at Nuremberg,[26] liability was neither determined nor excused through the existence of an order where perhaps unrealistically the judicial thinking preferred to measure a higher moral choice as the determinant of individual liability.[27]

Ethnic hate propaganda was significant in promoting and propagating the recent genocidal violence in the Balkans and in Rwanda. The insidious pervasiveness of such hate propaganda highlights the scope of actors involved in achieving such violence, from people who poison the pen to those who pull the trigger. This understanding impugns any adaptation of an individual liability paradigm known at the nation-state level and narrowly transposed to the context of collective violence which is global crime.

In the context of the Nuremberg trials, the sheer magnitude of Nazi extermination waves contextualised the difficulty with the using of nation-state notions of liability in prosecuting global crimes. Particular to the Nuremberg trials was the *ex post facto* defense that argued it is improper to prosecute someone for an act legal at the time and place where the crime was said to be committed. This link between domestic law and atrocities of global dimensions demonstrates the moral as well as legal dangers in binding nation-state technologies of proof to crimes that are mass violations of human rights, undermining objectives of ending impunity through individual liability conditional on perverted law at the time of the offense. Despite the extraordinary nature of the criminality of mass atrocity, the approach of ICJ to the process of determining guilt or innocence remains captured by the *ordinary*. The new lenses necessary for perceiving proof contradictions from within the atrocity context, as opposed to working with the domestic criminal liability blinkers, are what we offer in Chapter 5.

It is logical to expect that juridical analysis and decision-making in the international criminal jurisdiction will require the type of expansionism which is elaborated on in Chapter 3. However, it is not clear whether this can be achieved by tinkering with or transforming criminal proofs at the level of domestic procedural traditions. Chapter 5 sets an agenda for solving these challenges without jettisoning established nation-state proof technologies while at the same time taking hybridisation and complementarity outside their current criminal procedural conceptions (foreshadowed in Chapter 2).

25 Gaeta, Paola, "The Defence of Superior Orders: The Statute of International Criminal Court versus Customary International Law," *European Journal of International Law*, 10 1, 1999, pp. 172–191.

26 Garraway, Charles, "Superior Orders and the International Criminal Court: Justice Delivered or Justice Denied," *International Review of the Red Cross*, 81 836, 1999, p. 178.

27 O'Sullivan, Carmel, *Killing on Command: The Defence of Superior Orders in Modern Combat*, London: Palgrave Macmillan, 2016, p. 26.

In any case, the end to impunity should be directed against everyone responsible for the mass harms that ICJ wants to avoid as much as punish. If this is to be achieved through prosecutions and trials, judicial reasoning must be assisted by more than abstractions of national jurisdictional legal fictions (see Chapter 3). Throughout this chapter, we briefly touch on the range of actors and their particular roles and contexts that comprise global crimes, as victims and perpetrators in the frame of a continuum of responsibility (and obligation) – for harm caused and for harm suffered.

The wider proof obligations flowing from the notion of a continuum of responsibility relative to that which applies in state-based jurisdictions with individualised proof predispositions, pressure prosecutors and judges to interpret proof requirements as flexibly as possible in order that the end to impunity will apply to any sufficient perpetrator brought before the courts, and for the benefit of any victim suffering harm. Because of the complex complicity cascade that needs to be considered in proving global crimes, this new approach to responsibility (and obligation) will not diminish the brutality of each atrocity or exculpate the aggressors responsible individually, as a result of understanding the phenomenon more collectively and in an interrelated frame. In fact, it better allows for recognising harm as a crucial factor in the apportioning of responsibility. We want proof technologies that contemplate rich contextual variants such as bystander innocence, reparations for victims, reconciliation, groupthink, reintegration of offenders, and the dual role of the international community as enabler of violence and as arbiter of right or wrong. In other words, the extension of the dominant discourse of nation-state criminal law to include contextual considerations like the silence of the majority, the complicity of the bystander, and the inaction of the international community enriches the new proof potentials proposed in the chapter to follow, even if it also demands more expansive thinking from lawyers and judges. Thereby a more principled and reasoned international criminal jurisprudence will facilitate the development of remedies that stigmatise active and passive involvement in mass atrocity, and also focus on the need to restore victims beyond harm and damage. This restorative aim, often overlooked in nation-state criminal law systems directed at retribution, makes international criminal justice unique as a process for measuring transiting and understandings of responsibility and obligation along a proof continuum.

Genocide – proving the unprovable?

Proving the intention to commit genocide has been a matter of much debate and controversy. Where individualised intention is concerned, there are two approaches advanced in the literature as relevant to the issue, the predominant purpose-based and the less-ascribed knowledge-based approach. The purpose-based paradigm has been judicially endorsed while the knowledge-based direction is an alternative way of conceptualising genocidal intention preferred by certain critical commentators to answer the limitations of the purpose approach. The tensions behind this *divergence* in methods for proving genocidal intention can in turn be ameliorated through the tort/crime hybrid proof technology that we advance in the following chapter.

Knowledge-based intention proofs, originally suggested by Professor Greenawalt are inspired by similar concerns expressed above by ICTR in stretching traditional *mens rea* requirements in ways which challenge the foundations of subjectivity. Greenawalt noted that intention in the international criminal law context was being transformed into a creature unrecognisable in its nation-state proof traditions. The factors driving this distortion center on the difficulty in attributing the guilty mental state to an *individual* where the crime of genocide is one that is committed *collectively*.

Further, he claimed that the enormity of the *actus reus* and *mens rea* of genocide under Article 6 of the Rome Statute make proof unlikely to be attributed in the *same way* to each person engaged in the genocidal enterprise. For instance, the subordinate primary perpetrator of the genocidal *acts* might not (and very often does not) have the specific *intention* to commit genocide in terms of intending the destruction of the social group as a *goal* (this is the position under the purpose-driven interpretation of genocidal intention). Critically the specific intention of genocide as a goal is often found at the leadership level, but leaders rarely physically perpetrate the act of genocide.[28] Therefore, if one were to use a purpose-driven interpretation of genocidal intention, some cases may demonstrate that the act will coincide with the mental state of those whose purpose it is to achieve, distanced from those who fire the torch. Knowledge-based proofs have been twisted to overcome the dissonance between purpose and perpetration through focusing on what the perpetrator (whether a subordinate or leader) *knew* at the time he committed the genocidal act. If the organisation as a whole shared the intention to commit genocide and so performed genocidal acts, the court can infer (under the knowledge-based approach) that the accused also carried this intention when he participated in such acts. Such an analysis draws closer to the dynamics of the genocide phenomenon than the purpose-driven approach which looks at the subjective goal of the accused, but even so relies on often tenuous constructions and inferences of knowledge through the imputations of purpose. Neither pathway to proof satisfactorily addresses the realistic questions of contribution and causation which underlie genocidal phenomena.

The dynamics of genocide

The provisions for genocide and individual criminal responsibility set out in Articles 6 and 25 of the Rome statute, read as follows:

28 Greenawalt, Alexander, "Rethinking Genocidal Intent: The Case for a Knowledge-Based Interpretation," *Columbia Law Review*, 99, 1999. Link: http://digitalcommons.pace.edu/lawfaculty/338/, pp. 2281: more specifically, the defendant subordinate can attempt to use *orders* from superiors as a defense to genocidal intention.

Article 6

For the purpose of this Statute, 'genocide' means any of the following acts committed with intent to destroy, in whole or in part, a national, ethnical, racial or religious group, as such:[29]

- a killing members of the group;
- b causing serious bodily or mental harm to members of the group;
- c deliberately inflicting on the group conditions of life calculated to bring about its physical destruction in whole or in part;
- d imposing measures intended to prevent births within the group;
- e forcibly transferring children of the group to another group.

Article 25 Individual criminal responsibility[30]

1 The Court shall have jurisdiction over natural persons pursuant to this Statute.

2 A person who commits a crime within the jurisdiction of the Court shall be individually responsible and liable for punishment in accordance with this Statute.

3 In accordance with this Statute, a person shall be criminally responsible and liable for punishment for a crime within the jurisdiction of the Court if that person:

    - a Commits such a crime, whether as an individual, jointly with another or through another person, regardless of whether that other person is criminally responsible;
    - b Orders, solicits or induces the commission of such a crime which in fact occurs or is attempted;
    - c For the purpose of facilitating the commission of such a crime, aids, abets or otherwise assists in its commission or its attempted commission, including providing the means for its commission;
    - d In any other way contributes to the commission or attempted commission of such a crime by a group of persons acting with a common purpose. Such contribution shall be intentional and shall either:
        - i Be made with the aim of furthering the criminal activity or criminal purpose of the group, where such activity or purpose involves the commission of a crime within the jurisdiction of the Court; or
        - ii Be made in the knowledge of the intention of the group to commit the crime;

29 Rome Statute, Article 6.

30 Rome Statute, Article 25.

- e In respect of the crime of genocide, directly and publicly incites others to commit genocide;
- f Attempts to commit such a crime by taking action that commences its execution by means of a substantial step, but the crime does not occur because of circumstances independent of the person's intentions. However, a person who abandons the effort to commit the crime or otherwise prevents the completion of the crime shall not be liable for punishment under this Statute for the attempt to commit that crime if that person completely and voluntarily gave up the criminal purpose.

4 No provision in this Statute relating to individual criminal responsibility shall affect the responsibility of States under international law.

Judicial interpretation of the necessary mental state favors the establishment of purpose over knowledge. The purpose-based approach to genocidal intent unrealistically demands that the individual perpetrator of the crime must act with the *goal* or *desire* to contribute to the partial destruction of the targeted social group or entity. In *Akayesu* the court determined that the perpetrator must clearly seek to produce the act charged.[31] The same was said in *Prosecutor v Krstic*[32] where the relevant mental state to commit genocide was to engage in an act with the *purpose* of destroying a human group. Further in the case of *Jelisic*, the Appeals Chamber held that the relevant genocidal intention was to aim to destroy a human group.[33] These cases establish that the predominant judicial interpretation of 'specific intention' is focused on the presence of a subjective *purpose or desire* to engage in the act of genocide.

Critical commentary regarding individualised purpose or desire recognises its unjust outcomes. The alternative knowledge-based approach cautions that a purpose-based standard not merely facilitates culpable perpetrators escaping liability for genocide, but perhaps of more jurisprudential impact it creates just the evidentiary problems that compel courts to squeeze ambiguous fact patterns into the specific intent paradigm.[34]

The purpose-based standard at the international level of genocide proofs reveals profound proof incompatibilities when requiring individual liability thinking to confront the collective features of global crime. That said, in deconstructing the particular limitations of the purpose-based approach it is not difficult to draw out general complications associated with any proof approach rooted in an individual liability tradition;

31 *Akayesu (Trial)*, para [649].
32 *Prosecutor v Radislav Krstic*, Case No. IT-98-33-T, para [568].
33 *Prosecutor v Goran Jelisic*, Case No. IT-95-10-A, para [46].
34 Greenawalt, 1999, p. 2281.

1 The purpose-based approach focuses on individualised guilt and does not account for the *hierarchical* nature of the aggressor group. The leader who commands the commission of genocide but who does not himself engage in active perpetration, and the subordinate who acts but does not necessarily desire the outcome of genocide, neither may incur liability under the purpose-based standard yet are both essential to the crime's commission.
2 The nature of genocide itself connoting the destruction of a substantial number of individuals within a social group necessitates collective action. Very often, evidence of an individual's purpose in the enterprise is difficult and almost impossible to ascertain. Rather it is the organisation's culture or its goals that best indicate proof of genocidal intention on the part of its members (see Chapter 6).
3 The purpose-based approach provides an unrealistic depiction of genocidal intention, as it does of the dynamics of genocide. This unreality vests in the conventional understandings of intention as linked to knowledge and purpose individually, temporally and spatially bound. It also falters when causation and coincidence are tortured into a series of events where the determinant mental states are, conveniently determined not as a collective endeavor but rather an individual moment of evil.

To apply problematic consequentialist understandings of intention, individualised and drawn from domestic proof technologies entirely foreign to encountering the dynamics of atrocity,[35] produces the distortions and strains suggested above. In reflecting on these we ask the reader to contemplate how such contortions could be minimised by looking at responsible perpetrators as operating somewhere (with others) on our continuum of responsibility. Importantly paralleled by the continuum of harm methodology, their criminal conduct devolves to victims coming in and out of the genocide phenomenon across histories of abuse. Writing at the time we do, it is heartless not to pause and consider the ethnic cleansing of the Rohingyas in Myanmar.[36] It would be impossible to advance a genocide case against an individual member of the military or the insurgent

35 Chapter 3 reveals ways in which intention is being distorted at the international level using the following cases to illustrate that point: *Public Prosecutor v Milan Martic*, Case No. IT-95-11-A; *Public Prosecutor v Milomir Stakic*, Case No. IT-97-24-T; *Public Prosecutor v Milan Martic*, Case No. IT-95-11-T; *Public Prosecutor v Dusko Tadic*, Case No. IT-94-1-A.

36 "UN human rights chief points to 'textbook example of ethnic cleansing' in Myanmar," UN News Centre, 11 September 2017: The crucial facts mentioned in the article include Zeid Ra'ad al-Hussein's statement to the UN Human Rights Council in Geneva, noting that the current situation cannot yet be fully assessed since Myanmar has refused access to human rights investigators. He cited reports of Myanmar authorities laying landmines along the border with Bangladesh and requiring returnees to provide 'proof of nationality,' an impossibility, given that successive Myanmar governments have since 1962 progressively stripped the Rohingya population of their political and civil rights, including citizenship rights.

separatists, or the expulsionist locals or the antidisestablishmentarian Buddhists without implicating state authority in denial and an international community wary of the return to army rule.[37]

Having presented the difficulties associated with an over-concentration on purpose as a proof technology, it is appropriate to explore a consideration of consequentialist analysis by imposing individual liability models on the collective reality of the genocidal experience.

Arbitrary and unjust outcomes

To illustrate how the use of the purpose-based approach to genocidal liability may lead to an arbitrary apportioning of guilt between culpable perpetrators, Greenawalt refers to a situation of 'administrative massacre' such as that presented by the Holocaust where a state deploys an entire bureaucracy and military chain of command to realise a genocidal plan. People played roles in the atrocity within different power dispersals but the legitimacy, authority and sanctimonious sagacity of the genocide needed the cover and motivation of institutional orderliness.

Where a person commits genocidal acts under orders, for instance, one might argue that the *very nature* of certain orders requires a subordinate to exercise a rational genocidal intent, in some moral frame. An example is where when the District Court of Jerusalem convicted Adolf Eichmann under an Israeli domestic offense against the law of nations prohibiting genocide, they rejected the plea of superior orders by stating that 'the very wide compass of [Eichmann's] activities' testified to his intent. Although the court did not specify this interpretation, the proposition appears to argue that Eichmann's role in the collection and transportation of Jewish victims to death camps was so encompassing that any order he may

37 Fassihi, Farnaz, "World News: Myanmar Faces Outcry Over Crackdown – Military Push to Drive Rohingya Outdraws International Scrutiny and Militant Calls to Arms," *Wall Street Journal*, Eastern Edition, 2017, New York, states: 'The push by the Myanmar military to clear Rohingya villages and drive hundreds of thousands of members of the Muslim ethnic group into Bangladesh elicited censure on Wednesday (13th September 2017) from the United Nations Security Council . . . The council called on Myanmar to end the military operation, amid charges that the military leadership that runs the country alongside Nobel Peace Laureate Aung San Suu Kyi is pursuing a campaign of ethnic cleansing'; Robinson, Geoffrey, "East Timor Ten Years On: Legacies of Violence," *The Journal of Asian Studies*, 70 4, 2011, pp. 1007–1021, states: 'Maternus Bere, a commander of the pro-Indonesian Laksaur militia group, had been indicted for his role in the September 1999 killing of as many as 200 unarmed supporters of independence who had taken refuge in the Catholic Church in Suai . . . The Suai Church massacre was part of a shocking campaign of violence that followed a United Nations-organised referendum in which Timorese had voted overwhelmingly for independence from Indonesia'; Momah, Sam, *Nigeria Beyond Divorce – Amalgamation in Perspective*, Safari Books Ltd: Ibadan, 2013, Chapter 4 explains: 'Nigerian Military in Governance: The author gives a detailed analysis of the military coups and counter-coups within Nigeria from 1966 to 1999 and illustrates the instability and destruction they have caused to the country.' Ibadan, 2013, Chapter 4 explores.

have followed was equivalent to a directive stating, 'organise the destruction of the Jewish people.' In so many words, the German state at the time authorised and demanded genocide and the accused was positioned to be part of its facilitation. As such, Eichmann could not have performed his duties without directing himself towards their ultimate genocidal purpose, with the comfort of higher authority, but not exculpated by moral innocence overborne by a contrary criminal intent.[38]

However, in support of his knowledge-based approach Greenawalt projects that the above example depends too excessively and arbitrarily on the contingencies of Eichmann's specific role. Suppose instead that Eichmann was the head of a death camp and that his function was to oversee the daily killing of whichever prisoners happened to arrive. In this case Eichmann performed an assigned task in full knowledge that he was personally affecting the destruction of an entire people, but his specific duties required no particular attitude toward the identity of his preselected victims. In that instance it seems that the only way to demonstrate a specific genocidal intent under the purpose paradigm would be to show that Eichmann himself was personally motivated by a desire to participate in genocide. Yet even assuming such motives are demonstrable (as is unlikely to be the case in many instances of subordinate liability), or more importantly, satisfactory for nation-state proof technologies, judges are faced with legitimate questions as to whether Eichmann's own reasons for following orders should matter as a question of substantive principle, particularly given the extent to which his specific duties may be incidental to those motives.

Thus, it is clear in this reasoning, that the knowledge-based approach was developed in part to mitigate the injustice of allowing perpetrators who were clearly instrumental in the commission of genocide from escaping liability, as the nature of their individual purpose depended crucially on collective contingencies.

Evidentiary problems resulting in the distortion of specific intention

An additional problem in employing a purpose-based approach to intent sufficient for genocide is its failure to cater to the specific factual scenarios before it, and the subsequent manipulation of substantive legal principles by judges to make up for the *gap* that the dislocation between doctrine and daily dynamics creates. Greenawalt was particularly troubled by the ICTR's practice of presuming genocidal intent but at the same time doctrinally upholding the strict purpose-based version. Neither conceptually nor practically are they equivalent. The purpose-based approach is subjective[39] and looks at whether the accused had aimed to destroy a social group. By contrast, knowledge-based approaches consider whether the perpetrator acted in furtherance of a campaign targeting members of a protected group and knew that the goal or manifest effect of the campaign was the destruction of the group in whole or in part. It could be said

38 Greenawalt, 1999, p. 2281.

39 Because it requires that the accused has a cognitive appreciation of the purposeful outcome.

that the emphasis on knowledge prioritises more the context in which the perpetrator acted rather than constructing some strained presumption as to implied purpose. Yet the court in the seminal case *Akeyesu* suggested they were interchangeable standards for intention. That case gave judicial endorsement to the purpose-based approach for proving intention:

> Genocide is distinct from other crimes inasmuch as it embodies a special intent or *dolus specialis*. Special intent of a crime is the specific intention, required as a constitutive element of the crime, which demands that the perpetrator clearly seeks to produce the act charged. Thus, the special intent in the crime of genocide lies in 'the intent to destroy, in whole or in part, a national, ethnical, racial or religious group, as such.'[40]

Yet, in the subsequent parts of the judgment, the Trial Chamber curiously held that:

> It is possible to deduce the genocidal intent inherent in a particular act charged from the general context of the perpetration of other culpable acts systematically directed against that same group, whether these acts were committed by the same offender or by others.[41]

Despite the insistence that the highest level of specific intent is required to establish genocide, and that this intent should be inextricably represented in a purposeful determination to bring about the criminal conduct, the proof technology envisaged as sufficient could employ a deduction from the context of similar acts perpetrated against the same victims by anyone. The only logic that might join this thinking is that context generates knowledge which makes purposeful conduct the only interpretation of the accused's actions and the intent which drove them. Even so, if knowledge is conceded to be probative, it is in this thinking constructed for the crime in question out of similar behaviors in other similar settings. Hardly an individualised and subjective forensic!

The court reasoned that in the absence of a confession from the accused, his intent can be induced from total context. These contextual *facts* include the scale of atrocities committed, their general nature, located in a region or a country where similar contexts occurred. Furthermore, the intent to produce genocidal conduct may be proved by behaviors that deliberately and systematically targeted victims on account of their membership of a particular group, while excluding the members of other groups.[42] In this vein, the Chamber referred to the Trial Chamber I of the International Criminal Tribunal for the former Yugoslavia where it was held that specific intention for genocide:

40 *Akayesu (Trial)*, para 498.
41 *Akayesu (Trial)*, para 523.
42 Ibid.

> may be inferred from a number of facts such as the general political doctrine which gave rise to the acts possibly covered by the definition in Article 4, or the repetition of destructive and discriminatory acts. The intent may also be inferred from the perpetration of acts which violate, or which the perpetrators themselves consider to violate the very foundation of the group – acts which are not in themselves covered by the list in Article 4(2) but which are committed as part of the same pattern of conduct.[43]

This passage outstrips the foundations of the purpose-based approach by replacing what was once a subjective test with contextual inference based on the accused's associations and the knowledge that can be imputed from similar behavior. The implications of the dicta in *Akayesu* support genocidal intention established by virtue of the fact that a perpetrator participates in a genocidal campaign.[44] As observed by Greenawalt, the use of circumstantial evidence to demonstrate *mens rea* is not unique to genocide prosecutions before international tribunals, but the ICTR's standard suggests that courts should impute specific intent largely by virtue of the fact that a perpetrator participates in a genocidal enterprise, which begs the question as to whether the specific intent standard is unrealistic at the individual level, for crimes which are essentially collective and differentially cognisant. More than unrealistic, specific intent has become perverted at the international level, thus encompassing degrees of proof incompatible with its domestic qualifications, a high level of subjectivity and a direct link between act and consequences.

Drawing from this object-oriented judicial reasoning it matters little which of the purpose or knowledge approaches to proof of criminal mental state is preferred. The judges pay lip-service to a high order specific intent, consistent with nation-state notions of criminal proof for the most serious crimes. Yet, in extrapolating essentially individualised proofs to situations of complex collectivised criminality they admit that because of proof challenges in genocide we have earlier identified, judicial reasoning can do little more than revert to the broadest inferential proof terrains more compatible with the establishment of negligence, than intent. Subjective knowledge is the inevitable casualty.

Substance over form

In support of the move away from the purpose-based approach, another compelling argument focuses on the *actualities* of judicial discretion when deciding on *mens rea*.[45] Essentially this view suggests that while judges at the national level are governed by the proof of the accused's individualised mental state from his words

43 *Akayesu (Trial)*, para 524.

44 Greenawalt, 1999, p. 2282; and Kim, Sangkul, *A Collective Theory of Genocidal Intent*, Asser Press and Springer: Berlin, 2016, p. 29.

45 Kim, 2016, p. 83.

and deeds (often through admissions and confessions), judges at the international criminal court and tribunals, especially in the context of genocide crimes, tend to look at contextual and circumstantial evidence in establishing the same level of intention. Thus, the knowledge-based approach would simply give effect to what the international criminal courts are known to practice in substance, recognising the flexible manner in which actual knowledge is inferred.

At the national or the international level, judges cannot forensically tap the accused's thought processes and brain impulses. All technologies for proving mental state are to differing degrees, inferential projects. It is just that where subjectivity is respected at the national level there are firm limits on how much inference can be relied upon.[46] A good example of this is the genuine struggle to reconcile actual knowledge with that constructively or reasonably inferred. At the international level, because of the exigencies of such collectivised and dynamic crime contexts, specific intent is the noose with which harmonisation strangles any determining of collectivised responsibility (see Chapter 2). Rationalising this jurisprudential incompatibility by conceding its impossibility, international criminal judicial reasoning at once reaffirms the subjective mantra and retires to inferential proof technologies using purpose and knowledge as stepping stones along the path.

Paradoxically, from employing the words and actions of genocidal context to satisfy proof technologies for mental states at the national level, while reiterating problematic affirmations of menal state subjectivity that are required in nation state proof tests, international judges conflate 'words and deeds' with ways of thinking. Expanding on nation-state inductive proof platforms for the subjective which amount to little more than inferring intent,[47] international judges almost universally add another point of reference which can be represented by such phrases as 'a context of violence' or 'surrounding circumstances of massacres.'[48]

46 Papacharalambous, Charis, "Group-Based Imputation and the International Criminal Law Discourse – Individuals and Associations as International Criminal Wrongdoers," *Beijing Law Review*, 4 4, 2013, pp. 129–136: this work argues that collective agency is resurfacing within International Criminal Law (ICL) discourse; its genealogical traces can be found in socio-legal contexts such as systemic theories of liability, victimisation-centered approaches and criminal policy models transforming traditional criminal law provisions into 'combat norms'; Baker, Dennis J., "Reinterpreting the Mental Element in Criminal Complicity: Change of Normative Position Theory Cannot Rationalize the Current Law," *Law & Psychology Review*, 40, 2016, link https://ssrn.com/abstract=2683971 – this article provides a comprehensive analysis of secondary forms of liability and the complexities associated with mental states. It also seeks to define and limit the boundaries of imputed knowledge; Buell, Samuel and Griffin, Lisa, "On the Mental State of Consciousness of Wrongdoing," *Law and Contemporary Problems*, 75, 2012, 133–166 – this article seeks to illustrate the issues with imputation of mental states in the corporate context.

47 Jordash, Wayne, "Joint Criminal Enterprise Liability: Result Oriented Justice," in William Schabas, Yvonne MacDermott and Niamh Hayes (eds), *The Ashgate Research Companion to International Criminal Law*, Ashgate: Aldershot, 2013, pp. 160.

48 *Édouard Karemera and Matthieu Ngirimpatse v The Prosecutor*, Case No. ICTR-98-44-T, para [1482].

This development is particularly important for our argument that the contextual uniqueness of global crimes demands a new and liberated approach to proving responsibility (broken free of liability), detailed in the chapter to follow.

For criminal law at the national level, inferring *mens rea* to a limited degree involves the consideration of the relevant context. That context, however, is *closely connected to the actor and his action*. The actor's intentions are discovered by locating this particular action within a broader pattern of actions and reactions, by relating it to an end and by relating that to its own wider context in a strictly causal chain. Attention is primarily given to a *particular action* and the *wider context* that belongs to or surrounds the action. Even so, there are determined parameters which ring-fence inferential confirmation of otherwise subjective mental states from their objectively established counterparts. Subjective and objective recklessness are cases in point.[49]

Yet, the context and surrounding circumstances from which international judges infer genocidal intent far exceed such individualistic and subjective boundaries of a specific actor and his action. Moreover, the pattern of judicial analysis of genocidal intent exercised by international judges reveals that the probative importance of this category of *circumstantial* evidence is so colossal as to almost obviate the first two reference points of *words and deeds*. The heavy reliance on contextual/circumstantial evidence has damaging implications (measured against rationality and consistency) for the individualistic approach to genocidal intent in general, and for the purpose-based approach in particular.

In conclusion

If there is a subtext in this chapter, it is the call to take the analysis of proving global crimes beyond some preferential argument for knowledge over purpose rooted in nation-state conventions. We adopted this duality somewhat as a stalking horse for our more fundamental contention that the reinvigoration of international criminal jurisprudence does not lie in weeding a better path to compatibility with nation-state proofs. In picking up an academic debate one approach over another, we reveal the stark need to jettison a rigid (if soon distorted) nation-state harmonisation in jurisdictional compatibility, not in principled terms (as discussed in Chapter 2) but rather in structuralist ascription forming strained proof technologies.

Chapter 1 sets out the normative framework of ICJ and Chapter 2 is a plea to recognise these expansive principles beyond the incompatible stringencies of nation-state proof technologies that this chapter reveals as incapable of substantiating global crime responsibility against international criminal justice demands.

49 Heming, Andrew, "Reasserting the Place of Objective Tests in Criminal Responsibility: Ending the Supremacy of Subjective tests," *University of Notre Dame Australia Law Review*, 13, 2011, pp. 69–112; Cunningham, Sally, "Recklessness: Being Reckless and Acting Recklessly," *Kings Law Journal*, 21, 2010, pp. 455–467.

It is true that a knowledge-based approach may sit better with our case in the next chapter for a tort/crime proof hybrid, but that is not to limit the purpose of this chapter. It may well be that as Article 30 of the ICC Statute shows, there is still room for the knowledge-based concept of genocidal intent, as ***knowledge*** is the preferred subjective element applicable to the ***circumstantial*** facts. That said, the advocates of the knowledge approach are not confident enough to tackle the conundrum that *actual* knowledge can never be proved, rather it is only approached through differing degrees of circumstantial inference that substitutes for the mind of the accused. In global crime this is an enterprise confronting the minds and conduct of many at different locations of responsibility somewhere between principle perpetration and empathy with the purpose.

The time for tinkering of this sort is over. If proof technologies in international criminal justice were crafted for purpose then purpose would be evidenced through the concept of the campaign (aggregated thinking) and knowledge would be established not from the individual understanding of a single offender but from the natural appreciation of what contexts displayed and what participants could not deny, no matter what the level of contribution. From this perspective, our suggestion that proving global crimes demands engaging a continuum of responsibility and obligation is much more in touch with the behaviors ICJ is attempting to prevent and from which it is attempting to protect.

It is not foreign in state-based criminal law traditions, to talk of continuums. The intersection of the act with the mental state to establish coincidence often takes the form of a series of individual actions onto which mental state can be imposed at appropriate junctures.[50] But this thinking is made artificial from the requirements that individual liability must locate on a particular act, at a documented time and place, indicting a particular offender, for harming a particular victim. As such, this construction is naïve when applied to responsibility for global crimes where many individuals may engage in campaigns to exterminate communities and cultures, involving acts in different spatial and temporal zones, considered to substantiate through inference the intent of several indicted individuals who have combined to achieve the atrocity.

In the chapter to follow it will be advanced that global crimes need proofs that do not arise out of the consequences of denial. We have seen in the genocide judicial narrative the unacceptable victory of pragmatism over principle where specific intent is expressed (if not respected), its achievement is deemed impossible, and courts revert to proofs akin to criminal negligence and say they satisfy specific intent. In the next chapter, we will provide a way out of this incongruity.

50 Sullivan, G.R., "Cause and the Contemporaneity of *Actus Reus* and *Mens Rea*," *Cambridge Law Journal*, 52 3, 1993, pp. 487–500: the author seeks to explore why the court, confronted by a lack of temporal coincidence between *actus reus* and *mens rea* might nonetheless impose liability because on analysis the coincidence requirement is held to be satisfied in substance and in form; Sarch, Alex, "Knowledge, Recklessness and the Connection Requirement Between *Actus Reus* and *Mens Rea*," *Penn State Law Review*, 120 1, 2015, pp. 1–34.

Offenders sit somewhere on a proof continuum which can be established through aggregation and contribution, not purpose and knowledge. Both purpose and knowledge can be contextually calibrated not to qualify individual responsibility but to make acceptable punishment for culpability. And the relationships between individual offenders along the proof continuum become a genuinely contestable consideration. No longer would it be necessary to exclude superior orders or command responsibility through moral barriers, because the connections between parties on the continuum would confirm rather than confuse the sharing of individual responsibility, thinking that tort does not reject.

A final repost, before we address the detail of our hybrid approaches is the simple recognition that civil penalties have conveniently infiltrated nation-state and international criminal law.[51] With this in sight the crime/civil distinction is no functional barrier to what will be developed in the pages to follow.

51 Dyson, Matthew, *Comparing Tort and Crime – Learning from Across and Within Legal Systems*, Cambridge University Press: Cambridge, 2015, pp. 276.

5 Hybrid proof technologies

Introduction

The argument which follows is the empirical meat of our proposed approach to proving criminal responsibility for global crimes which will facilitate a more principled and rational international criminal law jurisprudence. In reading this chapter and reflecting on the two chapters which have preceded this analysis, it is important not to see our critique of current prosecutorial interpretation and judicial reasoning around atrocity trials as simply a case against expediency. Neither are we only suggesting that international criminal justice as enunciated in the Rome Statute Preamble necessitates a form of judicial creative-thinking that inevitably results in the application of limited proof technologies as they are currently distilled in ICL (see Chapter 2). While both these critical themes cannot be avoided, we have a more positive, and we hope more lasting, critical intention. As was made clear in the introduction to Chapter 4, international criminal justice is beyond the blameworthiness of the individual and it is not to be discounted as some utopian adventure responding to massive social necessity. Any new jurisprudence for international criminal law that is developed through deductive reasoning by judges not pragmatically outcome-driven, will grow from understanding a *new justice mission* (see Chapter 6) applied to the proof of individual responsibility for *new crime* worlds (see Chapter 4), with the assistance of *new frames of principle* aligned in a more reasoned form with the demands for punishment and peace-building (see Chapter 1) that ICJ manifests.

In Chapter 3, by exploring how international criminal law jurisprudence has expanded the interpretation of responsibility (via nation-state liability) through forms of secondary participation we sought to highlight the tensions arising between evidentiary issues associated with the collective nature of international crimes. In their mission to achieve just outcomes, relative to the complex aspirations of the Rome Statute Preamble (see Chapter 1), judges and prosecutors seem to be making law on a case-by-case basis and, as such, producing what might be little more than outcome-oriented justice, on the run.

To sophisticate this critique, and invite a more rational, predictable and principled international criminal jurisprudence, we argue through the remainder of the book, that rather than stretching the already contorted secondary criminal law liability tests extracted and adapted from domestic jurisdictions to suit the collective perpetration and victimisation of international crimes, a fresh juridical reasoning must be adopted. Its elaboration in this and the next chapter better corresponds with the unique proof requirements of global crimes and the need to determine individualised criminal responsibility in situations of collective perpetration and mass victimisation. The danger inherent in current judicial reasoning is that the fundamental principles which underlie the national proofs of secondary, participatory and collective liability, already strained as these are to suit proof demands of crimes where the perpetrators are consequentially connected, will be more sporadically and circumstantially determined, exposing the accused to innumerable grounds of liability without predictable and consistent interpretation.

Instead, it will be demonstrated that prosecutors and judges should adopt a more fit-for-purpose approach towards liability in the global crime context drawing inspiration from other areas of the law, such as tort, that are concerned with responsibility where it is a collective phenomenon involving complex chains of contribution and causation. That view is advanced for the following reasons:

- in its most general sense international criminal jurisprudence should develop in a rational, predictable and principled fashion not circumscribed by technologies which have been developed for contexts of responsibility and conclusions of justice not compatible with global crimes and international criminal justice aspirations;
- even in the context of harmonisation or hybridity, international criminal law and procedure can recognise the proof requirements of any legal doctrinal field if they are compatible with the purpose of establishing individualised criminal responsibility in a collective setting (see Chapter 2);
- international criminal jurisprudence should develop appreciating the unique collective and participatory features of global crimes, particularly atrocity crimes (see Chapter 4), as well as the broader restorative aims for international criminal justice (see Chapter 1);
- the collective nature of perpetration and victimisation means that there will be particular challenges in establishing criminal responsibility as set out in Article 25 of the Rome Statute (see Chapter 3);
- the focus on the heinous conduct which international criminal prosecutions address naturally means that judicial decision-making will consider the nature and scope of harms inflicted on victims (context and circumstance of the crimes), before the sentencing stage and prior to the determination of responsibility;
- to date, technologies of proof adapted from domestic criminal jurisdictions for the international context have produced distortions in favor of conviction;
- reasons for this may reside in the much wider aims of international criminal justice, which include protection from, and restitution of, harm and damage, the bread and butter of tort determinations;
- particularly, determining the criminal mental states of secondary participants is gradually shifting away from proof of actual subjective knowledge and agreement, and more toward what risks and consequences might be reasonably foreseeable from the circumstances in which original crimes are committed;

- tort proof principles consider the importance of contribution and the significance of proportionate responsibility;
- tort also is more interested in the actions causing harm and their damaging consequences; and finally
- tort has conventions concerning the proof of causation and the significance of objective negligence that appear to reflect the trend in judicial decision-making in international criminal trials of individual liability.

The selection of tort as our comparative doctrinal field for exploring new proof technologies reflects:

- the Preamble's specific interest in harm prevention and victim restitution, along with punishment and deterrence; and
- the recognition that in areas of contribution and participation tort faces not dissimilar proof challenges as does criminal law and procedure when determining guilt and apportioning responsibility, but does so with concepts of aggregation and contribution well-tuned to reflect the collective nature of perpetration and victimisation in global crime.

Additionally, as the discussion in the next chapter of trends in corporate criminal responsibility and criminal association reveal, tortious reasoning around contribution and aggregation are already making significant inroads into the criminal proof technologies of domestic juridical reasoning and legislative creativity.

There is scholarship identifying the common histories between tort and crime elements, and the sharing of fundamental proof concepts.[1] For instance, the concept of vicarious liability for an employee's tort is comparatively relevant when looking at joint criminal enterprise (JCE) and the manner in which responsibility can be imputed, servant to master. It is ultimately argued that the requirements to impose vicarious liability on the employer for an employee's tort more accurately mirror the approach taken (unstated) by the ICC judges when imposing responsibility under JCE at the international level. Additionally, given the contentious concept of a 'substantial effect on the commission of the crime' as a requirement for aiding and abetting at the international level, we propose instead using tortious contribution and aggregation as proof technologies which are compatible with the obligation dimension of responsibility. For reasons later to be explained, this tortious perspective adds to reasoned legal analysis by providing a fuller and more accurate picture of the illegal act and its key participants. In explaining our model, the body of this chapter (concomitant with the critique in Chapter 3) will be dedicated to JCE reinterpreted in terms of vicarious liability and aiding and abetting reinterpreted as material contribution.

1 Dyson, Matthew, *Comparing Tort and Crime – Learning from Across and Within Legal Systems*, Cambridge University Press: Cambridge, 2015.

As suggested above, an alternative and more convincing way to test secondary liability through JCE as applied to global crimes is via the lens of vicarious liability in Tort.[2] It has long been established that an employer may be vicariously liable for an employee's tort or criminal conduct if certain conditions are met. Before going into the analysis of how the substantive limbs of criminal mental state confirming blameworthiness remain relevant to the international criminal context through such a tortious interpretation, it is first necessary to consider the feasibility of introducing tortious concepts into criminal law.

Joint criminal enterprise and vicarious liability

At the national level, the applied need for just outcomes and their influence on the parallel development of legal principles in crime (punishment) and tort (harm resolution) is prominently revealed through vicarious liability (VL) reasoning. Therein, economic and policy considerations have largely driven the shift of liability (in the domestic context) from employees to employers who are determined to have 'control' over their delegates. At the international level (as elaborated on in Chapter 1) the victim-focused aims of the Rome Statute strongly suggest that courts must produce practical justice outcomes for the protection and compensation of victims. This imperative and its attainment increases (or if failed endangers) the legitimacy of the court in the eyes of the victims, and minimises the criticism that ICJ is little more than a political tool controlled by the powerful hegemonic west.[3] Such a critique is apposite when in any joint criminal liability scenario limited in its interpretation, authority figures who initiate and perpetrate the crime might be too far removed in a causation sense, thereby escaping responsibility. In answer to this, transferring VL principles to a JCE scenario can be supported by the need to achieve practical justice outcomes in terms of the ways in command structures perpetration is delegated in global crime settings and is consistent with the roots of vicarious liability in nation-state tort and criminal law.[4] In addition, merging the VL concept of *appreciable risk* into a JCE criminal proof reasoning is supported at the international level by its adoption in the *Karemera* case reflecting the recognition of *risk* by the accused to be sufficient grounds for culpability in criminal law as in tort.

2 In a number of national jurisdictions vicarious liability is recognised in criminal law, governed by strict principles of delegation. Here we are suggesting a more flexible approach as presented in tort responsibility determinations from master to servant, focusing on the neighbour approach to obligation.

3 "African Leaders Plan Mass Withdrawal From International Criminal Court," *The Guardian*, 31 January 2017. Link: www.theguardian.com/law/2017/jan/31/african-leaders-plan-mass-withdrawal-from-international-criminal-court; Withnall, Adam, "Gambia Pulls out of 'Racist' ICC amid Fears of Mass Africa Exodus," *The Independent*, 26 October 2016.

4 *R v Powell & English* [1999] 1 AC 290; *Lister and others v Hesley Hall Limited* [2001] UKHL 22; *Bazley v Curry* [1999] 2 S.C.R. 534; *Home Office v Dorset Yacht Co Ltd* [1970] 2 All ER 294; McBride, Nicholas, and Bagshaw, Roderick, *Tort Law*, Longmans Law Series, Pearson Education Limited: London, 5th edition, 2015.

Thus, to justify the proposed tort/crime hybrid in terms of improved proof technologies, the following analytical themes will be highlighted:

1 evidentiary considerations and the need for practical justice;
2 a principled approach to determining responsibility via causal links based on risk; and
3 the unique aims enunciated in the Rome Statute, compatible with Continental Civil law traditions which amalgamate criminal and tort law paradigms.

Evidentiary considerations and the need for practical justice outcomes

The explanations for vicarious liability and the formulations of its legal tests are largely based on the need for a principled and realistic approach to meet policy requirements regarding the allocation of responsibility for damage[5] and to obtain practical justice outcomes. Canvassing the origins of vicarious liability, the economic considerations both in the master/servant relationship and the harm that its careless or criminal performance can inflict, are obvious. For example, a *deep pockets* reasoning justifies vicarious liability on the basis that the victim of the tort should have a financially viable defendant (the employer) to materially compensate for her damage.[6] In other words, there may well eventuate unfairly constrained restitution possibilities when an employee's individual perpetration is used as a shield against responsibility for damages further up the discretionary chain.[7] This consideration of qualified responsibility is particularly important where employers or supervisors are in an actual and practical position to pay compensation for the harm that their delegation has enabled. Additionally, such a *relative blame* reasoning suggests that since someone has suffered damage from a harm caused in the execution of employment, the employer by virtue of having engaged the employee under identifiable and delegated terms of service should remedy the damage instead of placing the burden of loss on an indigent employee and thereby depriving the victim of restitution.[8] Coincidently in this reasoning, there needed to be counteracted the practical proof impediments where in some cases, responsibility may be difficult to pass down the line due to problems in identifying the particular employee responsible.[9] With these considerations prevailing, it is evident that the driving rationales behind the creation of

5 Jordash, Wayne, "Joint Criminal Enterprise Liability: Result Oriented Justice," in William Schabas, Yvonne MacDermott and Niamh Hayes (eds), *The Ashgate Research Companion to International Criminal Law*, Ashgate: Aldershot, 2013, pp. 160. Stahn, Carsten, and Sluiter, Goran, *Emerging Practice of the International Criminal Court*, Vol. 8 of Legal Aspects of International Organization, Part III Prosecutorial Policy and Practice. Brill: Leiden, 2009.

6 *Lister*, paras [13]–[20]; McBride and Bagshaw, 2015, p. 910.

7 *Lister*, para [66].

8 *Lister*, paras [16]–para [20], McBride and Bagshaw, 2015, p. 910.

9 Neyers, Jason, "A Theory of Vicarious Liability", *Alberta Law Review* 43, 2005, pp. 287–326, here p. 295.

VL were pragmatic in nature, responding to the needs of justice viewed broadly in terms of victim restitution, which resonates with the aspirations of the Rome Statute Preamble (see Chapter 1).

Further, in the development of tortious responsibility there has always been much judicial resistance to leaving victims without remedy or recourse, as to do so would undermine the court's credibility in the eyes of those it is meant to protect. Again, such concerns are mirrored in the victim interest dimensions of the Rome Statute, which bolster the court's legitimacy through the satisfaction of valid victim interests. Extending the court's obligation to consider and where possible compensate for the harm consequences of responsibility along with apportioning criminal liability as would be the limit of its remit in domestic traditions, further strengthens legitimacy claims through victim satisfaction. Thereby, the requirement in international criminal justice to restore victims following the harms caused through global crime approximates the central aim of a successful tort prosecution and further endorses the arguments in favor of proof transferability.[10]

Similar policy motivations directing the rationales for determining delegated liability JCE at the national level are heavily based on consequentialist considerations that crimes committed by groups often escalate to more serious offenses or their collectivity increases the likelihood of secondary crimes being committed as a result of ongoing or future group action. So crafted, the protection of society justifies creative interpretations of association, delegation and contribution. Compatible approaches to collective culpability as aggravation are now also commonly prominent in national criminal sentencing principles. Where the principal perpetrators of crimes cannot be identified except up the chain of delegation and where victimisation occurs on a massive scale,[11] it would be even more pragmatically justifiable to hold individuals at the leadership level responsible for international crimes if they contributed to or controlled their commission, in similar fashion to the ways that the master/servant relationship joins responsibility for those who operationally produce harm. Were it not so, victim communities will doubt the actuality of international criminal justice if they are left without judicial recognition of their suffering, undermining both the procedural and outcome legitimacy of the victim-focused aims in the Rome Statute.[12] It is the tactical impunity of the leadership in the collective perpetration of atrocities which has a much greater negative impact on victim safety than could be counterbalanced by the random prosecution of small fish. In addition, the impression by victims that the powerful are above the law undermines any credibility in the end to impunity aspiration, which, unrealistic as it may be in practice, is the central *call to arms* of the ICJ trial model.

10 Findlay, 2013, Chapter 6.

11 Duraj, Erinda, "The Rights of Victims under International Criminal Justice," *Academic Journal of Business, Administration, Law and Social Sciences*, 1 2, 2015, pp. 102–114.

12 UN General Assembly, Rome Statute of the International Criminal Court (last amended 2010), 17 July 1998, Preamble.

A principled approach to imposing liability via causal links based on risk

The national courts have often cited *fairness* as the basis for vicarious liability. The courts have reasoned that 'it is right and just that the person (employer) who creates a risk bears the loss when the risk ripens into harm.'[13] This recognition of risk reflects the ICC's approach to imposing joint liability on the accused for the commission of a secondary crime by the principal perpetrator (see Chapter 3). As mentioned above, the courts have based their determination of whether the secondary crime was reasonably foreseeable on an objective evaluation of *risk* that the secondary crime would occur as a result of the primary crime as a natural and foreseeable consequence (see *risk analysis*, Chapter 3).[14]

In the context of vicarious liability, the employer is viewed as having introduced the risk of harm (through employment) into the community and if he possesses the administrative control and supervision capabilities to prevent or reduce the risk of the harm occurring and fails to do so, he should be responsible for consequent damages.[15] Further, it has been held that fairness demands where there is an 'obvious and manifest risk' of harm being inflicted by a third party for whom another party is responsible, the latter owes a personal duty of care to those who may suffer damage.[16] Similarly, in *Karemera* the ICC cited the accused's leadership position and the open and notorious manner in which the secondary crimes were committed to show that the risks of the secondary crimes were obvious and manifest. Therefore, the use of the risk analysis by the ICC courts can be paralleled with the aforementioned tortious principles confirming the concept of fairness.

What this line of reasoning offers international criminal law jurisprudence is a method for linking sufficient contribution to apparent risk. It avoids the necessity to prove that the accused was part of the criminal enterprise, provided he can be determined as *responsible* through his position relative to the perpetrator, and the extent to which he is responsible to manage the perpetrator's exercise of discretion. Coincidence here would be established by accepting the criminal conduct as a series of acts, into which the accused's responsibility for control (or neglect thereof) intersects with the necessary mental state prior to the commission of the primary crime. Regarding causation, it is the accused's supervisory authority and the discretion he transfers to the perpetrator which contributes to the outcome, even if that may not be considered under nation-state crime causation rules to be anything but the history against which the perpetrator and those in the enterprise would be said to cause the crime.

13 *Bazley v Curry* [1999] 2 S.C.R. 534, paras [30]–[31].

14 In determining risk, the courts have looked at the historical and statistical coincidence between the occurrence of the primary and secondary crimes.

15 *Bazley*, para [33].

16 *Home Office v Dorset Yacht Co Ltd* [1970] 2 All ER 294 at p. 305.

The unique aims of the Rome Statute that support removing traditional domestic law divisions between criminal and tort law

Although Continental civil law jurisdictions like Spain and Germany have systems which mix criminal and tort law processes, academics have often identified some fundamental distinctions between the two even in such traditions. This distinction between two doctrinal fields of law, connected as they are through victimisation, might act conventionally to confound the possibility of a tort/crime hybrid, even limited as we suggest, to proof technologies. But Chapter 2 establishes such distinctions are not indelible because of harmonisation which incorporates doctrinal domains of proof in the same way that it melds criminal procedure traditions. International criminal law must reflect an enunciation of justice which, unusual in domestic traditions, pays equal weight to harm in the determination of responsibility, and as such confronts the proof of crimes manifestly different in the senses of contribution and causation than could be imagined in domestic criminal justice. Further, as Chapter 6 will establish, harmonisation argues for the tort/crime hybrid in revolutionary approaches to the proof of corporate liability and association with criminal organisations, by using applications of contribution and aggregation to prove criminal cultures and relational criminality. In this context, tort and crime proofs are already in sync at the nation-state level when facing new crime contexts.

Not dissimilar to common law appreciations of the tort/crime divide, the distinction between criminal law and delict in Germany relates to their respective functions – the primary function of delict being to decide who should bear the loss and thus *compensate* the victim, while criminal law under the German *preventative theory* has an essential purpose to protect legal interests of the community at large and current and future victims through punishment and the threat of punishment.[17]

Consistent with the tortious aims of restitution, under the Rome Statute,[18] Art 75 concerns reparations to victims for the damage, loss or injury they suffer. The section essentially seeks to compensate for the harms inflicted by crime, thereby injecting a conscious tortious dimension into determining responsibility.[19]

17 Hellwege, Phillip, and Wittig, Petra, "Delictual and Criminal Liability in Germany," in Matthew Dyson, *Comparing Tort and Crime: Learning Across and Within Legal Systems*, Cambridge University Press: Cambridge, 2015, Chapter 4.

18 Rome Statute, Article 75 (1) states: 'The Court shall establish principles relating to reparations to, or in respect of, victims, including restitution, compensation and rehabilitation. On this basis, in its decision the Court may, either upon request or on its own motion in exceptional circumstances, determine the scope and extent of any damage, loss and injury to, or in respect of, victims and will'; See also, Rome Statute, Article 75(2) which states: 'The Court may make an order directly against a convicted person specifying appropriate reparations to, or in respect of, victims, including restitution, compensation and rehabilitation.'

19 Note that the word 'compensation' in Art 75(1) has historical links to tort.

With this in mind, the Preamble of the Rome Statute states that important among the goals of the ICC is to 'put an end to impunity for the perpetrators of these crimes and thus to contribute to the prevention of such crimes.' Ending impunity is both punitive for the past and present, and protective for the future. In declaring motivations for responsibility and punishment through international criminal law as preventative and not narrowly punitive the ICC is exhibiting similar punishment justifications as those advanced in the German tradition, and thereby opening up opportunities for harm for be considered at the proof and not just the punishment stage, comparable with civil law predispositions.

Under Spanish law, although the two systems of crime and tort seem to have been integrated procedurally and substantively,[20] academics have preferred a distinction between the purposes of the two. Their reasoning is that tortious liability is of an economic or patrimonial nature while criminal liability is personal.[21] In the international criminal law context, the two directions are merged – the accused is often part of an executive machine or holds leadership positions, therefore (as mentioned above) he/she has the economic capacity to compensate the victims and further, he/she is likely to have the requisite control over or to have contributed to the criminal enterprise, so that it can fairly be said (through employing a risk-analysis approach) that such persons are responsible for the harms suffered as well as for the crime committed. These higher-order accused often make determinations which lead to individualised criminal responsibility and harm for wider political and economic purposes. Incorporating liability for harm with accountability for the damage that criminal harm delivers, supports an argument in favor of the merging of tortious and criminal determinations of responsibility for atrocities in the international jurisdiction. Obviously, the court's understanding of these crimes is from a victim harm perspective, required by the Preamble, in addition to the more conventional community retribution paradigm.

Having briefly canvassed the feasibility of the proposed crime/tort hybrid, we will now anticipate criticisms of this proposition, particularly the potential lack of moral blameworthiness if the tort/crime hybrid could be advanced as undermining the place of criminal law within the merger, and the procedural criticism of developing the law beyond the bounds of permissible doctrinal distinction, which we have already tackled but which might benefit from reiteration for those who remain unconvinced.

Criticisms of the merged approach in employing vicarious liability of an employer for an employee's crime

As a preliminary, the rationales for employing vicarious liability to prove criminal conduct in this hybrid atmosphere are two-fold and bear many similarities to the

20 Dyson, Matthew, "Civil Law Responses to Criminal Judgments in England and Spain," *JETL*, 3, 2012, pp. 308–339.

21 Dyson, Matthew, *Comparing Tort and Crime – Learning from Across and Within Legal Systems*, Cambridge University Press: Cambridge, 2015, p. 227.

foundations of vicarious liability for tortious conduct. Where an employer promotes an enterprise carrying with it certain risks and those risks materialise and cause injury, it is fair that, having created the enterprise and the risk, the employer should bear responsibility for the loss. Holding the employer vicariously liable might have the deterrent effect of persuading employers who control real harm potential to exercise a greater degree of care in relation to the appointment and supervision of employees.[22] Therefore, the courts (in tort actions) have acknowledged that the employer is blameworthy but only to the extent that he creates a *risk to the community* for engaging in his enterprise.

Generally, at the national level, there is *no moral blameworthiness* required on the part of the employer when apportioning responsibility for damage – vicarious liability shifts legal liability, not moral fault for the commission of the crime which causes harm. In *Lister v Hesley Hall*, *John Doe v Bennett* and *Bazley v Curry*, all of which concern sexual assaults committed by priests or care-givers on children under their charge, the employers were held vicariously liable for the acts of abuse and thus obliged to pay damages for the injuries suffered by the victims. Yet, moral blameworthiness for the abuse was in no way imputed onto the employers – the latter's fault lay solely upon giving the employee an opportunity to cause the damage or contributing to the risk of the damage occurring.

Transposing to the international level the position of the employer onto an accused tried before the ICC who holds a leadership position in the criminal enterprise, reveals the utility of a tort/crime hybrid for the purposes of satisfying proof. As mentioned above, vicarious liability transfers legal liability not moral blameworthiness back up the responsibility chain. Those who cannot break free criminal liability from moral considerations may criticise adopting a tortious approach as diminishing the moral blameworthiness or culpability of the accused within a form of responsibility imposed in the proposed extension. In these terms, the vicarious imposition of responsibility might be viewed as downplaying moral blameworthiness for the commission of crimes, rendering criminal responsibility less reprehensible and as such at odds with the heinous nature of the crimes prosecuted and demeaning retributive rationales.

A simple dismissal of this concern can be found in the wording of the Rome Statute. Despite the constant emphasis on the unimaginable nature of the crimes which the ICC will consider, there is no extant link in the language of the Statute between responsibility and blameworthiness. Responsibility leads to punishment for deterrent, protective and restorative outcomes. There is no express interpretation of responsibility as existing within a natural law moral framework. The end to impunity is a positivist aspiration, and as such the protection and restoration of victims could be interpreted as a utilitarian enterprise, and the significance of atrocity interpreted in distinctly realist language.

At the same time, it is not helpful to diminish the moral approbation that should flow from a determination of responsibility for one of the four global crimes.

22 *Various Claimants v The Catholic Child Welfare Society and Others* [2010] EWCA Civ 1106, para [64].

As such within the ICC context the tort/crime hybrid will function to hold the accused *responsible in some way* (vicariously) for the secondary crimes committed by his subordinates, but in so saying is this type of responsibility sufficient to recognise the individual reprehensibility of atrocity crimes and thereby denounce the harm caused in moral terms?

As mentioned earlier, and revisited here for completeness, the other criticism of the tort/crime hybrid which we foresee is whether this approach to proof goes beyond the bounds of permissible doctrinal development. Despite confidence in meeting this concern in Chapters 2 and 4, we here reiterate this is not the case. Against the distortions of crime proofs revealed in Chapter 3, it would be disingenuous to claim that the hybrid is advanced as some tenuous expedient. The difficulties faced by the international courts in deliberating on JCE III crimes due to the collective nature of these offenses and often the resultant lack of evidence of subjective foresight on the part of the accused means that the international judges are regularly unable to hold the accused criminally liable for the secondary crimes committed unless they stretch existing criminal law proof requirements.[23] Working within such proof limitations no doubt produces profound frustrations in making those most morally responsible pay the price for their actual culpability. A crucial purpose of the tort/crime hybrid is to create a new form of responsibility better suited to the international criminal context where evidentiary issues surrounding subjective foresight, the accused's actual knowledge and the identity of the principle perpetrators are presently confounding reasoned proof. The introduction of tortious evidential technologies in compatible areas of tort and crime proof deliberations (such as causation) will enable responsibility to be determined in a manner more appropriate to the articulation and perpetration of global crimes. The gloss on top of such transmogrification is that the hybrid will better complement the aims of ICJ covering harm and victim restoration through a responsibility – a damages nexus that talks tort language.

If the hybrid approach is said to downplay moral blameworthiness, we respond that determining JCE through vicarious liability impugns the superior accused for the *risk* he created through that criminal enterprise. Thereby, if criminal responsibility were to attach as a result of delegated conduct, somewhat like strict liability then no moral blameworthiness of a criminal nature would be determined. To avoid such implication, even though we retain that moral blameworthiness is not essential to responsibility, it could be required of the accused to establish that despite all due diligence on his part, the secondary crime would still have occurred. This proof of alternative motivation would avoid scapegoating a higher-order accused for all secondary offenses committed by his subordinates and infuses blameworthiness into the resultant responsibility, emphasising its more individual criminal character.

23 See the adoption of 'objective foreseeability' and the broad framing of the common intention by the ICC judges. We have already canvassed (in Chapter 3) the various negative implications of the 'objective' approach including judicial subjectivity in decisions, object-oriented justice, the disregard for the underlying principles of parasitic liability etc.

The inspiration for this justification (or excuse) derives from the Continental civil law approach. If the ICC judges are to adopt the close connection/integration tests in lieu of (or along with) the foreseeability test (as later argued), there must be a means by which the accused can declare his innocence beyond delegated conduct. In this regard, a possible defense to criminal responsibility allegations would be to allow the accused to establish that despite the secondary crime being committed by his subordinates he had taken *adequate* measures for preventing its occurrence or that the secondary crime even so was inevitable – an assertion of *due diligence*. This challenge to the proof of the prosecution case is similar in style to s. 831 of the German Civil Code (BGB) and resonates with notions that resist liability without fault (such as absolute liability in common law).[24] If the ICC were to adopt this consideration of vicarious liability, its legal reasoning and decisions would reflect the fundamental values of domestic and international criminal law, as elaborated and enhanced in the Rome Statute, endorsing a presumption of innocence (even in situations of reversed onus). Further, it would give effect to the Preamble's interest in deterrence,[25] as deterrence is based on sufficient blameworthiness on part of the accused, and a defense which denies blameworthiness also undermines the existence of a rational choice to commit the crime, on which deterrence relies. Further, as common law regarding strict liability has developed, strict liability presumptions regarding knowledge do not relieve the prosecution from disproving a denial of knowledge by the accused, and a denial of consequent blameworthiness.

Continuing to sophisticate the consideration of blame and harm, vicarious liability does not always exonerate the responsibility of the employee in favor of the employer. Often, if the employee is deemed the primary perpetrator then the employer may be held liable as a secondary party, or vice versa. In tort, such analytical contortions are avoided through considerations of contribution.[26]

An objection to the *due diligence* answer to vicarious liability is Neyers' argument that it is illogical to say that the employer is at fault and therefore vicariously liable for his employee's harm, if the employer would be able to escape from vicarious liability by proving that she was without fault.[27] This criticism wrongly presumes we suggest that the due diligence purports to nullify the employer's (or accused's) fault confronted by the fact that the employer (or accused) created a risk to society that is objectively determined and cannot be overturned through justification or excuse. While fault through risk remains, the due diligence justification is available only when it is shown that despite the employer (or accused) forming the risk, the secondary crime would nevertheless have occurred. In other words, there was no prevailing and operating causal link between the

24 Giliker, Paula, "Vicarious Liability or Liability for the Acts of Others in Tort: A Comparative Perspective," 2 *JETL* 1, 2011, pp. 31–56 at 36.

25 Rome Statute, Preamble.

26 Bermingham, Vera, and Brennan, Carol, *Tort Law Directions*, Oxford University Press: Oxford, 2016, p. 234.

27 Neyers, p. 294.

employer's risk generation and the actual crime. In such thinking the employer located the perpetrator/employee in a position where they could choose to commit the crime, and that represented the risk involved. However, the actions of the perpetrator could in certain circumstances make the employer's risk simply the history in which the eventual crime was caused. Further, in a scenario where the employer (or accused) provides adequate safeguards against the commission of torts (or secondary crimes) then it suggests that the risk posed by the organisation facilitating the crime would have been reduced and as such, responsibility (based on risk-creation) should be adjusted accordingly. What due diligence obviates is an allocation of blame for the crime if not responsibility for the risk. More importantly, in the context of international criminal law, the risk aversion excuse has important practical protective ramifications in terms of managing potential harm.

Remembering the atrocious crimes dealt with by the ICC, for the prosecution to prove prima facie that the leader was at fault (even if it is a contributory fashion) we argue should not ignore counter evidence that the accused can raise to his otherwise apparent blameworthy role. Not to do so would negatively reinforce responsible risk minimisation on the part of superior participants and this would be against the Preamble's protective commitments.

How will the hybrid operate?

Having established the reasons for adopting the tort/crime hybrid in the context of JCE III crimes, the substantive limbs of vicarious liability as proof technologies necessitate elaboration under the following heads.

Substantive limbs[28] of vicarious liability – how they are open for merging

Substantive proofs of vicarious liability

The requirements for the proof of tortious vicarious liability, in brief, are as follows:

1 Employment of the employee by the employer.

In tort, there are two main tests used to determine if the tortfeasor is an employee; the *control test* and the *integration test*. In relation to the control test, the employer must have governed the actual performance of the work and how it was to be done by the employee. Factors to be considered under this test are: (i) the extent to which the employer controls the details of the work, (ii) whose equipment is used and (iii) the power of the employer to dismiss the employee.[29]

28 Under common law traditions.

29 Witting, Christian, *Street on Tort*, 14th Edition, Oxford University Press: Oxford, 2015, p. 626.

Alternatively, under the integration test the tortfeasor must to a large extent be integrated into the business of the employer, acting as an integral part of the employer's business and not an accessory to it. Exceptions to the requirement of employment have been conceded so long as there is a relationship that is akin to employment.

2 The tort or crime must be committed in the course of employment or within the scope of the employee's employment.

This limb requires the court to determine on the facts the scope of the employment and whether the tort or criminal act fell within that scope. Central to this determination are questions of whether the tort was: (i) incidental to the scope of employment;[30] (ii) closely connected to the scope of employment;[31] (iii) performed in furthering the employer's business or benefits the employer in some way;[32] or (iv) inherent in the nature of the business.[33] If the tort or crime was committed when the employee was acting in a separate and independent way from what was authorised by the employer then no vicarious liability would be imposed. Some cases have also suggested that the courts may take an evaluative approach to consider whether the acts complained of are so closely connected with what the employee was employed to do that it would be fair and just to hold the employer vicariously liable.[34] The courts have also looked at: (i) whether the wrongful act was authorised by the employer or (ii) whether the tortious or criminal act was a wrongful and unauthorised mode of doing some act authorised by the master.

The proposed merging of tortious vicarious liability and JCE III requirements

As seen from above, tort law has long recognised that an employer may be vicariously liable for an employee's tort/criminal conduct if the tort/crime occurred *during the employee's employment* and fell within his *scope of employment*. At the international level, an accused could be responsible if the general nature of his organisation (governmental or otherwise) was to promote genocidal killings, as well as rape committed by his soldiers during these killings. Under this approach, the criminal organisation would be akin to a criminal enterprise in a business context, the accused/leader being the employer and the principal perpetrator being the employee. The objective foreseeability test (JCE III) can be substituted with

30 *Century Insurance Co Ltd v Northern Ireland Road Transport Broad* [1942] 1 All ER 491 per Lord Wright.

31 *Joel v Morison* [1834] EWHC KB J39, per Park B.

32 *Rose v Plenty* [1976] 1 WLR 141, per Lord Denning.

33 Witting, Christian, *Street on Torts*, Oxford University Press: Oxford, 2015, p. 63.

34 *Lister*, at para [28]; McBride and Bagshaw, p. 898.

the tortious *integration* test in determining whether the primary perpetrator is employed[35] by the accused who is likely to be the superior in the criminal organisation.[36] Moreover, the common intention (JCE III) will be substituted with an inquiry as to whether the primary perpetrator's secondary crime fell within his scope of employment in the criminal organisation.[37] The facts of *Karemera* will be used to illustrate this approach.

As noted in other places *Karemera* was a case where the primary crime was to commit genocidal killings and there was overwhelming evidence of systematic, widespread, and targeted killings perpetrated by the *Interahamwe* (Karemera's subordinates) throughout the genocide against Tutsis (which evinced genocidal intent). The prosecution satisfied the proofs in Art 6 (a) of the Rome Statute which states:

> Article 6: For the purpose of this Statute, 'genocide' means any of the following acts committed with intent to destroy, in whole or in part, a national, ethnical, racial or religious group, as such: (a) Killing members of the group; . . .

In addition to genocidal killings, Karemera's subordinates had also performed the systematic rape and sexual assault of Tutsi women throughout Rwanda which would constitute the secondary crime to the primary offense. This secondary crime fell under Article 7(1)(g) of the Rome Statute:

> Article 7: 1. For the purpose of this Statute, 'crime against humanity' means any of the following acts when committed as part of a widespread or systematic attack directed against any civilian population, with knowledge of the attack: . . .
>
> (g) Rape, sexual slavery, enforced prostitution, forced pregnancy, enforced sterilization, or any other form of sexual violence of comparable gravity; . . .

Assuming the intention and the knowledge requirements in Art 6(a) and Art 7(1)(g) of the Rome Statute respectively are met, the subordinate who takes on the legal character of the 'employee' within the vicarious liability approach would have committed a crime punishable under the Statute. The proof question is the extent to which *employer-type* responsibility can be imposed under Art 25(3)(a) which reads as follows:

35 In the context of criminal association 'employment' could be taken to equate with authority over, control, delegation and direction.

36 Under the 'integration test' the tortfeasor must to a large extent be integrated into the business of the employer. In other words, the tortfeasor must be an integral part of the employer's business and not an accessory to it.

37 This limb requires the court to determine on the facts the scope of the employment and whether the tort or criminal act fell within the scope. Factors to be considered are whether the tort was: (i) incidental to the scope of employment, (ii) closely connected to the scope of employment, (iii) performed in furthering the employer's business or benefits the employer in some way, or (iv) inherent in the nature of the business.

> Art 25: 3. In accordance with this Statute, a person shall be criminally responsible and liable for punishment for a crime within the jurisdiction of the Court if that person: (a) Commits such a crime, whether as an individual, jointly with another or *through another person*, regardless of whether that other person is criminally responsible
>
> (emphasis added)

Arguably, the proof technologies envisaged in the Rome Statute provide room for a tortious approach to imposing responsibility on the accused by means of vicarious liability. Particularly Art 25 envisages that, 'a person shall be criminally responsible and liable for punishment of a crime . . . if that person commits such a crime . . . through another person.' Under vicarious liability, a tort (that is to be read in our proposal in similar fashion to a secondary crime in the ICC context) is deemed to fall within the scope of employment (discretionary responsibility superior to inferior) if it contributes towards benefiting the organisation's purpose or orchestrates an inherent risk of the organisation perpetrating the harm. As such, with reference to the international context, the accused or leader who motivates and manages a criminal organisation for the primary purpose of genocidal killings would be responsible for his subordinates who perform killings as he commits the crime through his subordinates, or enables delegations of power for such perpetration without countervailing due diligence. In these terms the killings by the subordinates benefit the interests of a criminal organisation and advance its purpose. However, in the case of secondary crimes (like rape), the accused commits such crimes through his subordinates whereby in commanding the latter to engage in the work of the criminal organisation (to perform genocidal killings), there is an *inherent risk* of rape occurring, and this risk is a consequence of delegated authority rather than direct instruction.

The first requirement under the vicarious liability approach is to ask whether the principle perpetrator falls within the accused's employment (or delegated organisational authority). In this regard, and we are comforted by this logical outcome, the *integration* test replaces *objective foreseeability* under the current JCE III approach. According to the integration test, the principal perpetrator must be to a large extent integrated into the accused's criminal enterprise (through delegated authority) and cannot merely be an accessory to its commission. On this point, the court in *Various Claimants v Catholic Child Welfare Society and others* held that in the context of a Christian institution, there is a quite exceptional level of control exercised by the order over its brothers. The whole of a brother's life is under the control of his superiors. The order decides who serves where, when and how. The closest secular comparator would be the military services.[38] Similarly, in the *Karemera* case, the soldiers who were the principal perpetrators of the secondary crime of rape and sexual assault on the Tutsi population were clearly integrated in the criminal enterprise (to perform the genocidal killings of the Tutsi population) overseen by the accused who was its leader. The question then

38 *Catholic Child Welfare Society and others*, p. 5.

remained whether systematic rape could be viewed as a consequence of delegated authority. On the facts of the case Karemera, acting on behalf of the Interim Government, ordered an "*opération de ratissage*" in Bisesero against the Tutsi population in June 1994. The trial chambers held that the prosecution proved beyond a reasonable doubt that Karemera requested assistance from the operational *secteur* commander in Gisenyi, the commander in Kibuye, and the *préfet* of Kibuye to facilitate this killing operation. Furthermore, he also expressly called for the support of the *communes* surrounding the Bisesero hills in conducting the cleanup operation. The Trial Chamber found that a large number of militia and *gendarmes* traveled from Kibuye to Bisesero in late June to participate in attacks against Tutsis, thus supporting the initiation of the killings at Karemera's command. It was therefore held that the mass slaughters of Tutsis were taking place in Kibuye *préfecture* at the instigation or with the approval of the authorities constituting by and with the accused.[39] The authority of Karemera to control the soldiers was shown by his ability to command their activities, and by virtue of their orders to perform the killings required by Karemera's 'killing operations' meant that they were integrated into the accused's organisation, for the purposes of the crimes that eventuated and including consequential crimes that were contemplated in his delegation of authority.

The second requirement in the vicarious liability proof model is whether the crime was committed in the course of employment or within the scope of the soldier's engagement. Again, the test of *common intention* under JCE III liability will be substituted with an investigation of whether the crime fell within the scope of employment (or organisational delegation). *Lister v Hesley Hall*, in holding the employer vicariously liable, stated that culpability will be imposed where the tort in question constituted a particular risk which was inextricably linked to the employer's type of business or where the risk is one which experience shows is inherent in the nature of the business.[40] In *Mattis v Pollock*, a nightclub had hired a bouncer who was accustomed to manhandling resistant customers. The owner of the nightclub routinely encouraged the bouncer to be aggressive in the discharge of his duties. During one incident, a customer of the club fought the bouncer, producing violent retaliation. The court held that the owner of the nightclub was vicariously liable for the injuries inflicted on the customer by the bouncer. Significantly, the court stated that 'bouncers perform functions of barring and ejecting unruly patrons by use of reasonable force, the employment and encouragement of a violent bouncer therefore enhanced the risk of injury to customers that is generated by the friction and confrontation inherent in the enterprise of running a nightclub.' As such, the violence fell within the broad scope of employment and was an inherent risk of the employer's delinquent business culture. Similarly, in *Karemera*, the accused was responsible for planning and organising the destruction of the

39 *Édouard Karemera and Matthieu Ngirimpatse v The Prosecutor*, Case No. ICTR-98-44-T, para [1234].

40 *Lister*, para [65].

Tutsi race, and the accused in contributing to the primary crime, had enhanced the risk of sexual assaults and rapes occurring as secondary crimes due to the tendency of soldiers to use violence against individuals and to dehumanise them in the process, particularly through sexual assault. The rapes and sexual assaults would likewise fall within the broad scope of the accused's enterprise and were positioned in the general nature of delegation. Relating back to the Trial Chamber's determination in the *Karemera* case, it held that in the context of genocidal killings, the secondary crimes of rape and sexual assault were 'open and notorious' or 'widespread' in nature.[41] This conclusion confirmed that the secondary crimes represented an inherent risk promoted by the accused in the achievement of his general criminal enterprise.

Having established that Karemera will be vicariously liable for the secondary crimes of rape and sexual assault, the inquiry moves to determine whether there is a possible defense (justification or excuse) for liability (responsibility). To this end, the court must consider whether despite the secondary crime being committed by Karemera's subordinates, he had taken measures for preventing its occurrence or that the secondary crime would have been committed in any event, despite whatever he did. In this regard, Karemera claimed that he sent a report to the Minister of Defence to sanction those soldiers who left the warfront and came back to rape women and pillage. The Trial Chamber assigned no weight to this piece of evidence as the accused never entered this report or any additional proof to support his claim into evidence. Furthermore, the alleged report was not mentioned in the accused's closing brief or during his final argument. However, had Karemera tendered any such evidence it would not have relieved him of vicarious liability as the measures taken by the accused directed against the secondary crimes should be for that purpose preventative in nature and not reactive. This condition means that at the time the orders were given by the accused to perform genocidal killings, sufficient measures had to be in place to prevent the commission of the secondary crimes.

Implications of adopting the tort/crime hybrid for the proof of JCE III

As identified in Chapter 3, there are several contentious issues with the ICC's current approach to proving JCE III liability: the use of objective foreseeability, the wide framing of the common intention and the imposition of liability on the accused for crimes committed by non-JCE members. Having applied the *Karemera* reasoning to the substantive limbs of vicarious liability, we now explain how the proposed tort/crime hybrid alleviates the problems associated with JCE III liability in the international criminal law context as currently struggled with.

41 *Édouard Karemera and Matthieu Ngirimpatse v The Prosecutor*, Case No. ICTR-98-44-A, para [627].

Objective foreseeability

The purpose of the objective foreseeability test under JCE III liability is to link the secondary participants in the crimes who have instigated, permitted or tolerated the physical commission of the offenses by their subordinates, down the line to the perpetrator. As such, the test allows for levels of perpetration (the senior level and the execution level) to be causally connected. With regard to the senior or leadership defendants who have 'no blood on their hands,' they derive liability for the crimes committed based on considering how the mind of the ordinary person in their circumstances must have foreseen the secondary crimes likely to be committed.[42] Similarly under the integration test of the tort/crime hybrid, the link between the secondary perpetrators of the offenses at the senior or leadership level and the principal perpetrators at the execution level is made through answering whether the principal perpetrator was an integral or integrated member of the leader's criminal organisation. If the answer is yes, then liability on the part of the accused arises out of this relationship between the parties, similar to that of the delegated employee.

Alluded to in the earlier parts of this chapter, one important implication of adopting the tort/crime hybrid is that the accused determined vicariously liable for the crime, is not (unlike in JCE III proofs) held jointly criminally responsible. This outcome is justified as in cases where the courts have used objective foreseeability, because proof of the accused's subjective foresight of the secondary crime is absent. In such circumstances, there is no evidential support for establishing the knowledge-based link between the accused and the principal perpetrator which is criminal in nature or which connotes moral blameworthiness. The tort/crime hybrid on the other hand provides a principled approach to the proof of liability balancing the evidentiary realities faced by the courts in holding the leadership of the criminal enterprise responsible for the crimes committed down the line of delegation, without ignoring the mind of the superior offender at least insofar as he created the risk of harm. A hybrid approach also allows for recognising variegated degrees of responsibility through the extent of contribution. This proof technology is important (as it is with determining damages) for apportioning punishment in sentencing on a more rational and subjective basis, rather than fictionalising uniform blameworthiness deserving equal penalty.

The imposition of liability on JCE members for non-JCE members' crimes

Another difficulty with the ICC's current approach to JCE III liability as detailed in Chapter 3 is the imposition of joint liability on JCE members from the alleged crimes committed by non-JCE members. Traditionally in domestic criminal justice traditions, courts imposed joint liability based on the close cooperation

42 Sliedregt, van Elies, "The Curious Case of International Criminal Liability," *Journal of International Criminal Justice*, 10 5, 2012, pp. 1171–1188 at 1174.

between one member of the JCE and the principal perpetrator in order to further the common intention. This close cooperation constituted the ***sufficient link*** between the JCE member and the principal perpetrator at the execution level.[43] In the factual context of global crimes (see Chapter 4) the difficulty with this approach is an absence of a sufficient shared mental state or common intention between the JCE member and the principal perpetrator of the secondary crime who acts outside the knowledge or purpose of the enterprise but should be deemed responsible through some other proof extension. There are also serious coincidence and causation issues entangled in this proof paradigm. Any inference of liability beyond the JCE, but reverting back to it without common purpose or reasonable foreseeability, while remaining reliant on more remote connections, undercuts the fundamental association principle underlying joint criminal enterprise. Specifically, this thinking removes the need for the common intention (or natural and reasonable foreseeability) to be shared or inferred jointly between all participants designated within the enterprise. By bridging the liability of the perpetrator through proof technologies beyond what binds the enterprise this approach almost irretrievably strains the establishment of coincidence and causation. Against such contention, the tort/crime hybrid provides a solution to this problem by shifting the inquiry from one of mental state to one of conduct between the parties, more realistically relegating mental state to the context of an original delegation wherein the party removed from the perpetration had a duty to avoid risk occurring even where he had no direct intentional or reasonably foreseen connection with the eventual criminal purpose.

Under our proposed approach, the integration test merely asks whether the parties have conducted themselves so as to form an employer–employee type of relationship or whether they acted in a way which would allow the courts to infer that a relationship ***akin to employment*** existed. This determination of delegated connection producing risk of harm would constitute the necessary link between the accused who is at the leadership level and the removed principle perpetrator who although contributing to the criminal organisation of the accused, is so structurally remote that he cannot be said to share a common mental state with the accused, or even be naturally foreseen beyond a prevalent risk. It is the delegation through frameworks of organisation and association which provides the necessary connection to the primary perpetrator, rather than some specious assertion of foreseeability no matter how remote. The risk at the heart of the tort technology can be much more generally understood than some assumed conclusion that a particular crime might be a natural and reasonable consequence of a remote association. The benefits of this approach can be seen in the case of *Prosecutor v Nikola Sainovic*, where one accused Ojdanic was the Chief of the General Staff and exercised command and control over all units and organs of the VJ. The Bosnian-Serb leadership including this accused had shared the common intention to advance the deportation and the forcible transfer of

43 *Karemera (Trial)*, para [345].

non-Serbs, and during the implementation of the common intention, crimes were committed by individuals who did not participate directly in that common intention binding the JCE members (such as the army, the Bosnian-Serb police, Serb paramilitary groups, Bosnian-Serb armed civilians and even unidentified individuals). The court referred to the close cooperation between the JCE members and the principal perpetrators to hold the JCE members jointly liable for the secondary crimes. We suggest that the tort/crime hybrid in shifting the inquiry to an investigation of conduct and the risk of harm, would determine liability in a more principled way by avoiding almost-fictional distortions of some presumed connected mental state.

In this regard, the army, police and paramilitary groups constitute the principal perpetrators who through the mass killing of non-Serbs could be said to constitute an integral part of the accused's criminal organisation. Via the lines of delegation which flowed beyond the common purpose and down to more peripheral but still related delegates, vicarious liability enables the imposition of responsibility for the crimes committed by these groups, even though the senior officials had not directly, through knowledge actual or imputed, connected to the common purpose of the crime in question. However, the hybrid proof test would exclude armed civilians and unidentified individuals as there would be no basis to hold that these groups were integral to the accused's criminal organisation or that they shared a relationship akin to employment with the accused.

Further, in the case of *Martic* the court confirmed Milan Martic's responsibility was as a JCE member for crimes that were carried out by non-JCE members who belonged to associated hierarchical organisations, such as the police or the military.[44] The court based its reasoning on the fact that perpetrators of the crimes (the JNA, the TO and the Milicija Krajine) were 'under the control of the other members of the JCE.' The case is a further instance where the ICC judges contrived the mental states of the senior participants as somehow transferring through delegation (and inadvertently employing the tort approach) by focusing on the conduct of the principal offenders, and on the nature of the organisation and general association. This thinking can be distilled back down to concerns for delegation, contribution and aggregation. Under the tort/crime hybrid approach, the control exercised by the accused would mean that the police and the military could be deemed to operate within an employment-like relationship down from Martic in his criminal organisation. As such, the necessary link between the leadership level and the execution level is formed and justified more convincingly using the tort/crime hybrid than the JCE III/non-JCE distortion.

Wide framing of the common intention under present proof frames.

Lastly, as mentioned in Chapter 3, the ICC judges have permitted a wide framing of the common intention shared between JCE members as a method of hurdling

44 *Martic (Appeal)*, paras [187]–[188] and [438].

proof limitations. Again, in *Martic* the court alleged that the accused was a participant in the JCE, with the common intention widely defined as 'the forcible removal of a majority of the Croat, Muslim and other non-Serb population from approximately one-third of the territory of the Republic of Croatia and large parts of the Republic of Bosnia and Herzegovina.' Similarly, in *Kupreskic*[45] the accused was charged with adhering to the common plan for the execution of the 'cleansing campaign in the village.' At the time of this case, the wide framing of the common intention led to almost any secondary crime potentially falling within such a broad conceived collective mental state. When compared even with JCE proofs in domestic jurisdictions satisfied by natural consequence conclusions, this approach to common intention over-extends the reach of joint criminal liability, by even removing the tenuous measures of the natural and foreseeable. The tort/crime hybrid obviates this extension as it forces a consideration of the scope of the criminal enterprise rather than artificially constructing the common intention of the parties. The necessity to address such proof fictions is revealed even in the discourse employed by the relevant judicial narratives. How can *common intention* ever be satisfied when its proof fails to enquire into the shared subjectivity of perpetrator and superior accused? The limitations of the current proof technology focus on the nature of the criminal enterprise and how the actors within it have conducted themselves so as to derive the scope of the organisation and the manner in which the parties associated contributed to its goals. If the leaders have historically permitted rapes and destruction of property to occur in conjunction with genocidal killings, then these crimes would be included within the scope of the enterprise as they were once authorised by the accused. This sounds like similar fact evidence in a realm for which it was never intended. Replaced by tort proof technologies, even if these crimes were not so authorised, the accused might be held vicariously liable for them if they were inherent in the nature of the criminal enterprise or closely connected to the scope of the criminal enterprise as would be the analogy with generally delegated employment duties and the risks that flow therefrom. Arguably, (as posited in the context of the *Karemera* case), crimes such as rape and sexual assault would be considered inherent risks closely connected to the scope of the accused's criminal organisation which aims at genocidal killing. This is due to the violent nature of the criminal organisation which endeavors to inflict physical and psychological harm on its victims. Thus, the tort/crime hybrid offers a principled framework for imposing liability on the accused without over-extending common criminal intention proofs.

Aiding and abetting and tortious contribution

Having explained and demonstrated the applicability of the tort/crime model for JCE proofs, the discussion now shifts to aiding and abetting. As mentioned in Chapter 3, the main controversy associated with aiding and abetting at the

45 *Prosecutor v Kupreskic et al*, Case No. IT-95-16-T.

international level is found in the causation requirement, that being whether there was some specific direction by the accused regarding the consequences of the assistance he provided and whether the assistance was sufficiently substantial to ensure the commission of the consequent crime. To encapsulate the point, there are two main casual *tests* applied to determine aiding and abetting liability – *specific direction* and *substantial contribution* to the crime. The ICTY and ICTR case-law on point might be criticised as a haphazard application of the *specific direction* requirement, at times using it inter-changeably with *substantial contribution* or leaving the requirement out of consideration altogether. Additionally, the courts' reasons for variegating the causation requirement to suit the specifics of certain difficult cases relate to the fact that the accused was at times geographically or temporally remote from the crimes. This reasoning led to the need to modify the substantive causal requirements to compensate for the accused's assistance being remote and abstract. Interpreted very generally, causation so established has been criticised as uncertain and disconnected from domestic principle previously applied though international criminal law jurisprudence. To address such concerns, and consistent with our tort/crime hybrid theorising, we suggest an alternative consideration of causation that finds its roots in the concept of tortious contribution. Such an approach naturally flows from the similarities between causation tests required to establish liability for aiding and abetting (i.e. sufficient contribution) and exceptions to the *but-for* test under tort (i.e. material contribution to injury, material contribution to risk).

Avoiding the contentious concepts of *specific direction* and *substantial contribution* through this analysis means that responsibility for aiding and abetting under international criminal law would be imposed when the accused assists, encourages or lends moral support to the perpetration of a certain specific crime (murder, extermination, rape, torture, wanton destruction of civilian property, etc.) and this support has a *substantial effect* upon the perpetration of the crime.[46] The specific direction and substantial contribution considerations inevitably enter the equation where the term *substantial effect* is used to connect the act of the accused to the crime's occurrence. Yet, in so doing, there is no formal proof requirements in straining temporal or spatial relationships to also establish substantial effect.

Before elaborating on our alternative position, it is first necessary to evaluate which current test is preferable (specific direction or substantial contribution) in terms of more accurately capturing the aims of the *substantial effect* requirement and thereby avoiding the complexities of selecting between the tests in order to somewhat-problematically establish proof. Since the standard required of aiding and abetting is based on substantial effect, a case could be made to introduce concepts such as material contribution to the injury/crime understanding, or to the risk of the crime occurring in setting a threshold causal link between the act of the accused to the commission of the crime. In simpler terms, the prosecution

46 *Prosecutor v Blagoje Simic*, Case No. IT-95-9-A, paras [156]–[160].

would have to show that the accused through his assistance, encouragement or moral support had materially contributed to the crime or had contributed to the *risk* of the crime occurring. The reasons for adopting this approach are that the *material contribution to risk* test would allow the courts to determine liability where the act of the accused was far removed from the actual crime committed in terms of it belonging to a long chain of conduct by other individuals or in terms of it being geographically or temporally remote from the crime. This reasoning would do away with the *Perisic* predicament which involved the courts applying the specific direction only when the accused is remote from the crime. Under the new approach, regardless of whether the accused was remote or proximate to the crime, the central issue is if he had materially contributed to the risk of the crime occurring through his assistance, encouragement or moral support. In addition, the material contribution test more accurately represents aiding and abetting situations at the international level as it does not require even more legally fictitious determinations of sufficient coincidence in order to hold the accused *totally* liable as he would be if he acted as the sole perpetrator.

The situationally grounded causation question in the global crime context where perpetration is complex and collective should be whether tortious (harm-oriented) notions of material contribution can be reconciled with substantial effect in international criminal law. From this point it is more logical to appreciate our analytical method. The argument for a more principled and rational international criminal jurisprudence is based on the conviction that synergies between the proof technologies in crime and tort hold out the prospect of establishing individual liability (responsibility) in a manner that better reflects the collective dimensions of perpetration and victimisation in international criminal law. As Chapter 1 argued international criminal justice is concerned to punish those guilty of atrocities, to prevent atrocities in future and to recognise and restore the damage caused by atrocities where possible. The emphasis on damage restitution and appreciating its collective nature chimes in well with tort law's purposes. Moreover, the required proof outcome of *responsibility* as set out in the Rome Statute permits tortious considerations to enter the legal analysis at the international level set free of narrow liability concerns (see Chapter 1). Taking this synthesis further, it is both logical and useful to apply particular features of tort proofs such as material contribution to test their preferred relevance for general causal notions such as substantial effect which merge both tort and crime causation determinations. In addition to these more attractive proof mechanics, we will put the case in Chapter 6 that the tort/crime transition exerts practical weight behind the argument that judicial reasoning in international criminal jurisprudence is challenged by the opportunity for a more original vision and mission to achieve international criminal justice in ways clearly conceived by the Rome Statute Preamble.

Before delving into the application of the material risk test, the following justifications are posed for adopting this preferred approach: (i) contribution as causation – an objective inquiry, (ii) accounting for multiple actors within causation determinations, and (iii) distributing costs and contribution concerning harm.

Contribution as causation – an objective inquiry – contribution and morality?

As mentioned in the earlier parts of this chapter, one of the main concerns about substituting tortious for criminal proof concepts is the view that the latter is concerned with moral blameworthiness while the former is generally not. However, when analysing whether criminal causation requirements can be replaced by tortious proofs, we say the argument against based on the absence of determining moral blameworthiness does not hold weight. The difference between causing a *substantial effect* under criminal law and *materially contributing* under tort need not amount to determining a difference between committing, or not committing a moral wrong.[47] The proof question in both cases (crime and tort) is one about conduct, not of morality, and the subsequent determination of causation would be settled in the same way if the facts of the case were compatible. The argument about diminishing moral blameworthiness by employing contribution rather than seeking complete liability (which in reality is a legal fiction where secondary offending occurs) does not come into consideration in determining cause. Rather, if at all, it may be an issue, but we say a more genuine one, when it is recognised that others may have contributed to differing degrees in causing the criminal conduct. Finally, causation is about criminal conduct and not about the moral mental state that an offender may (or may not) direct to his actions.

In *Furundžija*[48] the functions performed by Drosihn in his employment as a gas technician were an integral part of the supply and use of the poison gas, but this alone could not render him liable for its criminal use even if he was aware that his functions played such an important role in the transfer of gas. Without influence over the supply of the poisonous gas, he was not guilty through secondary participation. In other words, *mens rea* alone is insufficient to ground a criminal conviction based on aiding and abetting where there needs to be assistance sufficient to act as a causal element.[49] Moral blameworthiness is not a factor of contributing to causation in the absence of the necessary knowledge of what was to follow. Hence, the criticism that moral blameworthiness separates criminal law from tort, we reiterate, does not apply in the specific example of causation, which focuses proof on conduct.

However, these arguments do not solve the issue of whether material contribution is in substance equivalent to substantial effect. To determine whether by using the term substantial effect the ICC judges really mean material contribution we will examine multiple actors within causation.

Accounting for multiple actors within causation

Continuing from the previous point, the appeals chamber in the *Blaskic* case stated perhaps misleadingly, that proof that the conduct of the aider and abettor had a

47 Dyson, Matthew, *Unravelling Tort and Crime*, Cambridge University Press: Cambridge, 2014, p. 269.

48 *Prosecutor v Anto Furundžija*, Case No. IT-95-17/1-T.

49 *Furundžija (Trial)*, p. 223.

causal effect on the act of the principal perpetrator was not required to establish the offense. This reasoning is not strictly accurate, and what the court should have held was the aider and abettor's act need only have a *substantial effect* upon the perpetration of the crime. Thus, proof of a prevailing causal or consequential relationship between the conduct of the aider and abettor and the commission of the crime, or proof that such conduct served as a *condition precedent* to the commission of the crime, is not required, particularly if several actions comprised the cause.[50] This definition of substantial effect goes to the essence of causation in aiding and abetting and avoids the difficulty of balancing substantial contribution and specific direction.

The test for causation in both modes does not depend essentially on the subjective mental states of the parties involved, except as constructed courtesy of the ordinary person having foreseen consequentialist outcomes. Additionally, the test is centrally analogous to a *but-for* analysis. The aider and abettor need not have been the sole cause for the occurrence of the crime. The term substantial effect is potentially broad enough to include contribution to the crime (material contribution to the act) but also contribution to the risk of the crime occurring (material contribution to risks). The last point is the one of most interest to our present discussion. Where material contribution to injury from a tortious perspective refers to a form of cumulative causation in which of the two acts committed, neither can be said to be the but-for cause of the plaintiff's injury or harm, though the breach must have at least made the injury worse than it would otherwise have been.

> In a hypothetical case where a claimant develops a disease resulting from cumulative exposure to a noxious substance, only part of which is attributable to the defendant's breach of duty, it is unnecessary to demonstrate that the victim would not have suffered the disease at all, but for the accused's contribution to the breach. The prosecutor must only prove that the breach of duty made a material contribution which falls outside the *de minimus* range. At this stage the comparison between material contribution and substantial effect is most convincing as both are exceptions to but-for causation and require contribution that is beyond de minimus so that it would be justified and sensible to impose liability.[51]

However, arguably the tortious concept of material contribution is much more complex, as seen in the UK case of *Holtby v Cowan* (actualising the above hypothetical) where the claimant had developed asbestosis from occupational exposure to asbestos dust over a period of several years during which he had worked for different employers. The court held that each employer would only be held liable for a part of the claimant's total disability and divided the responsibility between them on a 'time-exposure' basis. As noted above in the current criminal law proof thinking around aiding and abetting under international criminal law, once aiding and abetting responsibility is imposed there is no calibration within

50 *Prosecutor v Tihomir Blaskic*, Case No. IT-95-14-A, para [48].

51 Lunney, Mark, and Oliphant, Ken, *Tort Law: Text and Materials*, Oxford University Press: Oxford, 2013.

that liability according to the 'causative' role of the accused. In other words, we do not speak of one accused having aided and abetted the crime *more or less* than another accused. If there are two aiders and abettors, they will be criminally responsible each in an absolute sense. This criminal causal model arguably fails to cater to situations where there are multiple aiders and abettors, exhibiting different degrees of involvement in the eventual crime, or when the aider and abettor is merely one contributor within a criminal chain of events.

The flexibility of the substantial effect test allows for what constitutes contribution to be often determined by an exercise of common sense, meaning that in a specific case one aider and abettor may be substantially relevant to the commission of a crime while another aider and abettor along the criminal chain who is not so associated with the former might be deemed less relevant but still effective. The acts of both accused would be determined independently and the substantial effect requirement could be met by both but the responsibility for aiding and abetting under current criminal proof technologies currently is not divisible between them, whereas applying tort law, material contribution is a much more malleable concept viewed in a different light to the requirements of criminal causation.

Conditioned by criminal law causation, it might seem strange to say that all the defendants had materially contributed to the resultant harm. Taking *Holtby* for example, defendant A's tort is estimated to have a 60 percent time contribution to the plaintiff's harm and defendant C's tort 30 percent and defendant D's only 10 percent, and as such then how can it be convincingly argued that D had materially contributed to the harm? The diminishing involvement measure is only one way of understanding tort responsibility, primarily designed to calibrate portions of damage. In determining initial responsibility, it is the collective contribution of these defendants that led to the long-term sickness, asbestosis. Hence each provided a material contribution to the ultimate harm. The responsibility is shared if the damages are divided.

To further understand the utility of this thinking let's interrogate a hypothetical case reflecting common responsibility concerns in the international criminal context:

> The accused A provides funds and equipment to C who then transports this equipment to E and F who under the separate instigation of G shoot H and J. The situation of potential responsibility is complex insofar as there could potentially be three groups of aiders and abettors – A who contributes the resources for the commission of the crime, C who transports the equipment from A to E and F, and finally G who directly instigates the shooting of H and J. Excluding for the present purposes of determining causation, the mental states of the accused, a strong case for criminal conduct is possible, resting on all of the group's actions substantially effecting the commission of the crime. Even in the absence of but-for reasons of criminal causation, the individual contributions of each accused is clearly above *de minimus.* If they were each to be charged and held in their own ways responsible for the shooting of H and J, this determination would rest on aiding and abetting in

> its different contexts and forms. In current proof terms responsibility would not be shared but targeted to each individual. It is clear from the reality of their singular and collective action, any individualised form of liability does not reflect well the responsibility spoken of in the Preamble that in this case so clearly aggregated between the different accused.

Were a tortious notion of contribution and its relationship to responsibility adopted, instead of ending the discussion of criminal responsibility at *whether* the accused had aided and abetted the crime, it would be possible to continue to the question of *how much* he had aided and abetted the crime *relative to other actors* involved in its commission. This inquiry should not be confined to the participation and proportion of one individual's contribution because it might be the case, as it usually is at the international level, that multiple individuals have contributed to the commission of what makes up complicated criminal conduct.

Distributing costs of harm

Adopting the above approach complements the dual purpose of the ICC to deter and punish as well as restore and compensate victims. By distributing aiding and abetting liability, costs for harm can be more appropriately apportioned. In a restorative/compensatory environment there is little justice in demanding that each aider and abettor totally compensate the victims of a crime for the total harm suffered, when the crime is a chain of events. The unrealistic absolutist interpretation of secondary responsibility, in this sense, cannot satisfy the Preamble's harm and damages aspirations in a context of metered justice.

The substantive limbs of aiding and abetting and how they are open for the hybrid proof approach

As noted on a variety of earlier occasions, in the case of *Perisic*, Momčilo Perišič was the top military officer of the Yugoslav Army. He was charged with aiding and abetting the crimes of murder, inhumane acts and attacks on civilians in Sarajevo by providing substantial assistance to the VRS. Along with other support, it was alleged that Perisic had provided logistic and personnel assistance and thus aided and abetted the crimes perpetrated by the VRS during its takeover of Srebrenica in 1995. As mentioned in previous discussions of these facts, in focusing on whether *Perisic* had given specific direction amounting to aiding and abetting the court defused the prosecution case by concluded that the VRS was not an organisation whose actions were criminal per se. Instead, the Appeals Chamber determined the VRS rather than being a criminal organisation was an army fighting a war.[52] As such the charges for aiding and abetting were not substantiated because the assistance was not given for the commission of crimes.

52 *Prosecutor v Momcilo Perisic*, Case No. IT-04-81-A, para [57].

Applying the material risk test, liability will be imposed if the accused assisted, encouraged or gave moral support to the perpetration of a certain specific crime and this support represented a *material contribution* to the perpetration of the crime, irrespective of the general purposes of the over-arching criminal enterprise. It is important to note that by excluding the specific direction requirement, the court in this case would not be limited to determining whether Perisic had *specifically* directed resources to the crimes said to be assisted and the causal determination would thus not be confined by contextual considerations such as whether the VRS was an organisation whose sole and exclusive purpose was the commission of crimes, and whether the strategic command endorsed a policy of assisting VRS crimes. Such an interpretation focusing on material contribution as a measure of causal degree links the criminal conduct of the accused in the sense that he, individually, had some complementary mental state which would direct the consequences of his contribution in a manner that the court could determine significant.

A more distinct question relating to causation here is whether the accused had knowledge that the VRS was engaged in unlawful activities apart from their main goal which was to fight a war, and armed with this knowledge he continued to supply aid to the VRS forces. It is enough proof of causal contribution in the hybrid mode if the accused is aware of or had knowledge of the *essential elements* of the crimes that could be committed via his contribution, and aided and abetted so informed.

From this point, using *logistical assistance* as an indicator of causal responsibility, we consider whether the requirements for the proposed aiding and abetting hybrid proof approach have been met. In doing so, the following conditions must be satisfied: (i) knowledge of the essential elements of the crime, (ii) material contribution through the provision of assistance, encouragement or moral support to the perpetrator in the commission of the aforementioned crime, and (iii) a measurable proportion of responsibility for causing the eventual harm.

Returning to the facts of *Perisic*, the logistical assistance suggested to satisfy aiding and abetting included assistance through the provision of weapons and ammunition, technical experts, training, medical support, fuel and operational support enabling the Pretis factory to produce weaponry for the VRS army. Regarding knowledge of the essential elements of the crime we differ from the Trial Chamber's reasoning that in part relied on concluding the unlawful acts were inextricably linked to the war waged by the VRS as it constituted part of its 'war strategy.' Only in such circumstances did the court deem the accused had knowledge of the crimes being committed by the VRS and their essential elements. However, the requirement of knowledge about crimes in general to which aid would be applied was substantiated by Perisic being provided with information, from a variety of sources, detailing the VRS's criminal behavior and discriminatory intent. This information related to acts of violence against Bosnian Muslims perpetrated in the Bosnian and Herzegovina theater of war. More importantly, Perisic had *specific* knowledge of the killing and wounding of civilians and/or persons not taking active part in the hostilities.[53]

53 *Prosecutor v Momcilo Perisic*, Case No. IT-04-81-T, para [1631].

For purpose established through knowledge, it was necessary to ground material contribution via the provision of assistance, encouragement or moral support to the perpetrator in the commission of the crime charged. On the contentious issue of causation, it is crucial to note that the VRS had also obtained a measure of assistance from sources other than Perisic and the VJ General Staff. As such and in domestic common law parlance, this raises the question of whether the contribution was *material*. Arguably, in the context of global crime (see Chapter 4) causation must not be viewed in such a myopic way. The question of material contribution requires consideration in a broader sense as the collectivity of the perpetration and victimisation demands. On the facts of the case, Perisic not only provided weaponry but military advice and financial assistance which kept the VRS army in operation.[54] This clearly meant that Perisic materially contributed to the crimes committed by the VRS as the VRS had served the dual-purpose goals of fighting a war *and* committing unlawful acts. In such a situation and courtesy of the concept of 'material,' the defense in our view should not be allowed to discriminate between the VRS's purposes (legitimate or otherwise) nor should the atrocities be ignored because they were committed under the pretense of war. Further, the *but-for* or *substantial* proof hurdles erected in domestic criminal causation proofs, if sufficient to enable this accused to avoid responsibility, would defeat the broader purposes of the Preamble.

Having established that Perisic had (or had not) materially contributed to the crimes by the VRS, the next issue to be considered would have been the extent of his contribution relative to other actors within the criminal scheme. Unfortunately, this question is confined to the hypothetical as the Trial Chamber had not directed itself to the matter in its fact-finding inquiry and as such, coming to a decision will be a speculative enterprise. To advance the tort/crime hybrid we work from the limitations of the court's reasoning around relative contribution. Assuming that enough evidence is available to advance the required proofs in both crime and tort approaches, the guiding considerations for the court would be to look at the following factors: (i) whether the preliminary requirements of *mens rea*, *actus reus*, coincidence and causation are present, (ii) the closeness of the contribution to the commission of the offense (e.g. a provision of weapons is more remote than the supervision of the killings itself), (iii) the level of control the actor had in the commission of the crime, and (iv) the degree of knowledge of the crime potentially committed as a result of the aiding and abetting. Against all of this, the aggregation approach makes it possible to avoid artificial determinations on whether the accused was the individual driver of causation.

Implications of adopting the tort/crime hybrid in aiding and abetting

The following implications arise from the application of our tort/crime hybrid approach to proofs of secondary liability and participation:

54 *Perisic (Trial)*, para [1598].

- the material contribution test allows the issue of causation to be asked and answered in a broader way;
- the test also considers the collective nature of international crimes which might include accused who are remote from the crimes' commission; and
- the test for establishing liability does not change according to the remoteness of the accused from the crime. Instead this factor might be understood in accessing the role of the accused relative to other contributors along the chain.

As to the first implication, the question to be answered by the court is no longer whether the accused had specifically directed his contribution to the crime but whether he materially contributed. This approach will allow flexibility in the court's reasoning in comparison to prevailing evidentiary difficulties with current criminal proof technologies dealing with participation and secondary parties. Further, the hybrid model is useful in situations which involve multiple actors along the chain of causation, as often the accused's contribution is merely one part of a series of events leading to the crime that is not specifically directed to the perpetration, yet might constitute a material contribution. For example, in *Perisic*, the evidence could not establish that the specific weapons used in committing the principal crimes charged, originated from logistical assistance overseen by Perisic. As such, the specific direction requirement would fail, and liability would not be established in those terms. However, under the material contribution model, liability is looked at in a more expansive and inclusive sense to involve the numerous other forms of practical assistance which substantially facilitated the perpetrators' crimes (e.g. provision of financial resources, advice etc). Hence, the approach through the tort/crime hybrid no longer suffers from the restrictive and artificial condition imposed by specific direction requirements. Further, the tort/crime hybrid provides a principled methodology for weighing the contribution of each actor within the criminal chain leading up to the crime committed and thereby offers a reasoned way of apportioning the compensation sums owed by each of the accused to victims of the resultant crimes. The importance of this outcome cannot be overestimated. If the ICC is to avoid allegations of scapegoating blame down the line of authority, it must adopt a model which seeks to impose responsibility in a reasoned and justified manner depending on the accused's level of participation in the crime, and its aggregated contribution and complex, contributory causation.

The final and most vital implication of the model is that it provides a balance between the retributive and restorative concerns of the court in determining responsibility at the international level. As revealed in *Perisic*, the courts were reluctant to impose liability where the accused was geographically and temporally remote from the crime. This led to a decision to apply the specific direction test only where such remoteness exists, as a safeguard to excessive criminalisation, even if that risked endorsing the impunity of a senior officer, due to the narrowness of considering the context and purpose of the organisation that he assisted. Chapter 3, noting that this reasoning has been severely criticised, argued the applicable legal tests for responsibility should not depend on the remoteness of the accused.[55] This unhelpful emphasis on time and space rather than material contribution no matter when and where, is precisely the outcome the tort/crime model seeks to avoid.

Working the model

In sum, the necessities for proving aiding and abetting and joint criminal enterprise demonstrate convincingly the benefit of the tort/crime hybrid approach by:

- avoiding the excessive distortion of already-stretched criminal proof technologies regarding participation through causation, coincidence, knowledge, foreseeability, and
- satisfying the need to better address the expanded aims of ICJ in their harm-minimisation concerns.

In addition, this new approach gives rise to legal analysis which is more principled as well as practical. In this sense, the hybrid approach does not just make proof easier but more importantly it enables juridical decision-making to accord with international criminal justice aims, without rejecting principled consistency in favor of outcome-oriented pragmatism.

For instance, when it comes to considerations of remoteness that determine the quantum of compensation due from the harm caused by criminal victimisation, the test for aiding and abetting liability need not alter according to the context or circumstances surrounding the commission of the crimes (primary or secondary), but will remain consistent with realistic collective determinations of contribution to causation. In the context of global crime, where the senior participants may consciously rely on remoteness to conceal their involvement, it is vital that proof technologies do not fall foul of this conceit. The question of remoteness comes into play only after aiding and abetting responsibility has been determined, or criminal enterprise engagement established, and the court has to decide on the issue of compensation. Thus, where the accused is far removed from the crime it could be a factor persuading the court to reduce his contribution relative to other actors who were geographically closer to the scene of the crime, subject to other considerations such as control over the crimes commission.

This outcome is a logical consequence of proving causation through degrees of contribution rather than other more artificial proof technologies. As such, the need for a principled approach to international proof technologies is balanced against the concerns of justice, wary of imposing excessive liability on accused persons whose actual contribution to the crime, while sufficient in proof of cause and appreciation of risk, remains comparatively less than that of more directly connected perpetrators. This approach also means that the senior officers cannot

55 *Perisic (Appeal)*, para [70].

escape responsibility by hiding behind proofs of remoteness rather than actual contribution. Consequentially, impunity is more richly addressed and deterrence relative to realistic considerations of responsibility is more likely to take effect.

A more principled interpretation of individual responsibility at the international level in the form of a tort/crime model is undeniable. Selecting two of the most controversial criminal law proof concepts at the international level – JCE III, and aiding and abetting to elaborate and actualise the viability of the model – not only exposes the failings of the present approach (Chapter 3) but also provides a practical framework for the enhanced possibilities of a reasoned and principled international criminal jurisprudence. In brief, the proposed adoption of tortious vicarious liability for JCE solves the issue of objective foreseeability, imputed responsibility through non-JCE members and the broad framing of the common intention, by ensuring that there is a 'sufficient link' between the accused and the commission of the crime. Under the hybrid frame such a sufficient link may be established through 'employment' or 'integral involvement' in the criminal organisation paired with contextual consideration as to the risky and harmful nature of the organisation's culture (whether it condoned secondary activities such as rape or destruction when the primary aim was to kill). Responsibility is thus justified through the actual identified connection between the accused and the illegal act, not distorted by temporal or spatial gymnastics. Regarding aiding and abetting, the introduction of a tortious view on causation in the form of material contribution provides a fuller picture of the participatory criminal conduct as it allows for aggregation of responsibility. This expansionist consideration is crucial in the context of collective crimes as it apportions responsibility actuarially among perpetrators and avoids the criticism of punishing low-level scapegoats. In addition, judges and prosecutors are otherwise not required to distort sufficiency or specificity when direction and assistance are considered.

The tort/crime model provides a reasoned approach to attaching secondary and participatory responsibility for collective crimes which in turn qualifies as a rational and principled jurisprudence, even within the constraints of complementarity and harmonisation (see Chapter 2). It escapes the criticisms directed against current outcome-oriented juridical decision-making by focusing on contextual and common-sense appreciations of international criminal responsibility derived from harm-focused areas of law such as tort, with common causation and contribution considerations. Hence, the imputation of responsibility is not only principled but intuitive to law's audience. We assert that this commitment to the constituency of humanity through concerns for blame *and* harm is crucial for promoting the legitimacy of the ICC among the community of victims it is meant to serve and protect, with the service of judges and lawyers no longer called upon to be case-by-case magicians.

6 Vicissitude or vision?

Introduction

In a recent review of the landmark ICTY decision of *Tadic* (1995) Nouwen and Baker[1] suggest that the judgment represents a 'high water-mark' in judicial decision-making and legal reasoning that invokes natural law or appeals to morality to overcome perceived shortcomings in the positive law exercised in the judgments. Despite the importance of the case for international law at many levels, in a more pragmatic vein Richard Goldstone, the Tribunal's first prosecutor observed that it was 'highly unsatisfactory that someone at the level of Dusko Tadic [as opposed to a higher profile defendant] should face trial and those who incited and facilitated his conduct should escape justice.' As a caveat Goldstone explained that Tadic was the only accused available at the time to bring before the Tribunal 'when the judges, the media and the international community were clamoring for us to begin prosecution.'[2]

The Appeals Chamber in *Tadic* took the consideration of individual liability into new international realms:

> customary international law imposes criminal liability for serious violations of common article 3 . . . on the protection of victims of internal armed conflict, and for breaching certain fundamental principles and rules regarding the means and the methods of combat in civil strife.[3]

The full support of the ICTY by its political founders, the Security Council, meant there was no risk as there is today for the ICC, of an exit by member states for what may have been perceived as judicial over-reach.[4] In the ICTY contexts judges could propose radical legal interpretations of foundation principles without one eye over their shoulder to measure any adverse reaction from those most affected.

1 Nouwen, Sarah, and Becker, Michael, "Tadić v. Prosecutor: International Criminal Tribunal for the Former Yugoslavia," in Eirik Bjorge and Cameron Miles, *Landmark Cases in Public International Law*, Hart Publishing: Oxford, 2017, Chapter 16.

2 Scharf, Michael, "The Prosecutor v. Dusko Tadic: An Appraisal of the First International War Crimes Trial Since Nüremberg," Faculty Publications, Case Western University, Paper 371, 1997, pp. 876. http://scholarlycommons.law.case.edu/faculty_publications/371.

3 *The Prosecutor v Dusko Tadic*, Case No. IT-94-1-A, p. 134.

4 Nouwen and Becker, 2017, p. 28.

There was no precedent for the court's position on the applicability of customary international law, and indeed the dissenting judge in *Tadic* resiled on just that point. Through what could only be viewed as an eclectic selection of nation-state practice evinced in military manuals, as well as legislative implementations of the Geneva Conventions and Security Council Resolutions, the majority justified their reasoning to be fully warranted from the point of view of substantive justice and equity.[5] The then President of the Appeal's Chamber in *Tadic* later explained his commitment that judicial reasoning should change law.

> I pushed so much and we exploited the *Tadic* case to draw as much as possible from a minor defendant to launch new ideas, and to be creative . . . so I said to my colleagues, 'Why don't we jettison this stupid distinction,' [between international armed conflict and other forms of war] . . . 'we agree with you . . . but how can we create this criminal offence?'[6]

This audacious example of prosecutors and judges breaking new ground, against an absence of clear authority and even in neglect of facts, is not to the taste of those who believe the law is there to be served.[7] In the *Tadic* situation, and its political and historical context, the Appeals Chamber was not daunted by the silence of the law, or the apparent absurdity of legal distinctions when played out against the common horror of atrocity whatever the nature of the conflict. Recognising the dangers inherent in law-making as the juridical province, and preferring the support of a compatible jurisprudence, the *Tadic* approach modeled judicial reasoning in the service of wider goals when pursuing a novel and more universalised victim-centered global order. In this spirit, and in answer to substantivist reservations Akhavan suggests that the legitimacy of international criminal law and ICJ processes and institutions does not seem to turn on respect for the principle of legality – 'no one wins prizes for strict interpretation.'[8] Returning to a law v justice theme;

> for those who support prosecutions of these horrible crimes, the fulfilment of particularistic legal niceties may not be the sole test of 'legitimacy' and that 'justice may not always strictly comply with law'.[9]

At this point, as our analysis so far has established, we can claim history in the development of ICJ, for:

5 *Tadic (Appeal)*, p. 135.

6 Cassese quoted in Hoffman, Tamas, "The Gentle Humanizer of Humanitarian Law – Antonio Cassese and the Creation of the Customary Law of Non-International Armed Conflicts," in Carsten Stahn and Larissa van den Erik (eds), *Future Perspectives on International Criminal Justice*, TMC: Acer Press, 2010, pp. 58, 64, 68.

7 Ohlin, David, "Three Conceptual Problems with the Doctrine of Joint Criminal Enterprise," *J. Int'l Crim. Just.*, 5 1, 2007, pp. 69–90 at 72.

8 Nouwen and Becker, 2017, p. 28.

9 Alvarez, Jose, "Nuremberg Revisited: The *Tadic* case," *EJIL* 7, 1996, pp. 245–264 at 264.

- juridical activism
- outcome-oriented juridical decision-making
- juridical reasoning driven by wide notions of social justice
- juridical rejection of constraint because of an absence of law
- juridical rejection of inappropriate legal distinctions
- juridical commendation of victim-focused and context-specific considerations of harm, and
- broad interpretations of determining responsibility.

At the same time, there is a genuine, and shared by us, concern that new visions for ICJ might remain untrammeled by the logic of a jurisprudence that represents a visionary recognition of ICJ as promoted in the Preamble, while recognizing and reforming the inadequacies of a more literalist approach bound to the reasoning of domestic criminalisation.

Concluding with this aspiration there are three intentions for this final chapter. Initially we will, against the empirical analysis presented in Chapters 3 and 5, expand the case for a reinterpretation of hybridisation, straddling much more than the principal nation-state criminal justice traditions. Particularly in the evidentiary arena, the new paradigm we advance is a resort to compatible tort law principles for overcoming the proof challenges identified in Chapter 4. Next, by employing recent approaches to the establishment of corporate criminal liability, it's argued that there is compelling precedent in some nation-state jurisdictions, when faced with uniquely novel proof requirement in *new crimes*, to employ influences from other legal proof frames. Associated with these developments, fresh approaches to proving membership of criminal organisations through associations will also be advanced as examples of radical proof departures. Taking the first two purposes for this chapter as arguably established we will round off with some speculation about how more appropriate trial technologies can complement the exceptional judicial mission that our interpretation of international criminal justice (set out in Chapter 1) requires.

Shifting the substantive paradigm of international criminal trials

The preceding chapters sought to highlight the evidentiary difficulties associated with proving mental states and acts committed by persons involved in international crimes. In particular, Chapter 4 has evaluated the extraordinary proof challenges exhibited in actioning the four crimes within ICC jurisdiction focusing on genocide prosecutions, the most problematic of them all. From that vantage point, the problematic evidential issues (and our proposed resolutions set out in Chapters 3 and 5) stem from the collaboration of multiple actors at different temporal and geographic locations contributing to the perpetration of international crime, along with the distinct consequences for victimisation. In Chapter 5, two approaches have been proposed to tackle these difficulties, the vicarious liability and material contribution models (tort/crime hybrid). In support of these approaches, it has been argued that *guilt* relating to the necessary criminal mental state should be reinterpreted as contributing to *risk* of the crime occurring under the proposed tort/crime hybrid. The analysis of the accused's role thus becomes much more contextual, and as such better aligned with the proof of responsibility, rather than the narrower niceties of criminal liability.

Having proposed the two alternative ways of viewing individual criminal responsibility through the lens of tort, we will now present a parallel instance of radical hybridisation which finds its roots in criminal organisation and corporate criminal liability proofs. For instance, as national jurisdictions became more aware of the criminal harms caused by the corporate personality, and the risks of serious victimisation arising from the activities of corporations, they were forced to go beyond conventional, individualised notions of criminal liability (as discussed below). Attaching liability to the corporate personality necessitated the creation of new concepts of mental state in particular, such as associating the corporation with perpetration via the criminal actions and purposes of individuals sufficiently identified, within their organisation. But even the *identification* approach (which could be viewed as a distortion of secondary liability principles) was not sufficient on its own to competently account for the corporation's liability.[10] Aggregation and contribution (from tort) have been advanced under the guise of establishing the criminal *culture* of the body corporate. Nothing like this development has been attempted in other contexts for proving collective liability. The precedent for the changes we advance in Chapter 5, if these are seen as revolutionary revisions of criminal proof technologies, are no more courageous (or some might say utopian) than the recent incursions into the proof of crimes by corporations.

The developments in corporate criminal liability might be seen as mirrored in recent approaches to proving criminal organisations and membership through association.[11] Broadly speaking, criminal organisations operate much like corporations, and in some cases, they are similar. Many of the accused brought before the ICC belong to organisations which are ranked and disciplined in nature with

10 Hanna, Don, "Corporate Criminal Liability," *Crim. L.Q.*, 31, 1988–1989, pp. 452–480 at 465: The article points to the size of Canada, necessitating that corporate operations are frequently very widespread. Hence, contesting the applicability of the identification approach which assumes that 'directing minds' can be found in different geographic locations; Parsons, Simon, "The Doctrine of Identification, Causation and Corporate Liability for Manslaughter," *Journal of Criminal Law*, 67 1, 2003, pp. 69–81 at 70: The article criticised the identification doctrine and noted the courts rarely provide guidance as to when the *actus reus* and *mens rea* or negligence of corporate officers could be identified or imputed to the corporation. The consequence of this thinking is that an expansive approach was taken by the courts when determining which officers could be identified with the corporation.

11 Schloenhardt, Andreas, "Mafias and Motorbikes: New Organised Crime Offences in Australia," *Current Issues Crim. Just.*, 19, 2008, pp. 259–282 at 278: This article provides a very comprehensive overview of organised crime laws in New South Wales, Queensland and South Australia. Criminal liability imposed via associations generally arising out of parties keeping company with known criminal group members whether formally or informally. The author observed that these laws targeting participation in or association with criminal organisations mark a considerable extension of criminal liability beyond the existing limits of inchoate and accessorial liability.

crimes being initiated at different levels of the hierarchy (from the executive to the bottom level). Thus, the same proof challenges are faced in large-scale corporate crimes at the national level, such as who should be taken to represent the organisation; whose mental state is relevant (or can be attributed to the company/organisation); and if mental state can and should be aggregated. For this reason, understanding the evolution of criminalising organisations through association and the development of corporate criminal liability in common and civil law jurisdictions could be instructive in developing a progressive model for criminal responsibility at the international level facing new crime contexts.

In the sections that follow we will selectively interrogate these two areas of recent trends in determining criminal liability. Both criminal organisations, and the criminal conduct of the corporate personality, in the jurisdictions identified below, required the courts, by interpreting conventional approaches in *actus reus* and *mens rea*, to offer adaptive constructions of proof which endeavored to accommodate the *thinking* of inanimate entities such as the organisation and the corporation. Appreciating the limitations of judicial creativity,[12] legislative revisions now offer new technologies for proving liability through methods such as aggregation and culture, more familiar, as we suggest in Chapter 5, to tort law. As with our analysis of global crimes in Chapter 4, the novel approaches discussed below are largely products of necessity in criminalising collectivities beyond the individual, by seeking out the combined actions of members and delegates.

Such is the first purpose for the empirical exploration of these original fields of liability: to expand on the thesis that new crimes demand new proof technologies. The second, and more complex aim is to take from this atmosphere of necessity, accommodation and invention the message that the jurisprudence surrounding these developments is less tangential and strained, offering a more holistic understanding of hybridisation and harmonisation. As foreshadowed in Chapter 2, the emergence of international criminal law cannot convincingly be constrained to some mix of the primary nation-state criminal procedural traditions. With new crimes before the courts, being deliberated in new contexts of justice, proofs of mental state, criminal conduct, causation and coincidence can be assisted by strategic borrowing from tort proofs in situations where these technologies better address the exigencies of new crimes.

12 Dixon, Nicolee, "Regulating Bikie Gangs," Queensland Parliamentary Library Research Brief No 2009/18, p. 14: The paper asserts that, for organised crime, the legislative developments criminalising associations are crucial as only legislative amendments can shift the burden of proving the innocence of the alleged association to the accused. Further, the statutory provisions (such as in South Australia) are complemented by increased police powers to enforce the laws. The use of legislation instead of judicial creativity in this area is driven in part by the need to promote consistency within this area of law which is problematic if the task were left in the judges' hands. For proving corporate crime, common issues involve evidential uncertainty which lead either to judicial reinterpretation of existing inadequate principle or corporations escaping liability despite their blameworthiness through the inability of corporate liability models to reflect the reality of modern corporate decision-making.

The substantive law in the following case-studies is taken from common law traditions. Besides the desire to simplify a holistic treatment of these two formative areas of proof development, this focus is arbitrary. For those seeking a wider and deeper understanding of comparable trends in Continental civil law traditions and hybrid jurisdictions Italy has developed some recent interesting approaches to criminalising organisations,[13] and China has advanced a reasoning that concerns itself more with the organisational entity rather than its members.[14] Since its anti-racketeering legislation post WWII, the USA has always had an interest in criminalising organisations, particularly through relationships between tax evasion and criminal enterprise.[15] With the notable exception of Germany, almost all the member states of the EU, and Norway and Switzerland have developed laws on corporate criminal liability.[16] Recently in Nigeria, a jurisdiction plagued by the criminal excesses of foreign corporations, the debate about corporate criminal liability as an actionable domestic offense has been lively.[17]

New crimes, new proofs

Recently, new crime *forms* (such as those perpetrated by the corporate personality or having emerged through the dynamics of organisations) have presented considerable complications in proving criminal liability. For instance, establishing the criminal mental state of the perpetrator when a crime is committed through the activity of a company or an organisation has seen judges and legislators attenuating

13 "Italian legislation on organized crime, corruption and money laundering," Library of the European Parliament, 11 October 2012. Link: www.europarl.europa.eu/document/activities/cont/201210/20121015ATT53636/20121015ATT53636EN.pdf.

Italian legislation against Mafia-type associations was recently codified by Legislative Decree No 159 of 6 September 2011, the *Codice Unico Antimafia*. Criminal penalties apply to membership of a criminal organisation of three or more persons. Harsher penalties are applied under Article 416-bis of the Italian Penal Code in the case of a *Mafia-type unlawful association*. This organisation is said to exist when participants use intimidation and the resulting conditions of submission and silence to commit criminal offences, or to manage or control, directly or indirectly, economic activities and concessions. The promotion, direction, participation and running of such criminal organisations can be punished with heavy penalties (in particular when there are aggravating circumstances such as in the case of an armed organisation.

14 Robinson, Allens Arthur, "'Corporate Culture' as a Basis for the Criminal Liability of Corporations," United Nations Special Representative of the Secretary-General on Human Rights and Business, 2008, p. 51.

15 Bradley, Craig M., "Anti-Racketeering Legislation in America," Articles by Maurer Faculty, 2006, Paper 160. Link: www.repository.law.indiana.edu/facpub/160.

16 Dubber, Markus, "The Comparative History and Theory of Corporate Criminal Liability," *New Crim. L. Rev.* 16 2, 2013, 203–240; Beale, Sara Sun, and Safwat, Adam, "What Developments in Western Europe Tell Us about American Critiques of Corporate Criminal Liability," *Buff. Crim. L. Rev.* 8 2, 2004, pp. 89–164 at 115.

17 Erhanze, Samson, and Momodu, Daud, "Corporate Criminal Liability: Call for a New Legal Regime in Nigeria," *Journal of Law and Criminal Justice*, 3 2, 2015, pp. 63–72 at 64–67.

individual and subjective *mens rea* by applying reasoning such as reversed onus for disproving consequentialist conclusions.

Playing with such core proofs of criminal liability to suit novel criminal characteristics is the story of international criminal law which we have so far enunciated. This trend was revealed in Chapters 3 and 5, with examples such as broadening the scope of the *common intention* of the parties to allow more secondary crimes to fall within that intention.[18] Similarly, in what follows we note how, by allowing the aggregation of corporate knowledge, intention can be satisfied as the decisions of senior staff combine to constitute corporate intent. Similarly with consorting within organisations the purpose of which is assumed to be criminal, legislators have criminalised the association of various individuals, requiring for mental state little more than a general knowledge of criminal purpose, or recklessness, as to whether such could be the case.

Where the proof technologies to satisfy the peculiarities of perpetration in these new crimes are deficient, the courts are more willing to look at the crime with the eyes of the ordinary person faced with simpler questions of harm and responsibility, and apply reasoning informed by *common sense*. In Chapter 3 we surveyed the *Tadic* case where the court considered the general context in which the secondary crimes occurred, concluding that the accused who was in a senior position in the offending organisation *must have known* that these ancillary crimes were being committed. Likewise, courts deliberating over corporate criminality, can now reflect on the prevailing culture of the body corporate and infer that the perpetrator of the crime 'reasonably' thought the corporate policy condoned his criminal contribution.

In an atmosphere where responsibility is drawn out of the broadest contexts of conduct and mental state sufficient for criminalisation, judges (and legislators) at the international and national levels have shown themselves to be creative with legal principle where the harm or damage in the case before them is extensive OR where the consequences of applying the law liberally outweighs any perceived injustice that would follow. In this manner, judicial reasoning endeavors to balance the limited substantive requirements enunciated in the Rome Statute against a process of establishing legal principles that prefer justice before form in a mundane context that accords with expansive notions of justice reflecting desires for victim-intuitive outcomes.

Chapter 3 provides ample evidence that judges are focused on *results-oriented* justice wherein common intention is interpreted broadly, and subjective foresight is diminished in favor of objective foreseeability as sufficient for criminal mental states. Regarding conduct, members of joint criminal enterprises are being found responsible for the behavior of non-JCE actors such as foot soldiers who could

18 *Prosecutor v Radoslav Brdanin*, Case No. IT-99-36-A, paras [407]–[408]. *Prosecutor v Radislav Krstic*, Case No. IT-98-33-T, paras [601], [611], [613]. See also: *Prosecutor v Blagoje Simic*, Case No. IT-95-9-T, paras [156]–[160].

never in any actual sense be said to share the common intention of their superiors.[19] In what follows, the application of aggregation, association and culture are controversial relative to conventional liability proofs, but they are advocated by legislators mindful of the wider community *consequences* of their decision.

In Chapter 5, it was argued that judges should be reflecting on tortious proof technologies to compensate for the proof limitations which emerge in the application of nation-state procedures. The following case-studies indicate that the evolution of both criminalised organisations through association, and corporate criminal liability through the influence of criminal cultures, represent *new laws* and new judicial interpretations more than some strained distortions of conventional proof technologies never meant to service these unique contexts of criminal perpetration. As with the historical transition from vagrancy laws to consorting, and now on to the anti-association crimes, perpetration is becoming envisaged well beyond an individual intending to harm an individual victim though some direct conduct. Such narrow interpretations of liability proofs hardly mirror the complex criminal machinations of corporations and organisations victimising whole communities, as explored in Chapter 4 with collectivised global crime.

New approaches to criminalising organisations and their membership

The criminalisation of organisations and association between individuals within a criminal group has recently found new political energy in Australian jurisdictions. Arguably, South Australia, Queensland and New South Wales have the world's toughest anti-bikie laws[20] which prevent the organisation and association of criminal individuals for illicit purposes deemed to be the rationale for the organisations concerned.

In South Australia, under the *Serious and Organised Crime (Control) Act 2008* ('OCCA'), the old offense of consorting was replaced with a new law of criminal association that prohibits technological communication such as telephone calls between individuals involved in the same proscribed organisation as well as meetings in person.[21] In terms of the OCCA, if a control order is made declaring the organisation as criminal, and the defendant is a member of the declared organisation, the order must prohibit that person from associating with others who through association are members of the declared organisation (s 14(5)(b)).[22]

19 *Prosecutor v Radoslav Brdanin*, Case No. IT-99-36-T, paras [354]–[370]. See also the analysis in Chapter 3.

20 Dixon, Nicolee, "Regulating Bikie Gangs," Queensland Parliamentary Library, Research Brief No. 2009/18, pp. 36–43; Hulls, Robert, Deputy Premier and Attorney-General, "Victoria's Tough Laws Best for Dealing with Bikie Gangs," Ministerial Media Statement, 15 April 2009.

21 Bartels, Lorna, "The Status of Laws on Outlaw Motorcycle Gangs in Australia," June 2009, Australian Institute of Criminology, Research in Practice, no.2.

22 In these situations, the onus of proof is reversed so that to answer the allegation of association the accused must prove a legitimate explanation for the association in question.

In considering whether or not to make a declaration, the Attorney-General may have regard to any of the following (s 10(3)):

i any information suggesting a link between the organisation and serious criminal activity;
ii any criminal convictions in relation to current or former members of the organisation, or persons who associate, or have associated, with members of the organisation;
iii any information suggesting that current or former members of the organisation, or persons who associate, or have associated, with members of the organisation have been, or are, involved in serious criminal activity (whether directly or indirectly and whether or not such involvement has resulted in any criminal convictions);
iv any information suggesting that members of an interstate or overseas chapter or branch of the organisation associate for the purpose of organising, planning, facilitating, supporting or engaging in serious criminal activity;
v submissions received from members of the public; and
vi any other matter the Attorney-General considers relevant.

Further, the general offense of 'criminal association' is specified in s 35 as follows:

> A person who associates, on not less than 6 occasions during a period of 12 months, with a person who is a member of a declared organisation or is the subject of a control order is guilty of an offense and liable to imprisonment for up to 5 years. The person must, on each occasion of association, know or be reckless about the fact that the other person is a member of a declared organisation or the subject of a control order;
>
> A person who has a prescribed criminal conviction and associates, on not less than 6 occasions during a period of 12 months, with another person who has such a conviction is guilty of an offense and liable to imprisonment for up to 5 years. The person must, on each occasion of association, know or be reckless about the fact that the other person had the relevant conviction.

However, certain forms of association will not amount to an offense unless the prosecution proves that the association was not reasonable in the circumstances (s 35(6)). These are associations:

1 between close family members;
2 occurring in the course of a lawful occupation, business or profession;
3 occurring at prescribed courses of training or education;
4 occurring at prescribed kinds of rehabilitation, counseling or therapy;
5 occurring in lawful custody or in the course of complying with a court order;
6 of certain prescribed kinds; or
7 where, under s 35(7), a Court disregards the association if the defendant can prove there is a reasonable excuse for the association, provided the defendant was not a member of a declared organisation, or subject to a control order, or had a prescribed criminal conviction at the time of the association.

In New South Wales, via the *Crimes Legislation Amendment (Gangs) Act 2006*, the pre-existing law of conspiracy was changed, or reinvented so as to criminalise organisations[23] that have either one of these shared objectives: (i) to profit from serious offenses, (ii) to engage in serious violence.[24] To that end, the NSW Legislation Review Committee noted that the concept of a criminal group in s 931J(1) is 'akin to a permanent or at least a long-term conspiracy,' which lasts for as long as three or more people maintain an association in pursuit of at least one of the criminal objectives listed in s 93IJ(1).[25] In contrast with conspiracies, however, there is no requirement of any specific agreement among the three or more people to commit particular (identifiable) crimes. Another notable feature of the legislation is the omission of leadership from the concept of a criminal group and participation in the offense. The legislature designed the new offenses to target a diverse spectrum of criminal groups and participants, not just those organisations with clear internal hierarchies. It appears that the legislature sought to criminalise a broad range of people who are directly and indirectly associated with criminal groups:[26]

> That offence targets a range of activities and people who work with criminal organisations, and obviously some of them will be members. They will wear the colours and have the tattoos. Others will wear tailored suits and appear to be the pinnacle of respectability. The offence targets those hiding in the background of a criminal enterprise and those who facilitate organised criminal activity. They may be accountants, bookkeepers. executives, or even lawyers who fudge records, launder money. construct sham corporate structures and hide assets. It also targets the front men. These are the so-called clean-skins, people with no criminal record who give criminals a legal front behind which to commit their crimes and minimise the risk of detection by law enforcement. They may be licensed hoteliers, real estate agents, smash repairers, pharmacists or public officials, who, in various ways, aid and abet ongoing criminal activity. And, of course, the bill targets the heavies – the people who actively commit ongoing criminal acts: the drug runners, the gun traffickers, the car re-birthers. the armed robbers and the stand-over men.[27]

In the *Crimes (Criminal Organisation Control Act) 2009* the Commissioner of Police can seek a declaration from a Supreme Court judge that a bikie gang is a declared criminal organisation. An eligible judge may make a declaration if they are satisfied that an organisation's members associate for the purpose of

23 Groups of more than three people.

24 Schloenhardt, 2008, p. 263.

25 "Legislation Review Digest, Legislation Review Committee, Parliament NSW Legislative Assembly," 2009, Sydney, NSW, p. 9.

26 Schloenhardt, 2008, p. 266.

27 Stewart, Terry, "New South Wales Legislative Assembly," *Hansard* 20 August 2006, p. 1142.

organising, planning, facilitating, supporting or engaging in serious criminal activity and that the organisation represents a risk to public safety and order in New South Wales. Once the organisation is declared, the Commissioner of Police may then seek control orders from the Supreme Court in respect of one or more persons on the basis that those persons are members of a declared criminal organisation and there are sufficient grounds for making the order. The controlled member will not be able to associate with another controlled member of that gang. If they do, they will risk two years in jail for the first offense, and risk five years for a subsequent offense.[28]

In considering whether or not to make the declaration, the eligible judge may have regard to any of the matters in s 9(2) (similar to those matters the Attorney-General considers in making a declaration under s 10(3) of the SA Act). These are, in brief: information suggesting a link between the organisation and serious criminal activity; any criminal convictions of current or former members; information suggesting current or former members are/have been involved in serious criminal activity; information suggesting that members of a chapter or branch in another jurisdiction associate for organising, planning, facilitating, supporting or engaging in serious criminal activity; any submissions received; and other relevant matters.[29]

The South Australia and New South Wales examples show the adaptability of legislatures and law enforcement agencies in their approaches towards policing new crimes. Subjective knowledge proofs are sacrificed in favor of inferential conclusions concerning purpose drawn from the conduct of association (with knowledge, or reckless as to whether the association could be objectively construed as criminal). Constructive knowledge and the imputation of agreement are now no longer required as association creates a series of inferences which shift to the defense to deny. And in some degree, association takes on similar connotations as it would in tort where responsibility is apportioned across the organisation because of how members contribute to the collective criminal purpose.

Schloenhardt notes the approaches taken by these jurisdictions signal a new trend towards criminalising persons for '*who they are*' rather than for '*what they do*' and have the appearance of revisiting the much-vaunted status offense created to address the exigencies of association in WWII at the sacrifice of actual knowledge and subjective intent.[30]

Under the South Australia OCCA, by focusing on the members' traits and their *propensity* or *susceptibility* towards crime, the law clearly penalises members for their status (passive) rather than the crimes they commit (active). In this sense, the proof of criminal conduct has been relegated to the consequentialist inferences drawn from people meeting in designated circumstances and with a mental

28 Rees, Nathan, Premier of NSW and Minister for the Arts, Agreement in Principle, Crimes (Criminal Organisations Control) Bill 2009 (NSW), NSW Legislative Assembly, *Hansard Online*, 2 April 2009.

29 Serious and Organised Crime (Control) Act 2008, Section 10 (3).

30 Schloenhardt, 2008, p. 260.

state as to knowledge which might be no more than peripherally reckless. The legal outcome might seem counter-intuitive for those trained to resist finding guilt by association without the support of subjective knowledge. As a political expedient, the anti-association laws claim their roots in common law consorting traditions but in a proof sense we are witnessing much more than adapting old laws to meet evolving criminal contexts.[31] Consorting was about individuals associating but with no necessary connection to the incriminating context of association and membership. In the new law organisations and membership have become the precipitators of risk in ways similar to behaviors and aggregations which may cause harm in a tortious sense.

Building on their history of criminalising consorting[32] New South Wales and South Australia directed their anti-association laws specifically at the perceived difficulty in prosecuting novel forms of criminal associations which had advanced from one-to-one criminal conversations into complex, multi-actor organisations. As highlighted by Schloenhardt,[33] criminal law and law enforcement are traditionally designed to prosecute and punish isolated crimes committed by individuals. The structure and modus operandi of criminal associations, however, like global crimes as we identified in Chapter 4, do not fit well into the individualised concept of criminal liability. Moreover, it is difficult to hold directors and financiers of organised crime responsible if they have no physical involvement in the execution of the organisation's criminal activities, or even physical associations with the perpetrators on the ground. Equally, those who are only loosely associated with a criminal gang and provide support on an ad hoc basis often fall outside existing concepts of inchoate and accessorial liability. Hence, this expansive model of anti-association crimes was developed and supported by proof technologies such as contribution and the diminution of the conventional prosecutorial criminal proof burdens concerning mental state, in favor of a reversed onus to disprove.

New approaches to criminalising corporations

In brief, the development of common law corporate criminal liability represents the creativity of courts and legislatures in adapting, borrowing and developing

31 Clarke, David, NSWPD, *Hansard*, Legislative Council, 7 March 2012, p. 9091: In the second reading speech for the Bill that introduced the new consorting law, the Hon. David Clarke (the Parliamentary Secretary speaking on behalf of the Minister for Police) said that the Bill modernises the offence of consorting, as well as extending and clarifying its application. The Government acknowledged that the existing consorting offence had 'been criticised for its potential application to everyday, innocent relationships which should not be the subject of prosecution.'

32 New South Wales Ombudsman, "The Consorting Law, Report on the Operation of Part 3A, Division 7 of Crimes Act 1900," 2016, p. 12 states: The offence of consorting was first introduced in New South Wales (NSW) in 1929 through amendments to the *Vagrancy Act 1902* in response to concern about Sydney's 'Razor Gangs.' Under the Vagrancy Act, it was an offence to habitually associate with reputed criminals, known prostitutes, or people convicted of 'having no visible lawful means of support.' The consorting laws remained unchanged until the 1970 repeal of the Vagrancy Act and the introduction of the *Summary Offences Act 1970*, which contained an amended offence of consorting.

33 Schloenhardt, 2008, p. 260.

new proof technologies to tackle novel developments in the criminal stratosphere. Gobert and Punch summarise the evolution of corporate law as it recognises criminalisation:

> When judges turned their minds to the question of whether a company could commit a criminal offence, they naturally looked to the applicability of existing criminal laws, principles and doctrines. These however, had been developed in cases involving natural persons. How to apply such distinctly human concepts such as *actus reus* and *mens rea* to an inanimate legal fiction was bound to tax the judicial imagination, and in retrospect, the judges might have been better advised to have accepted from the outset that fresh doctrines were going to be needed that took into account the unique characteristics of organizational entities.[34]

As discussed previously in the text, while the Rome Statute refers to the responsibility of natural persons, there has been extensive speculation on ways in which collective responsibility might be reconsidered so as not to offend that notion. One viable and compatible area for such interpretation is mirrored in the corporate personality, embodying the rights and obligations of the natural person.[35]

When confronted by the possible perpetration of crimes by corporations, as they did with the expansion of master/servant liability (see Chapter 5), common law jurisdictions adapted the vicarious liability approach to impose liability on companies for crimes committed by their members. This proof technology represented a measured attempt to marry pre-existing individualised proof technologies, originally borrowed from tort, to materialise and then criminalise the legal fiction of the corporate personality. Vicarious liability moderated through delegation obviated the requirement of *mens rea*, once the inescapable subjective determinant of an individual could now be passed up a hierarchy of delegated corporate officers, amalgamating them into a legal fictional personality. The novel proof challenge, as with approaches such as command responsibility and superior orders, was to sufficiently personalise and position responsibility from the individual lower-order actor, to the body corporate.

Post 1940s, the principle of *identification* was developed by the English appeal courts and largely replaced vicarious liability as the proof technology for revealing the mind of the company. Under this approach, the corporation could be liable for a crime if the state of mind of a *senior employee* was culpable. Despite meeting the traditional *mens rea* requirement in criminal law (as satisfied by the state of mind of the senior employee), this approach fails to recognise crimes that are committed at the lower levels of the organisational hierarchy (this commonly occurs

34 Gobert, James, and Punch, Maurice, *Rethinking Corporate Crime*, Cambridge University Press: Cambridge, 2003, p. 55.

35 Laufer, William, "Corporate Bodies and Guilty Minds," *Emory L. J.*, 43, 1994, pp. 647–730 at 709: Laufer recommends that the corporation should be viewed as an individual, thus the corporate culture model (which he advocates) asks the relevant question: whether a reasonable corporation like the one before the court will be taken to accept or encourage the conduct of its agent.

in the international criminal law context), and is equivocal about the degree to which necessary seniority is equated with identified degrees of delegation.

To resolve these issues, some common law jurisdictions like Australia have focused instead on the ***corporate culture*** of the firm. If the culture of the body corporate evinced some recognition and acknowledgment of the crime's occurrence, and thereby exhibited a tolerance of criminality as the company's ethos then criminal liability will attach.[36]

Another way of measuring corporate culture is through aggregation (developed later). In the US, aggregation of the mental state means that the courts will impose criminal liability where the total sum of mental states or acts by the company's members meets the legal requirements of the crime.[37]

Harking back to our advocacy for a tort/crime proof hybrid (see Chapter 5) it is useful to juxtapose the development of corporate liability at the national level with the similar developments in hybrid model. Focusing on England and Wales, and Australia, as we mentioned above, corporate criminal liability pre-1940s was imposed through finding vicarious liability on part of the accused-employer for the employee's act. The acknowledgment of corporate criminal liability based on the proof of vicarious liability involved a two-step process.[38] First, one should determine what constitutes the criminal conduct of the acts committed by an employee, and second, this ***conduct*** must be unconditionally transferred to the employer (corporation) by virtue of the legal employee–employer relationship, as determined through delegation. This proof technology (***originating as it did in tort law***) is compatible in the development of our tort/crime hybrid, tailoring comparably vicarious liability to suit the international crime context.

The introduction of vicarious liability into proving corporate crime and the academic controversy it has sparked, is significant for our purposes in this conclusion as it suggests a compromise between outcome-oriented concerns for justice emphasising fairness for victims above the accused in deferring to the consequentialist interpretation of justice at the international level which we explore in Chapter 1. These tensions between accused and victim interests, important now in the recognition of the extensive harm caused through corporate criminality, and as reflected in adjudicating international criminal law, are largely as a result of the novel nature of crime committed within a system of hierarchy or organisation typified by corporations and by military commands.

36 Robinson, 2008, pp. 10–18.

37 Cavanagh, Neil, "Corporate Criminal Liability: An Assessment of the Models of Fault," *J. Crim. L.*, 75, 2011, pp. 414–440 at 425 states: Under the aggregation doctrine, one combines all 'the acts and mental elements of the various relevant persons within the company to ascertain whether in total they would amount to a crime if they had all been committed by one person. Thus, a company can be criminally liable 'notwithstanding the absence of proof that any single agent intended to commit the offence or even knew of the existence of operative facts that led to the violation.'

38 Esakov, Gennady, "Corporate Criminal Liability: A Comparative Review," *City Univ. of Hong Kong Law Rev.*, 2, 2010, pp. 173–19 at 175.

In the corporate context, there are three main reasons (previously canvassed in other contexts) for the introduction of vicarious liability-style proofs reliant on delegation and contribution:[39]

- the corporation is likely to be better able to compensate the tort victim than the employee which is a relevant consideration in ICJ where responsibility for harm is a central justice determinant of responsibility. The cost of such torts can be dealt with, or insured against, as a price of doing business and thereby restitution is a more attainable outcome in outcome-oriented thinking;
- the corporation is in a better position than the employee to mandate that reasonable precautions be taken;
- the corporation engages the employee for economic gain, so it is fair that the law demand the corporation bear the losses occasioned because of the employment relationship, as the corporation will reap the benefits of the relationship; and
- because of the power asymmetry between the corporation and the employee, the onus is on the corporation to take responsibility for any criminal culture which may influence the exercise of the employee's delegation.

A similar reasoning could be attached to the problems associated with giving effect to command responsibility and other forms of superior direction in global crimes arising from military delegation.

The tort/crime hybrid already in play!

In proposing a shift towards tort proof considerations, it would be careless not to recognise that this comes at a cost to subjective proof traditions of criminal mental states. Against this worry we counter that the contortions revealed in Chapter 3 have already sacrificed this proof principle and much more in terms of subjectivity, irrespective of whether tort proofs are on offer. This compromised outcome is a logical result of employing proof technologies never designed to the special circumstances of global crime (see Chapter 4).

The lack of a culpable mental state requirement for the senior employee (representing the corporation) in the vicarious liability analysis led to the development of the identification principle in corporate criminal liability (as discussed above). However, identification fails to consider the fact that crimes within corporate organisations can originate from the lower levels of the corporate (or criminal) hierarchy (and in such situations the primary perpetrators or other officials down the hierarchical chain may possess and compound the relevant state of mind). Yet, if the executive has provided the conditions and opportunities for such crimes to

39 Fleming, John, *The Law of Torts*, Clarendon Press: Oxford, 2011, pp. 354–5.

occur at the lower level of the hierarchy then, as with joint criminal enterprise, liability should be apportioned to reflect such implication. In practice, it is difficult to identify any particular senior member who embodies all the requisite elements of the corporate crime (mind and conduct) and is in such a particular situation of delegation as to be responsible for criminal conduct and mental states actuated at lower levels of the corporate hierarchy. This is especially so in large organisations.[40] Identification proof technologies no longer reflect (if they ever did) the way in which corporate decision-making occurs. In many, if not most large companies, corporate policy is diffused throughout the management structure. It is simply not the case that modern multi-national corporate management works in a top-down manner and in the hands of individuals as assumed by the identification model. Nor does it reflect layers of complex decision-making and implication which may be lateral within hierarchies. This more disparate process of decision-making is particularly so where management frames for the sake of lateral accountability and compliance requirements decentralisation decision-making.[41] When applied in the international criminal law context, where collective liability is reconstructed through the agreement, knowledge or even foreseeability of combinations of individual minds, the problematic artificiality and unreality of constructs such as identification do not remedy intractable proof difficulties. Prominent among these is discovering individualised mental states and conduct out of delegation relationships, sufficient to hold both parties responsible in the same proportion and degree.

To resolve such issues, two common law developments, *aggregation* and *corporate culture*, offer a bridge between the responsibility of the natural person and the accumulation of sufficient conduct and mental states among persons in combination to satisfy conventional proof demands in tort, and ICL as the interpretations in Chapters 3 and 5 envisage.

Aggregation

The aggregation doctrine transposed to criminal responsibility finds interesting roots in US case law. Under developments in American jurisdictions, where the relevant criminal mental state is ***knowledge***, the knowledge acquired by employees within the scope of their employment is imputed to the corporation.[42] The corporation is in this way considered to have acquired the collective knowledge of its employees and is held responsible for their failure to act accordingly, provided that there is sufficient collective mental state to enable that transposition.[43]

40 Ntsanyu Nana, Constantine, "Corporate Criminal Liability in South Africa: The Need to Look Beyond Vicarious Liability," *Journal of African Law*, 55, 1, 2011, pp. 86–104 at 102.

41 Goode, Matthew, "Corporate Criminal Liability." Link: https://aic.gov.au/sites/default/files/publications/proceedings/downloads/26-goode.pdf, p. 4.

42 Cavanagh, 2011, p. 425.

43 *US v Time-DC Inc*, 381 F Supp 730 WD Va (1974).

It has been argued that aggregation offers an alternative and more intellectually satisfying basis for proof than the identification doctrine when constructing and imputing the criminal mental state of the corporation. Under aggregation, junior officials and other servants of the company can form part of the collective knowledge or mind of the company, and thereby more realistically reflect not only corporate decision-making but how and when legitimate (non-criminal) decisions are transformed into deviant determinations. Furthermore, aggregation has appeal in situations where no single individual within the company is in possession of all the facts or information that could satisfy knowledge about the act and carelessness as to its commission or otherwise.[44] Aggregation, therefore, represents a useful legal tool where the mental state of knowledge within a large corporate organisation is an amalgam of the understanding and purposes of employees up and down the hierarchy, as these may morph and change with the dynamics of corporate decision-making.[45]

With this said, aggregation in the US interpretation is limited to crimes where the *mens rea* requirement is mere knowledge or negligence in terms of what an ordinary person would not think and do. Aggregation does not apply to crimes that require intention. This would limit any direct transfer of the US position to international crimes under the Rome Statute which require intention. As we have argued, appreciating aggregation in conjunction with degrees of contribution (a tort measure of damages) would overcome any subjectivist distinction between crimes requiring strict intent and those satisfied by a lesser mental state.

Corporate culture

In 1993, the Standing Committee of Attorneys-General from Federal, State and Territory Governments of Australia delivered a report on corporate criminal liability which concluded that the *Tesco* identification principle was no longer appropriate in view of more diffuse governance structures and delegations to junior officers of corporations. The report instead favored the adoption of a mechanism of corporate criminal liability which recognised *independent corporate fault*. The main objective of the Committee was to develop a model of liability which as nearly as possible, adapted personal criminal responsibility to fit the modern corporation. The Code's approach clearly builds on a realist rather than a nominalist view of corporations that appreciates the body corporate as a much more complex and communal entity. The relevant amendments in the Federal Criminal Code put into legislative effect what criminal law commentators have been suggesting for some time – that a corporation is capable of intent, and that this can be found in the corporation's behavior demonstrating a measurable culture.[46]

44 Mays, Richard, "Towards Corporate Fault as the Basis of Criminal Liability of Corporations," *Mountbatten Journal of Legal Studies*, 2 2, December 1998, pp. 31–67 at 56.

45 Gobert and Punch, 2003, p. 58.

46 Wilkinson, Meaghan, "Corporate Criminal Liability: The Move Towards Recognizing General Corporate Fault," *Canterbury Law Review*, 9, 2003, pp. 142–178.

Subsequently, sections 12.3(1) and 12.3(2) in part 2.5 of the Australian Federal Criminal Code were passed to meet these legislative goals. Section 12.3(1) states that advertent fault (intention, knowledge or recklessness) will be attributed to a corporation that 'expressly, tacitly or impliedly authorized or permitted the commission of the offence.' Several (non-exclusive) means by which this authorisation or permission can be established are set out in s 12.3(2). The first two methods parallel the mechanism under the *Tesco* identification approach: the corporation will be liable through proof that the 'board of directors' or a 'high managerial agent' 'intentionally, knowingly or recklessly carried out the relevant conduct, or expressly, tacitly or impliedly authorised or permitted the commission of the offence.' Under s 12.3(2)(c) and (d), the corporation will be taken to have authorised or permitted the commission of an offense if it is proved that either a 'corporate culture' existed which directed, encouraged, tolerated or led to non-compliance, or, that the corporation failed to create and maintain a 'corporate culture' that required compliance (with the relevant provision).[47]

The Australian interpretation of *corporate culture* permits criminal liability to attach where it can be proven that 'a corporate culture existed within the body corporate that directed, encouraged, tolerated or led to non-compliance'; or 'the body corporate failed to create and maintain a corporate culture that required compliance.' Crucially, the expression *corporate culture* is defined to mean 'an attitude, policy, rule, course of conduct or practice existing within the body corporate generally or in the part of the body corporate in which the relevant activities take place,' meaning that the corporation can be sub-divided for the purposes of identifying corporate culture.

Factors relevant to whether a culture of non-compliance existed include 'whether authority to commit an offence of the same or a similar character had been given by a high managerial agent of the body corporate' and 'whether the employee, agent or officer of the body corporate who committed the offence believed on reasonable grounds, or entertained a reasonable expectation, that a high managerial agent of the body corporate would have authorised or permitted the commission of the offence.' Prosecutions of the corporation based on corporate culture will therefore be contingent on evidence of management's attitude to compliance from the individual accused of the misconduct. Objectively, reasonableness;

> will turn upon the real manner in which the corporation operates. Whilst it would be reasonable for an employee of a company which merely paid lip service to compliance to draw the inference that his illegal conduct would be permitted by senior officers, it would certainly be less reasonable for an employee to hold such a belief where the company had in place a genuine, efficient compliance system.[48]

47 Wilkinson, 2003.

48 Dixon, Olivia, "Corporate Criminal Liability: The Influence of Corporate Culture," in Justin O'Brien and George Gilligan (eds), *Integrity, Risk and Accountability in Capital Markets: Regulating Culture*, Hart Publishing: Oxford, 2013, Chapter 13.

In proof terms, the benefit of adopting such a corporate culture model is that it recognises companies are complex and may create group norms and systemic pressures which eventually lead to the commission of a crime.[49] In this respect the contextual forces *making the company* (express and implied) are as valid in proving criminal mental states as are the individualised knowledge and intention of a senior delegate. Criminal mental state evaluation in these terms more realistically addresses the corporate personality (which is the corporation as the natural person) as being a meeting of minds to create an attitude around action.

Arguably, the corporate culture model represents a feat in judicial and legislative innovation by translating the inquiry of the corporation's ethos which permeates the company's operations and locates corporate intent through company policy into a flexible but rational and tort/informed criminal proof technology. This approach makes the corporation liable for the wrongdoing it operationally can be said to have caused, facilitated or failed to deter. The example of corporate criminal liability thus illustrates the need for tailoring proof rules to address the nuances of the potential responsibility context wherein judicial decision-making is constructed, taking account of radical new features of criminal conduct and mental state. Alternatively, the inflexible application of traditional liability proof technologies in the face of new crimes inevitably leads to the distortion of those principles and logically inadequate outcomes which result as proof is removed even further from organisational or market practice. This corporate criminal responsibility case-study is advanced to buttress the need for reforming proofs in the prosecution and trial of international crimes that demonstrates a similar principled creativeness which organisational and corporate responsibility innovations demonstrate.

For instance, the nature of international crimes inevitably involves multiple actors within a hierarchy functioning much like a corporation or a criminal organisation. The question of specific mental state might become impossible to substantiate through conventional individualised proofs if the accused executive member is temporally and/or geographically far removed from the primary perpetrators of the crime. It might even be the case that where the primary perpetrators of the crimes are unknown to the accused and/or the victims, this anonymity complicates further the individualised proof of mental state. On the other hand, the corporate culture model provides a viable means of imposing liability based on the manner in which the criminal organisation operates within the broad control of the executive accused. This inquiry is contextually dependent on what the primary perpetrator perceived was the organisation's culture, with this perception crossing the threshold of reasonableness. So represented, this appreciation of responsibility crafted through aggregation in a cultural atmosphere that condoned the eventual perpetration and victimisation much better aligns with the second main field of international criminal justice, as expounded in the Preamble. A measure of the harm caused, and an apportioning of consequent damages becomes an empirically sound by-product of these proof technologies.

49 Wilkinson, 2003.

Vision

Returning to our reflections in Chapter 1 on the *justice* envisaged in the Preamble to the Rome Statute, it retains the following essentials:

- recognition that global atrocity crimes are an attack on humanity and as such victimisation, and legitimate victim interests are at the forefront of any international criminal justice constituency; therefrom
- blending retributive and restorative motivations; to produce
- outcome-orientations which will end impunity and bring peace and security in place of the ravages of global crime;
- obliging prosecutors and judges to achieve trial resolutions which go beyond determining guilt or innocence and apportioning punishment;
- considering the widest notions of responsibility for the perpetration of global crime and the damage wrought to victims and humanity; and
- ensuring that the harm caused by global crime will be recorded, and lessened as a result of international criminal justice intervention.

It is important to remember, in order to achieve the expectations set out in the Preamble, international criminal justice must be delivered through:

- determining ***responsibility*** and thereby appropriating tortious considerations of damage as well as criminal determinations of liability;
- consequentialist decision-making; and
- interventionist crafting of a new international criminal jurisprudence which is not only fit for purpose, but more likely to engender confidence from perpetrators and victims alike because it is principled, predictable and persuasive, not random, reactionary and for that, recused.

We have confirmed in Chapter 4, that to achieve international criminal justice as conceived in Chapter 1, international criminal prosecutions and trials need to proceed with the assistance of proof technologies which address the unique realities of global crime in terms of perpetration and victimisation. The collective nature of both is enough alone to radically distinguish these challenges for justice from any domestic crimes that exercise the decision-making capacities of nation-state courts.

Chapter 2 picks up from the pragmatic recognition in our preface that ICJ will always be a political project, and speculates on how the emergence of international criminal law through discipline-bound harmonisation or hybridisation is doomed to never achieving the new international criminal jurisprudence we regularly foreshadow as the text unfolds. Further, the limitations inherent in applying nation-state criminal law, which is neither concerned with responsibility nor held to account in peace-making or security terms, to the broader justice demands of international criminal trials is a recipe for strain and distortion. That strain is detailed in Chapter 3 through focusing on the current prosecution practices and judicial reasoning in the international criminal courts and tribunals over joint criminal enterprise and secondary liability.

Chapter 2 also interrogates the political compromise of complementarity and shows how the struggles over jurisdiction exacerbate a more principled approach to prosecution and trial, producing grave risks that international criminal justice will be held hostage by recalcitrant nation states, self-interested regional alliances, and neutered independent prosecution. Complementarity, we assert, need not suffer from its history of problematic jurisdictional applications if each level of contesting jurisdiction accepts the common indicia of international criminal justice service delivery through the prosecution and trial of global crimes, wherever this endeavor is located. International criminal justice, rather than struggles over jurisdiction, becomes a much more noble purpose for complementarity, so conceived.

The embedding of international criminal justice as the Preamble portends is the higher order vision we offer to prosecutors and judges charged with its service delivery. The more applied dimension of this endeavor is reflected through the stripping down of strained proof technologies in Chapter 3, and the invitation to explore compatible possibilities from tort law (Chapter 5) as these have already been revealed in recent approaches to criminalising organisations, and the corporate personality (Chapter 6). This is a vision for a much more principled trial practice through proof technologies purpose-applied to the exigencies of global crime and a new international contextualisation of criminal justice.

It is argued by a more pragmatic school of thought that consequentialist judicial reasoning in ICJ should not remain primarily influenced by the unique characteristics of global crime, nor the broader justice constituency and objectives which the Preamble expounds. Responding, in 'A Hierarchy of Goals for the International Criminal Court' Ford indicates[50] that despite Demaska's denial of anything but a retributive function for international criminal trials,[51] the most important goal for international trial justice is the prevention of violations of international criminal law. Even, however, if this priority is accepted, there is a wealth of argument to suggest that the end to impunity and its preventive consequences are deeply contingent on the political and pragmatic exercise of juridical discretion.[52]

50 Ford, Stuart, "A Hierarchy of the Goals of International Criminal Courts," *Minnesota Journal of International Law*, 27, 2017, p. 10.

51 Levitt, Justin, "Developments in the Law – International Criminal Law – II: The Promises of International Prosecution," *Harv. L. Rev.*, 114 7, 2001, pp. 1957–1982. The author notes that certain practices, like the use of plea bargains, can undermine retributive aims and that the punishments that international courts can give seem 'inadequate' for effective retribution given the 'moral magnitude' of the crimes; Harmon, Mark, and Gaynor, Fergal, "Ordinary Sentences for Extraordinary Crimes," *J. Int'l Crim. Just.*, 5 3, 2007, pp. 683–712. This paper argues that sentences from international criminal courts are too lenient given the magnitude of the wrongs; DeGuzman, Margaret, "Choosing to Prosecute: Expressive Selection at the International Criminal Court," 33 *Mich. J. Int'l L.*, 33, 2012, pp. 265–320 at 302: This author notes that many 'scholars who have studied the question' have expressed doubts about the ICC's ability to serve retributive ends.

52 Rudolph, Christopher, *Power and Principle: The Politics of International Criminal Courts*, Cornell University Press: Ithaca, N.Y., 2017, p. 6.

One writer,[53] accepting the politicisation of ICC critical decision-making suggests a vision for the court as a flexible actor on world politics, situated at the intersection of law, ethics and politics, rather than as a strictly legalist justice entity. In support of this position, Shklar's analysis of *legalist politics* is invoked. In particular she defends political trials in the following terms:

> political trials may actually serve liberal ends where they promote legalist values in such a way as to contribute to constitutional politics and to a decent legal order. The trial of major criminals by the International Military Tribunal at Nuremberg probably had that effect. To be sure, within a stable constitutional order political trials may be a disgrace, a reversion to the politics of repression, but it is not the political trial itself but the situation in which it takes place and the ends that it serves which matter. It is the quality of the politics pursued in them that distinguishes one political trial from another.[54]

Such trials can be the consequence of victors' justice, inventing new crimes to eliminate political enemies, but even if they cannot be defended on adherence to strict legal principle they find justification in political reasoning. These trials represent legalist means for eliminating unconscionable political power and its identities. Preferring to put mass atrocities within a practical political context rather than held up against lofty ideologies, Shklar iterates the legitimate purpose of political trials in dealing with threats to liberal values of tolerance and pluralism. These are political and not metaphysical concerns where law is a political action among others which may be occasionally applicable and effective, while often not so. The international criminal trial is not an answer to political contentions, nor can it be isolated from political purposes and struggles if we temper considerations of international criminal justice with a pragmatic realism.

Against this, Arendt contends that:

> The purpose of a trial is to render justice, and nothing else; even the noblest of ulterior purposes . . . can only detract from law's main business: to weigh the charges brought against the accused, to render judgement, and mete out due punishment.[55]

53 Anon, "International Criminal Justice between Scylla and Charybdis – The Peace versus Justice Dilemma Analysed through the Lenses of Judith Shklar's and Hannah Arendt's Legal and Political Theories," *Human Rights Review* (publication review), 2017.

54 Shklar, Judith, *Legalism: Law, Morals, and Political Trials*, Harvard University Press: Harvard, 1964, p. 145.

55 Arendt, Hannah, *Eichmann in Jerusalem: A Report on the Banality of Evil*, Penguin: New York, 2006, p. 53. Tismaneanu, Vladimir, and Lacob, Bogdan, *Remembrance, History and Justice: Coming to Terms with Traumatic Pasts in Democratic Societies*, Central European University Press: Budapest, 2015, p. 297.

That said, Arendt recognises in a consequentialist sense that perpetrators of atrocity crime may violate the order of mankind in such a unique way, and so harming an altogether different community so that the nature of the inevitable just outcome may be more extreme and more pressing. Here it seems absurd to ask which is more important as a focus for ICJ – humanity or justice. Any attempt to isolate justice from humanity, certainly in terms of the Preamble, puts at risk the judges' commitments to *political* justice (in terms of the ethics of humanity) and *legalist* justice (concerned with the punitive determinants of social action). Worse still might be the imputation that protecting humanity and pursuing justice as purposes for prosecutorial action and judicial reasoning are at odds. This type of reductionist thinking about the political and legalist nature of ICJ is unfortunately serviced by complementarity and discipline-bound harmonisation/hybridisation approaches as the sources of ICL. If it is argued that through the attempt to have ICL mirror domestic criminal law traditions, and the jurisdiction of ICJ governed by domestic primacy, then the unique requirements of global crime and the unique aspirations concerning the prosecution of international criminal responsibility will be down-played or ignored. The over-use of the domestic analogy when understanding the nature and consequences of ICJ has led to the proof distortions evinced in Chapter 3, but more worrying is the interest in what comprises ICJ has been side-lined in unhelpful debates about justice and peace.

Such a distracting duality *was* addressed head-on by Judge Song Sang-Hyun (the former ICC president):

> While the ICC's contribution is tough justice, not peace-making, its mandate is highly relevant to peace as well. The Rome Statute is based on the recognition that the grave crimes with which it deals threaten the peace, security and well-being of the world. The Statute's objective is to ensure their effective prosecution at the national or ICC level, putting an end to impunity and thereby . . . laying the foundation for a sustainable peace.[56]

What we see as reconciling the artificial duality of justice vs peace when structuring the judicial vision of ICJ is the value of human dignity and the condition of human plurality. When considering the intended outcomes of ICJ beyond idealism or liberal individual rights recognition, developing a method for unpacking a realist cosmopolitanism[57] becomes critical. In so doing, we are aware of the dangers inherent in consequentialist legal reasoning which can verge on sacrificing justice for peace. However, we would counter that so long as the protection of humanity is kept as the precious purpose of such consequentialism, then justice

56 Krzan, Bartlomiej, "International Criminal Court Facing the Peace vs. Justice Dilemma," *International Comparative Jurisprudence*, 2, 2016, pp. 81–88 at 83.

57 Beardsworth, Richard, "Cosmopolitanism and Realism – Towards a Theoretical Convergence?" *Millennium: Journal of International Studies*, 37 1, 2008, pp. 69–96.

will be the necessary context for judicial reasoning, and cosmopolitan values will inform the struggle for peace, security and well-being.

There is no doubt that the trial format for achieving such incorporeal justice aims creates the risk of another tension – focusing on the nature of a particular act under law while at the same time anticipating 'a grand gesture of legal renewal.'[58] International criminal justice triggered through the proof of global crimes moves between the local and the global in much more than jurisdictional terms. If ICL is to be true to some domestic roots of procedure than it cannot but recognise the temporal and the spatial in evaluating the responsibility and the damage to individual human subjects. At the same time, the cosmopolitan aspirations of protecting and compensating humanity will never entirely break free from power and politics. The atrocious and unimaginable has tested the capacity of criminalisation to present an acceptable and commensurate response on behalf of humanity. Compounding the operational and conceptual challenges attendant on the context for determining responsibility for such harm, the diversity of interests which comprise any global community invite conflicting interpretations of justice which would challenge the cosmopolitan authority of the courts. These cannot be mediated by adversarial argument. Throughout this text we have consciously avoided (and we might be criticised for so doing) the important role of the defense in achieving international criminal justice.[59] The logistical reason for this is simply the confines of monograph length. Against this is the prioritisation of *proof processes* which are juridical necessities in advancing the end to impunity. If the prosecution case does not reach initial sufficiency under the determinations of pre-trial review, then there is no trial justice to eventuate. The first stage in proof for ICJ is what Gordon and Werner refer to as translating concrete suffering into formal legal categories: imagining the unimaginable. But even if, with a much improved proof 'toolkit,' for practical or political reasons the prosecutor is not able to achieve her function in determining responsibility there still remains a higher order collective duty on the global community to respond outside the courtroom to the plight of victims whose rights and dignity have been so ferociously violated.

> In short, in keeping with the conflicted condition of cosmopolitanism as we have observed it (through the sectarian politicization of prosecutorial discretion to charge some massive perpetrators and not others), the particular practices of international criminal law and its grand gestures are in tension, undermining the aspiration to a positive programme of justice. As such the

58 Gordon, Geoff, and Werner, Wouter, "Between the Dog and the Divine: Resistance and Conventionalism in Cosmopolitanism," *Utrecht Law Review*, 13 2, 2017, pp. 28–38 at 35.

59 This topic has been comprehensively discussed by other academics; some relevant works consist of the following: Zyberi, Gentian, and Rohan, Colleen, *Defence Perspectives on International Criminal Justice*, Cambridge University Press: Cambridge, 2017; Fabian, Raimondo, *General Principles of Law in the Decisions of International Criminal Courts and Tribunals*, BRILL: Leiden, 2008.

> ICC appears to occupy the local site of suffering, but on the basis of a universalised code that floats freely above that site, a code that is otherwise unconnected and administered from afar.[60]

Even if our calls for rethinking the substantive, procedural and jurisdictional dimensions of trial-based international criminal justice were heeded and actioned, the *grand gestures* voiced out in the Preamble would not be entirely satisfied. Such is a failing of all forms of trial-based justice subject to juridical discretion, contextualised by dynamic and often overpowering political super-structures.[61] Recognising the ineffable limitations of trial-based justice whatever its jurisdictional out-play, the importance of locating within a responsibilised global community, the crucial and continuous collective duty to signify, value and protect humanity ravaged by global crime, is the message of international criminal justice beyond the courtroom. Judges can and must materialise this vision. But they can only do so much. International criminal justice, if it is to be attained, must see the responsibilities it demands returned to global civil society and personalised by each individual in humanity for the benefit of those whose capacity, common security, and self-worth are the core casualties of global atrocity.

60 Gordon and Werner, 2017, p. 33.
61 Rudolph, 2017, p. 67.

Bibliography

Books

Alexander, Larry, and Ferzan, Kimberly, *Crime and Culpability: A Theory of Criminal Law*, Cambridge University Press: Cambridge, 2009.

Ambos, Kai, *The Colombian Peace Process and the Principle of Complementarity of the International Criminal Court: An Inductive, Situation-based Approach*, Springer: Berlin, 2010.

Arendt, Hannah, *Eichmann in Jerusalem: A Report on the Banality of Evil*, Penguin: New York, 2006.

Ashworth, Andrew, *Principles of Criminal Law*, Clarendon Press: Oxford, 1991.

Bećirević, Edina, *Joint Criminal Enterprise*, Yale University Press: New Haven, 2014.

Benedetti, Fanny, Bonneau, Karine, and Washburn, John, *Negotiating the International Criminal Court New York to Rome, 1994–1998*, BRILL: Leiden, 2013.

Bermingham, Vera, and Brennan, Carol, *Tort Law Directions*, Oxford University Press: Oxford, 2016.

Billing, Fenella, *Right to Silence in Transnational Criminal Proceedings: Comparative Law Perspectives*, Berlin: Springer, 2016.

Çakmak, Cenap, *A Brief History of International Criminal Law and International Criminal Court*, Palgrave Macmillan US: New York, 2017.

Clarke, Kamari, *Fictions of Justice: The International Criminal Court and the Challenge of Legal Pluralism in Sub-Saharan Africa*, Cambridge University Press: Cambridge, 2009.

Damgaard, Ciara, *Individual Criminal Responsibility for Core International Crimes*, Springer-Verlag: Berlin Heidelberg, 2008.

De Vos, Christian, Kendall, Sara, and Stahn, Carsten, *Contested Justice: The Politics and Practice of International Criminal Court Interventions*, Cambridge University Press: Cambridge, 2015.

Dyson, Matthew, *Unravelling Tort and Crime*, Cambridge University Press: Cambridge, 2014.

Dyson, Matthew, *Comparing Tort and Crime – Learning from Across and Within Legal Systems*, Cambridge University Press: Cambridge, 2015.

Elliott, Catherine, *French Criminal Law*, Routledge: Oxford, 2001.

Findlay, Mark, *International and Comparative Criminal Justice: A Critical Introduction*, Routledge: Oxford, 2013.

Findlay, Mark, and Henham, Ralph, *Beyond Punishment: Achieving International Criminal Justice*, Palgrave Macmillan UK: Basingstoke, 2010.

Fleming, John, *The Law of Torts*, Clarendon Press: Oxford, 2011.

Gill, Aisha, and Anitha, Sundari (eds), *Forced Marriage: Introducing a Social Justice and Human Rights Perspective*, Zed Books: London, 2012.

Gobert, James, and Punch, Maurice, *Rethinking Corporate Crime*, Cambridge University Press: Cambridge, 2003.

Goy, Barbara, *International Criminal Responsibility before the International Criminal Court*, Martinus Nijhoff Publishers: Amsterdam, 2012.

Heller, Kevin, *The Nuremberg Military Tribunals and the Origins of International Criminal Law*, Oxford Scholarship Online, September 2011.

Horder, Jeremy, *Homicide Law in Comparative Perspective*, Bloomsbury Publishing: London, 2007.

Imoedemhe, Ovo Catherine, *The Complementarity Regime of the International Criminal Court: National Implementation in Africa*, Springer: Berlin, 2017.

Kim, Sangkul, *A Collective Theory of Genocidal Intent*, Asser Press and Springer: Berlin, 2016.

Knight, Charlotte, and Wilson, Kath, *Lesbian, Gay, Bisexual, and Trans People and the Criminal Justice System*, Palgrave Macmillan: London, 2016.

Knoops, Geert-Jan Alexander, *Mens Rea at the International Criminal Court*, Volume 10 of International Criminal Law Series, BRILL: Nijhoff, 2016.

Lunney, Mark, and Oliphant, Ken, *Tort Law: Text and Materials*, Oxford University Press: Oxford, 2013.

Marchuk, Iryna, *The Fundamental Concept of Crime in International Criminal Law*, Springer: Berlin, 2013.

McBride, Nicholas, and Bagshaw, Roderick, *Tort Law*, Longmans Law Series, Pearson Education Limited: London, 5th edition, 2015.

Meisenberg, Simon, and Stegmiller, Ignaz, *The Extraordinary Chambers in the Courts of Cambodia: Assessing Their Contribution to International Criminal Law*, The Hague: Asser Press: Berlin, 2016.

Mendes, Errol, *Peace and Justice at the International Criminal Court: A Court of Last Resort*, Edward Elgar Publishing: Cheltenham, 2010.

Mitsilegas, Valsamis, *Globalisation, Criminal Law and Criminal Justice: Theoretical, Comparative and Transnational Perspectives*, Hart Publishing: Oxford, 2015.

Momah, Sam, *Nigeria Beyond Divorce – Amalgamation in Perspective*, Safari Books Ltd: Ibadan, 2013.

Murphy, John, *The Evolving Dimensions of International Law: Hard Choices for the World Community*, Cambridge University Press: Cambridge, 2010.

Odom, Thomas, and Reimer, Dennis, *Journey into Darkness: Genocide in Rwanda*, Texas A&M University Press: College Station, 2005.

Ormerod, David, *Smith and Hogan's Criminal Law*, 13th edition, Oxford University Press: Oxford, 2011.

O'Sullivan, Carmel, *Killing on Command: The Defence of Superior Orders in Modern Combat*, Palgrave Macmillan: Basingstoke, 2016.

Raimondo, Fabian, *General Principles of Law in the Decisions of International Criminal Courts and Tribunals*, BRILL: Leiden, 2008.

Reichel, Philip, and Albanese, Jay, *Handbook of Transnational Crime and Justice*, Sage: Los Angeles, 2014.

Rudolph, Christopher, *Power and Principle: The Politics of International Criminal Courts*, Cornell University Press: Ithaca, N.Y., 2017.

Safferling, Christoph, *Towards an International Criminal Procedure*, 1st edition, Oxford University Press: Oxford, 2003.

Schabas, William, *Unimaginable Atrocities: Justice, Politics, and Rights at the War Crimes Tribunals*, Oxford University Press: Oxford, 2012.

Schlütter, Birgit, *Developments in Customary International Law Theory and the Practice of the International Court of Justice and the International Ad Hoc Criminal Tribunals for Rwanda and Yugoslavia*, BRILL: Leiden, 2010.

Shklar, Judith, *Legalism: Law, Morals, and Political Trials*, Harvard University Press: Cambridge, M.A., 1964.

Simester, Andrew, Spencer, John, Stark, Findlay, Sullivan, Robert, and Virgo, Graham, *Simester and Sullivan's Criminal Law*, Bloomsbury Publishing: Oxford, 2016.

Sliedregt, van Elies, *The Curious Case of International Criminal Liability*, Oxford University Press: Oxford, 2012.

Stahn, Carsten, and Sluiter, Goran, *Emerging Practice of the International Criminal Court*, Vol. 8 of Legal Aspects of International Organization, Part III Prosecutorial Policy and Practice, BRILL: Leiden, 2009.

Stark, Findlay, *Culpable Carelessness: Recklessness and Negligence in the Criminal Law*, Cambridge University Press: Cambridge, 2016.

Stover, Eric, *The Witness: War Crimes and the Promise of Justice in The Hague*, University of Pennsylvania Press: Philadelphia, 2005.

Tanaka, Yuki, McCormack, Tim, and Simpson, Gerry, *Beyond Victor's Justice? The Tokyo War Crimes Trial Revisited*, BRILL: Leiden, 2010.

Tibori-Szabo, Kinga, and Hirst, Megan, *Victim Participation in International Criminal Justice: Practitioner's Guide*, T.M.C. Asser Press: Heidelberg, 2017.

Tismaneanu, Vladimir, and Lacob, Bogdan, *Remembrance, History and Justice: Coming to Terms with Traumatic Pasts in Democratic Societies*, Central European University Press: Budapest, 2015.

Witting, Christian, *Street on Tort*, 14th edition, Oxford University Press: Oxford, 2015.

Zyberi, Gentian, and Rohan, Colleen, *Defence Perspectives on International Criminal Justice*, Cambridge University Press: Cambridge, 2017.

Journal articles and book chapters

Abass, Ademola, "Prosecuting International Crimes in Africa: Rationale, Prospects and Challenges," *EJIL*, 24 3, 2013.

Alvarez, Jose, "Nuremberg Revisited: The *Tadic* case," *EJIL* 7, 1996.

Anon, "International Criminal Justice between Scylla and Charybdis – The peace versus Justice Dilemma Analysed through the Lenses of Judith Shklar's and Hannah Arendt's Legal and Political Theories," *Human Rights Review* (publication review), 2017.

Baker, Dennis J., "Reinterpreting the Mental Element in Criminal Complicity: Change of Normative Position Theory Cannot Rationalize the Current Law," *Law & Psychology Review*, 40, 2016.

Baum, Lynne Miriam, "Pursuing Justice in a Climate of Moral Outrage: An Evaluation of the Rights of the Accused in the Rome Statute of the International Criminal Court," *Wisconsin International Law Journal*, 19 2, 2000–2001.

Beale, Sara Sun, and Safwat, Adam, "What Developments in Western Europe Tell Us about American Critiques of Corporate Criminal Liability," *Buff. Crim. L. Rev.*, 8 2, 2004.

Beardsworth, Richard, "Cosmopolitanism and Realism – Towards a Theoretical Convergence?" *Millennium: Journal of International Studies*, 37 1, 2008.

Beck, Susanne, "Intelligent Agents and Criminal Law—Negligence, Diffusion of Liability and Electronic Personhood," *Robotics and Autonomous Systems*, 86, 2016.

Bederman, David, "International Criminal Court – Appeals Chamber – Rome Statute – Article 17 – Complementarity – Article 19 – Challenges to Jurisdiction or Admissibility of a Case – Kenya," *Am. J. Int'l Law*, 106, 2012.

Bibas, Stephanos, and Burke-White, William, "International Idealism Meets Domestic-Criminal-Procedure Realism," *Duke Law Journal*, 59, 2010.

Birmingham, Peg, "Hannah Arendt's Philosophy of Law Approach to International Criminal Law," Georgetown Public Law and Legal Theory Research Paper No. 11–30.

Bocchese, Marco, "Odd Friends: Rethinking the Relationship Between the ICC and State Sovereignty," *New York University Journal of International Law and Politics*, 49 2, 2017.

Bohlen, Rachel, "Questioning Authority: A Case for the International Criminal Court's Prosecution of the Current Sudanese President, Omar Al-Bashir," *George Washington International Law Review*, 42 3, 2010.

Borda, Aldo, "Appraisal-Based and Flexible Approaches to External Precedent in International Criminal Law," *Leiden Journal of International Law*, 28 3, 2015.

Bradley, Craig M., "Anti-Racketeering Legislation in America," Articles by Maurer Faculty, 2006, Paper 160.

Brennan, James R., "Lowering the Sultan's Flag: Sovereignty and Decolonization in Coastal Kenya," *Comparative Studies in Society and History*, 50 4, 2008.

Brighton, Claire, "Avoiding Unwillingness: Addressing the Political Pitfalls Inherent in the Complementarity Regime of the International Criminal Court," *International Criminal Law Review*, 12 4, 2012.

Brubacher, Matthew, "Prosecutorial Discretion within the International Criminal Court," *J. Int'l Crim. J.*, 2 1, 2004.

Bucy, Pamela, "Corporate Ethos: A Standard for Imposing Corporate Criminal Liability," *Minnesota Law Review*, 75, 1991.

Bucy, Pamela, "Trends in Corporate Criminal Prosecutions," *Am. Crim. L. Rev.*, 44, 2007.

Buell, Samuel, and Griffin, Lisa, "On the Mental State of Consciousness of Wrongdoing," *Law and Contemporary Problems*, 75, 2012.

Burke-White, William, "Complementarity in Practice: The International Criminal Court as Part of a System of Multi-level Global Governance in the Democratic Republic of Congo," *Leiden Journal of International Law*, 18 3, 2005.

Caplan, Russell, "Professor Dworkin's Jurisprudence," *American Journal of Jurisprudence*, 22 1, 1977.

Cassese, Antonio, "Proper Limits of Individual Responsibility Under the Doctrine of Joint Criminal Enterprise," *J. Int'l Crim. J.*, 5 1, 2007.

Cavanagh, Neil, "Corporate Criminal Liability: An Assessment of the Models of Fault," *J. Crim. L.*, 75, 2011.

Ciorciari, John, and Heindel, Anne, "Victim Testimony in International and Hybrid Criminal Courts: Narrative Opportunities, Challenges, and Fair Trial Demands," *Virginia Journal of International Law*, 56 2, 2016.

CoCo, Antonio, and Gal, Tom, "Losing Direction," *J. Int'l Crim. J.*, 12 2, 2014.

Corradetti, Claudio, "The Priority of Conflict Deterrence and the Role of the International Criminal Court in Kenya's Post-Electoral Violence 2007–2008 and 2013," *Human Rights Review*, 16 3, 2015.

Cunningham, Sally, "Recklessness: Being Reckless and Acting Recklessly," *Kings Law Journal*, 21, 2010.

Damaska, Mirjan R, "What is the Point of International Criminal Justice?" *Chicago Kent Law Review*, 83 1, 2008.

Defrancia, Cristian, "Due Process in International Criminal Courts: Why Procedure Matters," *Virginia Law Review*, 87 7, 2001.

DeGuzman, Margaret, "Choosing to Prosecute: Expressive Selection at the International Criminal Court," *Mich. J. Int'l L.*, 33, 2012.

DeWolf, Harold, "Criminal Justice as Defense and Restoration of Community: Our Non-System of Criminal Justice," *Cumberland Law Review*, 7, 1977.

Dixon, Olivia, "Corporate Criminal Liability: The Influence of Corporate Culture," in Justin O'Brien and George Gilligan (eds), *Integrity, Risk and Accountability in Capital Markets: Regulating Culture*, Hart Publishing: Oxford, 2013, Chapter 13.

Drumbl, Mark, "Pluralizing International Criminal Justice," *Michigan Law Review*, 103 6, 2005.

Dubber, Markus, "Criminal Jurisdiction and Conceptions of Penalty in Comparative Perspective," *University of Toronto Law Journal*, 63 2, 2013.

Dubber, Markus, "The Comparative History and Theory of Corporate Criminal Liability," *New Crim. L. Rev.*, 16 2, 2013.

Du Plessis, Max, "Complementarity and Africa: The Promises and Problems of International Criminal Justice," *African Security Review*, 17 4, 2008.

Du Plessis, Max, "The Future of International Criminal Justice: Civil Society, Complementarity and the Case of South Africa," *African Security Review*, 19 4, 2010.

Duraj, Erinda, "The Rights of Victims under International Criminal Justice," *Academic Journal of Business, Administration, Law and Social Sciences*, 1 2, 2015.

Dyson, Matthew, "Connecting Tort and Crime: Comparative Legal History in England and Spain since 1850," *Cambridge Yearbook of European Legal Studies*, 11, 2009.

Dyson, Matthew, "Civil Law Responses to Criminal Judgments in England and Spain," *J. Euro. Tort L.*, 3, 2012, pp. 308–339.

Elliot, Catherine, "The French Law of Intent and Its Influence on the Development of International Criminal Law," *Criminal Law Forum*, 11 1, 2000.

Elliott, Catherine, "The *Mens Rea* Required of Secondary Parties," *Journal of Criminal Law*, 64 6, 2000.

Ellis, Mark, "International Justice and the Rule of Law: Strengthening the ICC through Domestic Prosecutions," *Hague Journal on the Rule of Law*, 1 1, 2009.

Erhanze, Samson, and Momodu, Daud, "Corporate Criminal Liability: Call for a New Legal Regime in Nigeria," Journal of Law and Criminal Justice, 3 2, 2015.

Esakov, Gennady, "Corporate Criminal Liability: A Comparative Review," *City Univ. of Hong Kong Law Rev.*, 2, 2010.

Ezennia, Celestine Nchekwube, "The Modus Operandi of the International Criminal Court System: An Impartial or a Selective Justice Regime," *International Criminal Law Review*, 16 3, 2016.

Farhang, Cliff, "Point of No Return: Joint Criminal Enterprise in Brđanin," *Leiden Journal of International Law*, 23 1, 2010.

Farrell, Norman, "Attributing Criminal Liability to Corporate Actors: Some Lessons from the International Tribunals," *J. Int'l Crim. J.*, 8 3, 2010.

Findlay, Mark, "Contemporary Challenges for the Delivery of International Criminal Justice: Where to the ICC?" in Arlie Loughnan and Thomas Crofts (eds), *Criminalisation and Criminal Responsibility in Australia*, Oxford University Press: Melbourne, 2015.

Findlay, Mark, "Harmonising Global Criminal Justice for Peacebuilding," in Kerry Clamp (ed.), *Restorative Justice in Transitional Settings*, Routledge, 2016.

Findlay, Mark, and Bohlander, Michael, "The Use of Domestic Sources as a Basis of International Criminal Law Principles," in Michael Bohlander, *Globalization of Criminal Justice*, Aldershot: Ashgate, 2010, pp. 69–92.

Findlay, Mark, and Ngare, Sylvia, "Sham of the Moral Court: Testimonies Sold as the Spoils of War," *Global Journal of Comparative Law*, 1 1, 2012.

Finlay, Lorraine, "Does the International Criminal Court Protect Against Double Jeopardy: An analysis of Article 20 of the Rome Statute," *U. C. Davis J. Int'l L. & Policy*, 15, 2008–2009.

Flynn, Colin, "Sentencing at the International Criminal Court A Practice in Search of a Rationale," PhD Thesis, University of Leicester, 2015.

Ford, Stuart, "A Hierarchy of the Goals of International Criminal Courts," *Minnesota Journal of International Law*, 27, 2017.

Fouladvand, Shahrzad, "Complementarity and Cultural Sensitivity: Decision-making by the International Criminal Court Prosecutor in the Darfur Situation," *International Criminal Law Review*, 14 6, 2014.

Gaeta, Paola, "The Defence of Superior Orders: The Statute of International Criminal Court versus Customary International Law," *EJIL*, 10 1, 1999.

Garbett, Claire, "The Truth and the Trial: Victim Participation, Restorative Justice, and the International Criminal Court," *Contemporary Justice Review*, 16 2, 2013.

Garkawe, Sam, "The Victim-Related Provisions of the Statute of the International Criminal Court: A Victimological Analysis," *International Review of Victimology*, 8 3, 2001.

Garraway, Charles, "Superior Orders and the International Criminal Court: Justice Delivered or Justice Denied," *International Review of the Red Cross*, 81 836, 1999.

Gevers, Christopher, "International Criminal Law: Recent Cases," *South African Journal of Criminal Justice*, 26 3, 2013.

Giliker, Paula, "Vicarious Liability or Liability for the Acts of Others in Tort: A Comparative Perspective," *J. Euro. Tort L.*, 2 1, 2011.

Gillet, Matthew, "Victim Participation at the International Criminal Court," *Australian International Law Journal*, 16 1, 2009.

Glasius, Marlies, "What is Global Justice and Who Decides? Civil Society and Victim Responses to the International Criminal Court's First Investigations," *Human Rights Quarterly*, 31 2, 2009.

Goodrich, Herbert F., "Foreign Marriages and the Conflict of Laws," *Michigan Law Review*, 21 7, 1923.

Gordon, Geoff, and Werner, Wouter, "Between the Dog and the Divine: Resistance and Conventionalism in Cosmopolitanism," *Utrecht Law Review*, 13 2, 2017.

Greenawalt, Alexander, "Rethinking Genocidal Intent: The Case for a Knowledge-Based Interpretation," *Columbia Law Review*, 99, 1999. Link: http://digitalcommons.pace.edu/lawfaculty/338.

Guilfoyle, Douglas, "Responsibility for Collective Atrocities: Fair Labelling and Approaches to Commission in International Criminal Law," *Current Legal Problems*, 64 1, 2011.

Hanna, Don, "Corporate Criminal Liability," *Crim. L.Q.*, 31. 1988–1989.

Harmon, Mark, and Gaynor, Fergal, "Ordinary Sentences for Extraordinary Crimes," *J. Int'l Crim. J.*, 5 3, 2007.

Harris, Whitney, "A World of Peace and Justice under the Rule of Law: From Nuremberg to the International Criminal Courts," *Washington University Global Studies Law Review*, 6 3, 2007.

Heath, J. Benton, "Human Dignity at Trial: Hard Cases and Broad Concepts in International Criminal Law," *The George Washington International Law Review*, 44 2, 2012.

Hellwege, Phillip, and Wittig, Petra, "Delictual and Criminal Liability in Germany," in Matthew Dyson (ed.) *Comparing Tort and Crime: Learning Across and Within Legal Systems*, Cambridge University Press: Cambridge, 2015.

Hemming, Andrew, "Reasserting the Place of Objective Tests in Criminal Responsibility: Ending the Supremacy of Subjective tests," *University of Notre Dame Australia Law Review*, 13, 2011.

Hoffman, Tamas, "The Gentle Humanizer of Humanitarian Law – Antonio Cassese and the Creation of the Customary Law of Non-International Armed Conflicts," in Carsten Stahn and Larissa van den Herik (eds), *Future Perspectives on International Criminal Justice*, TMC: Acer Press / Cambridge University Press: Cambridge, 2015.

Horovitz, Sigall, "International Criminal Courts in Action: The ICTR's Effect on Death Penalty and Reconciliation in Rwanda," *George Washington International Law Review*, 48 3, 2016.

Jackson, Miles, "Individual Criminal Responsibility," in Miles Jackson, *Complicity in International Law*, Oxford University Press: Oxford, 2015, Chapter 3.

Jain, Neha, "Perpetrators and Accessories in International Criminal Law: Individual Modes of Responsibility for Collective Crimes," *J. Int'l Crim. J.*, 13 4, 2015.

Jordash, Wayne, "Joint Criminal Enterprise Liability: Result Oriented Justice," in William Schabas, Yvonne MacDermott and Niamh Hayes (eds), *The Ashgate Research Companion to International Criminal Law*, Ashgate: Aldershot, 2013.

Jovasevic, Dragan, "International Criminal Courts: Between Law, Justice, Reconciliation and Rights of Victims," *Medjunarodni Problemi*, 63 4, 2011.

Kiyani, Asad, "The Antinomies of Legitimacy: On the (Im)Possibility of a Legitimate International Criminal Court," *African Journal of Legal Studies*, 8 1–2, 2015.

Klass, Alexandra, "Punitive Damages and Valuing Harm," *Minnesota Law Review*, 92, 2007.

Krebs, Beatrice, "Joint Criminal Enterprise," *Modern Law Review*, 73 4, 2010.

Krings, Britta, "The Principles of 'Complementarity' and Universal Jurisdiction in International Criminal Law: Antagonists or Perfect Match?" *Goettingen Journal of International Law*, 4 3, 2012.

Krzan, Bartlomiej, "International Criminal Court Facing the Peace vs. Justice Dilemma," *International Comparative Jurisprudence*, 2, 2016.

Kucher, Olena, and Petrenko, Aleksey, "International Criminal Responsibility After Katanga: Old Challenges, New Solutions," *Russian Law Journal*, 3 1, 2015.

Kyriakakis, Joanna, "Corporate Criminal Liability and the ICC Statute: The Comparative Law Challenge," *Netherlands International Law Review*, 56 3, 2009.

Laufer, William, "Corporate Bodies and Guilty Minds," *Emory L. J.*, 43, 1994.

Lazarev, Nikolai, "Hohfeld's Analysis of Rights: An Essential Approach to a Conceptual and Practical Understanding of the Nature of Rights," *Murdoch University Electronic Journal of Law*, 7 205, 2005.

Lehnardt, Chia, "Individual Liability of Private Military Personnel under International Criminal Law," *EJIL*, 19 5, 2008.

Lemarchand, René, "Consociationalism and Power Sharing in Africa: Rwanda, Burundi, and the Democratic Republic of the Congo," *African Affairs*, 106 422, 2007.

Leveau, Fanny, "Liability of Child Soldiers Under International Criminal Law," *Osgoode Hall Review of Law and Policy*, 4 1, 2014.

Levitt, Justin, "Developments in the Law – International Criminal Law – II: The Promises of International Prosecution," *Harv. L. Rev.*, 114 7, 2001.

Mannheim, Hermann, "*Mens Rea* in German and English Law – II," *Journal of Comparative Legislation and International Law*, 17 4, 1935.

Maogoto, Jackson, "A Giant without Limbs: The International Criminal Court's State-Centric Cooperation Regime," *U. Queensland Law Journal*, 23, 2004.

Mays, Richard, "Towards Corporate Fault as the Basis of Criminal Liability of Corporations," *Mountbatten Journal of Legal Studies*, December 1998.

Meernik, James, "The International Criminal Court and the Deterrence of Human Rights Atrocities," *Civil Wars*, 17 3, 2015.

Megret, Frederic, "What Sort of Global Justice is 'International Criminal Justice'," *J. Int'l Crim. J.*, 13 1, 2015.

Meijers, Tim, and Glasius, Marlies, "Trials as Messages of Justice: What Should Be Expected of International Criminal Courts?" *Ethics and International Affairs*, 30 4, 2016.

Mireille, Hector, "Enhancing Individual Criminal Responsibility For Offences Involving Cultural Property – The Road to the Rome Statute and the 1999 Second Protocol," in Nout van Woudenberg and Liesbeth Lijnzaad (eds), *Protecting Cultural Property in Armed Conflict*, BRILL: Leiden, 2010.

Moffett, Luke, "Elaborating Justice for Victims at the International Criminal Court," *J. Int'l. Crim. J.*, 13 2, 2015.

Morris, Madeline H., "Rwandan Justice and the International Criminal Court," *ILSA Journal of International & Comparative Law*, 5 2, 1999.

Ndahinda Mukwiza, F., "The Bemba-Banyamulenge Case before the ICC: From Individual to Collective Criminal Responsibility," *International Journal of Transitional Justice*, 7 3, 2013.

Neyers, Jason, "A Theory of Vicarious Liability", *Alberta Law Review*, 43, 2005.

Nouwen, Sarah, and Becker, Michael, "Tadić v. Prosecutor: International Criminal Tribunal for the Former Yugoslavia," in Eirik Bjorge and Cameron Miles (eds), *Landmark Cases in Public International Law*, Hart Publishing: Oxford, 2017.

Ntsanyu Nana, Constantine, "Corporate Criminal Liability in South Africa: The Need to Look Beyond Vicarious Liability," *Journal of African Law*, 55 1, 2011.

Ochi, Megimi, "The Concept of *Mens Rea* in International Criminal Law: The Case for a Unified Approach," *J. Int'l Crim. J.*, 11 4, 2013.

Ohlin, J. David, "Three Conceptual Problems with the Doctrine of Joint Criminal Enterprise," *J. Int'l Crim. J.*, 5 1, 2007.

Oidtmann, Raphael, "The Responsibility to Protect and The International Criminal Court—Protection and Prosecution in Kenya," *Cambridge Review of International Affairs*, 29 4, 2016.

O'Mahony, Jane, "'Not So Nice': The Treaty of Nice, the International Criminal Court, the Abolition of the Death Penalty – The 2001 Referendum Experience," *Irish Political Studies*, 16 1, 2001.

Papacharalambous, Charis, "Group-Based Imputation and the International Criminal Law Discourse – Individuals and Associations as International Criminal Wrongdoers," *Beijing Law Review*, 4 4, 2013.

Parsons, Simon, "The Doctrine of Identification, Causation and Corporate Liability for Manslaughter," *Journal of Criminal Law*, 67 1, 2003.

Petrig, Anna, "Negotiated Justice and the Goals of International Criminal Tribunals," *Chicago-Kent Journal of International and Comparative Law*, 8 1, 2008.

Plesch, Dan, and Sattler, Shanti, "Changing the Paradigm of International Criminal Law: Considering the Work of the United Nations War Crimes Commission of 1943–1948," *International Community Law Review*, 15 2, 2013.

Prorok, Alyssa K., "The (In)compatibility of Peace and Justice? The International Criminal Court and Civil Conflict Termination," *International Organization*, 71 2, 2017.

Rabin, Robert L., "The Pervasive Role of Uncertainty in Tort Law: Rights and Remedies Symposium: The Limits of Predictability and the Value of Uncertainty: Sixteenth Annual Clifford Symposium on Tort Law and Social Policy," *DePaul Law Review*, 60, 2011.

Rauschenbach, Mina, Staerkle, Christian, and Scalia, Damien, "Accused for Involvement in Collective Violence: The Discursive Reconstruction of Agency and Identity by Perpetrators of International Crimes," *Political Psychology*, 37 2, 2016.

Roach, Steven, "The Turbulent Politics of the International Criminal Court," *Peace Review*, 23 4, 2011.

Robinson, Geoffrey, "East Timor Ten Years On: Legacies of Violence," *The Journal of Asian Studies*, 70 4, 2011.

Saber, Mahmoud, and Sadeghi, Azade, "The Survey of Criterion of Gravity Threshold for Prosecution of Crimes in International Criminal Court: Comparative View on Other International Courts," *Majallah-i ḥuqūq-i taṭbīqī*, 6 2, 2015.

Sarch, Alex, "Knowledge, Recklessness and the Connection Requirement Between *Actus Reus* and *Mens Rea*," *Penn. State Law Review*, 120 1, 2015.

Sayre, Francis, "Criminal Responsibility for the Acts of Another," *Harv. L. Rev.*, 43 5, 1930.

Scharf, Michael, "The Prosecutor v. Dusko Tadic: An Appraisal of the First International War Crimes Trial Since Nüremberg," Faculty Publications, Case Western University, Paper 371, 1997.

Scheffer, David, "The Complex Crime of Aggression under the Rome Statute," *Leiden Journal of International Law*, 23 4, 2010.

Schloenhardt, Andreas, "Mafias and Motorbikes: New Organised Crime Offences in Australia," *Current Issues Crim. Just.*, 19, 2008.

Schwartz, Sarah, "Wartime Sexual Violence as More Than Collateral Damage: Classifying Sexual Violence as Part of a Common Criminal Plan in International Criminal Law," *University of New South Wales Law Journal*, 40 1, 2017.

Seshaliah, Shasthri, "Self-Referrals by States and Criminal Prosecutions before the International Criminal Court," *ISIL Yearbook of International Humanitarian and Refugee Law*, 11, 2011.

Sheffield, Kai, "Speak Softly and Carry a Sealed Warrant: Building the International Criminal Court's Legitimacy in the Wake of Sudan," *Appeal*, 18, n163, 2013.

Sigler, Mary, "The Boundaries of the Criminal Law. By R. A. Duff, Lindsay Farmer, S. E. Marshall, Massimo Renzo and Victor Tadros," *British Journal of Criminology*, 52 3, 2012.

Simmons, Beth, and Danner, Allison, "Credible Commitments and the International Criminal Court," *International Organization*, 64 2, 2010.

Sliedregt, van Elies, "The Curious Case of International Criminal Liability," *J. Int'l Crim. J.*, 10 5, 2012.

Stahn, Carsten, "Libya, the International Criminal Court and Complementarity," *J Int'l Crim. J.*, 10 2, 2012.

Stahn, Carsten, El Zeidy, Mohamed M., and Olásolo, Héctor, "The International Criminal Court's Ad Hoc Jurisdiction Revisited," *The American Journal of International Law*, 99 2, 2005.

Stephen, Christopher, "International Criminal Law: Wielding the Sword of Universal Criminal Justice?" *International and Comparative Law Quarterly*, 61 1, 2012.

Stewart, James, "The End of 'Modes of Liability' for International Crimes," *Leiden Journal of International Law*, 25 1, 2012.

Sullivan, G.R., "Cause and the Contemporaneity of *Actus Reus* and *Mens Rea*," *Cambridge Law Journal*, 52 3, 1993.

Tallgren, Immi, "The Sensibility and Sense of International Criminal Law," *EJIL*, 13 3, 2002.

Van Der Wilt, Harmen, "Corporate Criminal Responsibility for International Crimes: Exploring the Possibilities," *Chinese Journal of International Law*, 12 1, 2013.

Varaki, Maria, "Introducing a Fairness-Based Theory of Prosecutorial Legitimacy Before the International Criminal Court," *EJIL*, 27 3, 2016.

Werle, Gerhard, "Individual Criminal Responsibility in Article 25 ICC Statute," *J. Int'l Crim. J.*, 5 4, 2007.

Westmoreland, Robert, "Dworkin and Legal Pragmatism," *Oxford Journal of Legal Studies*, 11 2, 1991.

Wilkinson, Meaghan, "Corporate Criminal Liability: The Move Towards Recognizing General Corporate Fault," *Canterbury Law Review*, 9, 2003.

Reports and news

"African Leaders Plan Mass Withdrawal From International Criminal Court – Decision reached at African Union summit follows announcements by South Africa, Burundi and the Gambia that they plan to leave the court," *The Guardian*, 31 January 2017. Link: www.theguardian.com/law/2017/jan/31/african-leaders-plan-mass-withdrawal-from-international-criminal-court.

"African Union Backs Mass Withdrawal From ICC," BBC News, 2017. Link: www.bbc.com/news/world-africa-38826073.

Anna, Cara, "Why African States Have Started Leaving the ICC," *The Jakarta Post*, 2016. Link: www.thejakartapost.com/news/2016/10/21/ap-explains-why-african-states-have-started-leaving-the-icc-.html.

Bartels, Lorna, "The Status of Laws on Outlaw Motorcycle Gangs in Australia," June 2009, Australian Institute of Criminology, Research in Practice, no. 2.

Clarke, David, NSWPD, *Hansard*, Legislative Council, 7 March 2012.

"Democratic Republic of Congo – Situation in the Democratic Republic of the Congo," International Criminal Court. Link: www.icc-cpi.int/drc.

Dixon, Nicolee, "Regulating Bikie Gangs," Queensland Parliamentary Library Research Brief No 2009/18.

Fassihi, Farnaz, "World News: Myanmar Faces Outcry Over Crackdown – Military Push to Drive Rohingya Outdraws International Scrutiny and Militant Calls to Arms," *Wall Street Journal*, Eastern Edition, 2017.

Goode, Matthew, "Corporate Criminal Liability," 2016. Link: https://aic.gov.au/sites/default/files/publications/proceedings/downloads/26-goode.pdf.

Hulls, Robert, Deputy Premier and Attorney-General, "Victoria's Tough Laws Best for Dealing with Bikie Gangs," Ministerial Media Statement, 15 April 2009.

Human Rights Watch, "The War Within the War – Sexual Violence Against Women and Girls in Eastern Congo," Report, 2002.

Human Rights Watch, "'You Will Be Punished' – Attacks on Civilians in Eastern Congo," Report, 2009.

"Italian Legislation on Organized Crime, Corruption and Money Laundering," Library of the European Parliament, 11 October 2012. Link: www.europarl.europa.eu/document/activities/cont/201210/20121015ATT53636/20121015ATT53636EN.pdf.

Kaplan, Robert, "The Coming Anarchy," *The Atlantic Monthly*, 1994.

"Legislation Review Digest, Legislation Review Committee, Parliament NSW Legislative Assembly," Sydney, NSW, 2009.

Manson, Katrina, "ICC Rules Kenyatta Can Miss Part of Trial," FT.com, 18 October, 2013.

New South Wales Ombudsman, "The Consorting Law, Report on the Operation of Part 3A, Division 7 of Crimes Act 1900," 2016.

Rees, Nathan, Premier of NSW and Minister for the Arts, Agreement in Principle, Crimes (Criminal Organisations Control) Bill 2009 (NSW), NSW Legislative Assembly, *Hansard Online*, 2 April 2009.

Robinson, Allens Arthur, "'Corporate Culture' as a Basis for the Criminal Liability of Corporations," United Nations Special Representative of the Secretary-General on Human Rights and Business, 2008.

Security Council Press Statement on the contribution of courts and tribunals in the fight against impunity, 2012, SC/10700.

Stewart, Terry, "New South Wales Legislative Assembly," *Hansard* 20 August 2006, p. 1142.

"UN Human Rights Chief Points to 'Textbook Example of Ethnic Cleansing' in Myanmar," UN News Centre, 11 September 2017.

United Nations Population Fund, Child Marriage. Link: www.unfpa.org/child-marriage.

Ventures Africa, "How Armed Militia Groups are Fuelling Genocide in the Democratic Republic of Congo," November 2016.

Withnall, Adam, "Gambia Pulls out of 'Racist' ICC amid Fears of Mass Africa Exodus," *The Independent*, 26 October 2016.

Legislation

Australian Federal Crimes Act 1958 Sect 181.

Crimes Legislation Amendment (Gangs) Act 2006, New South Wales Australia.

Crimes (Criminal Organisation Control Act) 2009, New South Wales Australia.

Criminal Code of the French Republic (as of 2016).

England and Wales, Accessories and Abettors Act 1861 Art 8.

German Criminal Code in the version promulgated on 13 November 1998.

Legislative Decree No 159 of 6 September 2011, the Codice Unico Antimafia, Italy.

Rules of Procedure and Evidence, International Criminal Court (2nd ed., 2013).

Serious and Organised Crime (Control) Act 2008, South Australia.

UN General Assembly, Rome Statute of the International Criminal Court (last amended 2010), 17 July 1998.

Case-Law

Bazley v Curry [1999] 2 S.C.R. 534.

Century Insurance Co Ltd v Northern Ireland Road Transport Broad [1942] 1 All ER 491.

Chan Wing-Siu v The Queen [1985] AC 168, 177E-H.

Davies v Director of Public Prosecutions [1954] AC 378.

Decision on Ojdanic's Motion Challenging Jurisdiction: Indirect Co-Perpetration, Case No. IT-05-87-PT. See: Separate judgment of Judge Iain Bonomy.

DPP v Smith [1961] AC 290.

Édouard Karemera and Matthieu Ngirimpatse v The Prosecutor, Case No. ICTR-98-44-A.

Édouard Karemera and Matthieu Ngirimpatse v The Prosecutor, Case No. ICTR-98-44-T.

Francois Karera v The Prosecutor, Case No. ICTR 04-71-A.

Holtby v Cowan (Hull) Ltd. [2000] 3 All ER 42.

Home Office v Dorset Yacht Co Ltd [1970] 2 All ER 294.

Joel v Morison [1834] EWHC KB J39.
John Doe v Bennett [2004] SCC 17.
Lennard's Carrying Co Ltd v Asiatic Petroleum Co Ltd [1915] AC 705.
Lister and others v Hesley Hall Limited [2001] UKHL 22.
Mattis v Pollock [2004] 4 All ER 85.
Prosecutor v Anto Furundžija, Case No. IT-95-17/1-T.
Prosecutor v Blagoje Simic, Case No. IT-95-9-A.
Prosecutor v Blagoje Simic, Case No. IT-95-9-T.
Prosecutor v Goran Jelisic, Case No. IT-95-10-A.
Prosecutor v Jean Paul Akayesu, Case No. ICTR-96-4-T.
Prosecutor v Kupreskic et al, Case No. IT-95-16-A.
Prosecutor v Kupreskic et al, Case No. IT-95-16-T.
Prosecutor v Milan Martic, Case No. IT-95-11-T.
Prosecutor v Momcilo Perisic, Case No. IT-04-81-A.
Prosecutor v Momcilo Perisic, Case No. IT-04-81-T.
Prosecutor v Naser Ori, Case No. IT-03-68-A.
Prosecutor v Nikola Sainovic, Case No. IT-05-87-A.
Prosecutor v Radislav Krstic, Case No. IT-98-33-T.
Prosecutor v Radoslav Brdanin, Case No. IT-99-36-A.
Prosecutor v Radoslav Brdanin, Case No. IT-99-36-T.
Prosecutor v Tihomir Blaskic, Case No. IT-95-14-A.
Prosecutor v Vidoje Blagojevic and Dragan Jokic., Case No. IT-02-60-A.
Public Prosecutor v Dusko Tadic, Case No. IT-94-1-A.
Public Prosecutor v Milan Martic, Case No. IT-95-11-A.
Public Prosecutor v Milomir Stakic, Case No. IT-97-24-T.
R v Anderson; R v Morris [1966] 2 QB 110, 120B.
R v Becerra and Cooper (1975) 62 Cr App R 212.
R v Hyde [1991] 1 QB 134.
R v Mendez and another [2010] 3 All ER 231.
R v Powell & English [1999] 1 AC 290.
R v Rahman and Others (Appellants), [2008] UKHL 45.
Rex v Vincent Banka & Anor [1936] MLJ 53, per Huggard J.
Rose v Plenty [1976] 1 WLR 141.
Tesco Supermarkets Ltd. v Nattrass [1972] AC 153.
Thabo Meli and Others Appellants v The Queen [1954] 1 W.L.R. 228.
US v Time-DC Inc, 381 F Supp 730 WD Va (1974).
Various Claimants v The Catholic Child Welfare Society and Others [2010] EWCA Civ 1106, para [64].
Woolmington v DPP [1935] UKHL 1.
Yemoh & Ors v R. [2009] EWCA Crim 930.

Index

For Product Safety Concerns and Information please contact our EU representative GPSR@taylorandfrancis.com
Taylor & Francis Verlag GmbH, Kaufingerstraße 24, 80331 München, Germany

www.ingramcontent.com/pod-product-compliance
Ingram Content Group UK Ltd.
Pitfield, Milton Keynes, MK11 3LW, UK
UKHW011015180926
475701UK00004B/760

* 9 7 8 0 3 6 7 5 8 8 6 1 8 *